TRANSFORMING DEVELOPMENT: FOREIGN AID FOR A CHANGING WORLD

Edited by Jim Freedman

The practice of rich countries providing financial assistance to developing countries has become increasingly controversial. Foreign aid is now characterized more by its failures than its successes, making foreign assistance budgets easy targets for politicians. In academic and policy circles the claim is made that foreign aid has outlived its usefulness. The original essays in *Transforming Development* take a more optimistic view, and instead of foreseeing the end of foreign aid, show how it might be revived.

The essays in this volume argue that foreign aid is, first and foremost, a humanitarian enterprise. The contributors suggest ways to reform the practice of development assistance, including new approaches to development financing and novel strategies for increasing the effectiveness of foreign aid, maintaining that development assistance must continue to receive donor support.

This forward-looking collection is an ideal text for undergraduate and graduate courses in international development and a valuable resource for practitioners and policy-makers in the field.

JIM FREEDMAN is on leave from the University of Western Ontario, serving as an analyst in the Office of the Iraq Programme at the United Nations in New York.

Edited by Jim Freedman

TRANSFORMING DEVELOPMENT:
Foreign Aid for a Changing World

UNIVERSITY OF TORONTO PRESS
Toronto Buffalo London

© University of Toronto Press Incorporated 2000
Toronto Buffalo London
Printed in Canada

ISBN 0-8020-4193-0 (cloth)
ISBN 0-8020-8051-0 (paper)

∞

Printed on acid-free paper

Canadian Cataloguing in Publication Data

Main entry under title:

Transforming development: foreign aid for a changing world

Includes bibliographical references.
ISBN 0-8020-4193-0 (bound)   ISBN 0-8020-8051-0 (pbk.)

1. Economic assistance – Developing countries.   I. Freedman, Jim.
HC60.T697 2000   338.91′09172′4   C99-932563-9

University of Toronto Press acknowledges the support of the Canada
Council and the Ontario Arts Council for our publishing program.

University of Toronto Press acknowledges the financial support for its
publishing activities of the Government of Canada through the Book
Publishing Industry Development Program (BPIDP).

Canada

Contents

Acknowledgments

Financial support for the publication of this manuscript has been provided by the Canadian Consortium of University Programs in International Development (CCUPIDS) and from the Office of the Dean, Faculty of Social Sciences, University of Western Ontario. I would also like to acknowledge the personal and intellectual support that I have received throughout from Professor Cranford Pratt. Finally, fondest appreciation goes to Virgil Duff, executive editor at the University of Toronto Press.

TRANSFORMING DEVELOPMENT:
FOREIGN AID FOR A CHANGING WORLD

Introduction: Aid at the Forks

JIM FREEDMAN

In another year, perhaps, the foreign affairs minister's use of funds from the Canadian International Development Agency (CIDA) to reward a Liberal Party worker with a bogus contract (Wood, 1995) might have slipped by unnoticed as pork belly politics, but the year was 1995, a turning point for development assistance in Canada. A federal budget had just reduced Canada's foreign assistance by 20 per cent over three years. What might otherwise have been a politician's discrete prerogative was in this instance a gaffe illustrative of the government's lack of interest in the integrity of foreign aid. Shortly after Minister Ouellet proposed a parliamentary inquiry to explore the possibility of turning CIDA's budget even more explicitly away from international poverty alleviation and towards providing incentives for Canadian merchants to trade overseas he was caught with his hand in the till.

So many signposts like this point to the demise of foreign aid that one might expect the voices in this book to join other respectful eulogies in announcing its final days. But they do not. The dire predictions drawn from downward trends in aid flows and the nonchalance of politicians have led others to contemplate the corpse of the aid regime, already sallow from the departure of the Cold War. In this book, however, we attempt to provide an optimistic alternative, setting out terms for reconfiguring crucial aspects of the aid regime to enable its revival.

Most dire predictions about the future of foreign aid begin with the implications of the conclusion of the Cold War. For all the great expectations following the collapse of the Soviet Union, it was clear that the aid regime would suffer. There had always been an implicit relationship between the politics of superpower antagonism and paying for aid, as the domestic fears of Soviet bloc and capitalist countries were played against one another. Commercial interests joined political interests as foreign aid came simultaneously to provide a vehicle for nation states to secure not only allies but also markets. The humanitarian motive was, as ever, the blush applied to the face of these not so humanitarian objectives. The decline of the Soviets and the change in global affiliations that followed broke the curious alliance between foreign aid and the Cold War, as the political fears which had justified paying for most of it disappeared.

A common claim is that the job of foreign aid is done. The packages of foreign assistance once proffered to countries that might otherwise have been lured into the wrong camp succeeded in building alliances and in clearing the terrain for market economies and the aid regime can now be placed proudly on the shelf. Deep cuts to American aid budgets come with roughly this rationale (Zimmerman and Hook, 1996) and versions of it can be heard in Canada as well (see Pratt, 1994 for a summary).

Prevalent as it is, this is only one perspective and a restricted one at that, accounting for only a portion of what is happening among the twenty-one donor countries (members of the Organization for Economic Cooperation and Development's Assistance Committee). When the political tangle which had held aid hostage for so many years began to unravel in 1988, the ulterior ends then served by aid rapidly dissipated, setting the hostage free. In many places, aid was now free to become a very different regime, one more in keeping with the spirit of its charitable conception, more resolutely humanitarian (Stokke, 1996). It is impossible to understand much of the fate of foreign aid in the last few years without recognizing this trend.

Year by year, overall aid flows have indeed declined, but the decline is modest, somewhat over 10 per cent between 1996 and 1997. In 1998, this downward trend reversed and turned slightly upward as donor countries increased their aid contributions by 9 per cent from $51 billion to $63 billion. As a percentage of gross national product (GNP), aid flows increased in ten out of the twenty-one donor countries during 1996 and increased again during 1997 in thirteen of them. Sharp drops occurred in contributions from donors with large aid programs, especially those made by Japan and the United States to multilateral agencies. Such declines are dramatic, but they reflect only marginally upon the global commitment among donor countries to humanitarian assistance.

TABLE 1.1
Official development assistance (ODA) for ten major donors

	ODA as a percentage of GNP					
Group	1992	1994	1995	1996	1997	% Change 1996–7*
Group 1						
Denmark	1.02	1.03	0.96	1.04	0.97**	+3.3
Netherlands	0.86	0.76	0.81	0.83	0.81	+2.7
Group 2						
Sweden	1.03	0.96	0.77	0.82	0.76	−5.9
France	0.63	0.64	0.55	0.48	0.45	−3.8
Group 3						
United Kingdom	0.31	0.31	0.28	0.27	0.26	−2.2
Germany	0.38	0.34	0.31	0.32	0.28	−10.9
Canada	0.46	0.43	0.38	0.31	0.36	+20.8
Group 4						
Italy	0.34	0.27	0.15	0.20	0.11	−45.2
United States	0.20	0.15	0.10	0.12	0.08	−35.5
Japan	0.30	0.29	0.28	0.20	0.22	+9.6

Source: OECD (1996a, 1997, 1998)
*Account is taken of both inflation and exchange-rate fluctuations.
**Denmark introduced a new system of national accounts in 1997 that led to an upward revision of GNP and which, combined with other technical factors, caused a downward adjustment of the final ODA/GNP ratio to 0.97 in 1997.

Table 1.1 shows foreign aid as a percentage of GNP for ten major donors in five separate years and the trends suggest four different scenarios for this period. Groups of donors can be discerned for each.

- *Group One.* A few donors, including Denmark and the Netherlands, have maintained their high level of aid disbursements, even increasing disbursements in certain cases.
- *Group Two.* A second group has not maintained the same level of aid as a decade ago, but even with cuts to aid disbursements the countries in this group, including Sweden and France, still maintain respectable levels of foreign assistance.
- *Group Three.* A third group may never have had high levels of aid by comparison with the first two, but their aid budgets, such as they

are, have remained partially intact and have been only partially affected by the trends in the United States and Japan. Germany, the United Kingdom, and Canada fall squarely within this group.
• *Group Four.* A final group includes those countries, like the United States and Japan, whose aid budgets have dropped significantly in the last five years to levels well below previous commitments. Because of the large sums disbursed by this latter group of countries, there is a temptation to allow the trends of this group to testify to the negative prospects for aid internationally.

This might be the case if the decline in contributions from the United States and Japan were indicative of global aid flows, but they are not. Donors in the other three groups have either maintained a relatively high level of aid disbursements or preserved the level of a decade ago. Among the donors in these three groups, aid is poised to take advantage of the freedom from constraints that formerly bound it to special interests in the Cold War and to preserve its compassionate agenda. Among some of these countries one can even see a renewed or stronger inclination to allow aid genuinely to be shaped by the interests of recipients. The actions and budgets of this group of donors suffice to preserve if not promote what Olav Stokke calls humanitarian internationalism (Stokke, 1996: 22).

Instead of demise, then, there is a bifurcation into separate policies driving aid in two directions. Aid is poised at the forks, branched in two tines, and it is here at this branch that the essays in this book are situated.

Most essays on the future of foreign aid can be found at these forks, discerning a direction down one path or the other. Along the pessimistic path lie essays nurtured in the soils of nations in which the severest cuts occur. These essays tend to generalize from the instances in North America and Japan to world disenchantment with aid. Their role is to explore the meaning of an incontestable trend, to chart the substitution of new trade channels for aid flows and the rise of private flows in tandem with the decline in public ones, and to divine the consequences. This confident pessimism can be found, not surprisingly, among American writers, whose government trends most markedly take this direction (Hook, 1995, 1996; Kawakami, 1993; Lumsdaine, 1993).

But the essays presented in this volume join more sanguine appraisals (Stokke, 1996; Hewitt, 1994) in looking down the other path. Nurtured in Canadian soil, this collection lies outside the ambit of fin-desiècle concerns about the decline of U.S. aid and aid's new orientation towards prying markets open throughout the globe. It is also removed, geographically and philosophically, from the World Bank's pro-market credo, with its vision of spare market place channels taking the place of diplomatic and foreign assistance channels. To be sure, Canada's federal budget may seem to favour the yoking of aid to ulterior motives. But as Cranford Pratt demonstrates in Chapter 2, this is accompanied by a great wringing of hands and an inclination to nurture new ideas for making aid serve compassionate ends. Lacking the heavy weight of American policy implications and in spite of its budget cuts there remains in Canada a continued inclination to reconfigure aid rather than to chart its demise. The fact that most of the authors in this volume write from within Canada means, in part, that they write outside the pale that colours the future of aid as a function of American policy. It also means that the argument at the hub of the particular arc these essays describe is the notion that foreign aid, in spite of its derelictions, has always been the precursor to global government.

For all the guises it has assumed, development assistance has been the avant-garde ground on which experiments transpire as the world gropes for a transnational polity. Political and economic competition among nations makes this theme difficult to discern, especially at a time when the decline of the Soviets has turned this experimental terrain into an American parade ground. It remains, nevertheless, an implicit feature of nearly all aid agendas.

The national interests of the United States and other countries will continue to occupy this experimental ground, despite the lip service paid to humane internationalism. Players' motives are rarely free of ulterior motives. Development assistance programs in Russia conspicuously play a rogue's game, since the short-term aim of almost all aid to Russia has been self-serving, anticipating political and financial paybacks when Russia stabilizes. Yet an implicit, longer term humanitarian agenda of protecting civic institutions against the threats of irresponsible leaders can also be detected. There is a fine line between humane intervention and political meddling, a line that Gerry Helleiner draws in Chapter 4. Crossing this line violates sovereignty. Yet, while doing so is one of the skeletons in aid's closet, it is also, in the end, its implicit objective. By withholding loans international donors hold leaders hostage – Yeltsin in Russia and Bhutto in Pakistan – and one might properly argue that the policies of international lending institutions have effectively kept the Yeltsin regime in check. They certainly had a significant hand in deposing Madame Bhutto. While overstepping its prerogatives, the international donor community has nonetheless prevented the populations in Russia and Pakistan from suffering more than they might otherwise have done.

The broad theme of this book can be summed up thus: development assistance is an ongoing experiment, a terrain of policy inventions. From this perspective, many of aid's failures may appear as positive steps in an experimental process. In a recent monograph, Roger Riddell assumes a position that has become only too familiar among the critics of foreign aid. He chides aid for its contradictions and for having too many objectives. Aid, he says, has become so laden with aspirations that it satisfies no one (Riddell, 1996). Nothing could be truer, and yet the diversity of aid's agendas, while betraying a lack of consistency and the meddling of too many chefs, is its strength, since it is through these objectives that well-meaning planners invest their highest ideals in the process. No one project is simultaneously capable of preparing a traditional economy for a market, pulling large numbers of households out of a poverty trap, increasing the productivity of crops and local industry, balancing benefits between the genders, and promoting good governance and human rights at regional and national levels. But development assistance will weather these contradictions and eventually benefit from trying many different strategies to see how they work. This is how experiments proceed: the evolution of ideas thrives on diversity. The aid game, confused and scattered as it is, builds a base of possible dénouements that widen the scope of its possibilities.

Paradoxically, many of aid's failings have potential for creating something that has never existed: some form of world government. Evolutionary paths are strewn with the detritus from trials and errors; the process is wasteful and inefficient. But the evolution of an idea or an organism feeds on the multiplication of possibilities.

As the bulk of international economic transactions grows, there is the risk that they will dwarf national ones and progressively displace aid regimes. Development assistance from national agencies may then decline, not only in scale but also in stature and reputation, and as the world obsession with competitiveness continues unabated, the place of civic consciousness risks shrinking into a small and renegade idea. This is an unsavoury prospect. The idea of a global civic consciousness needs to stay mainstream, and aid is the vehicle by which the globalization juggernaut will be tempered and eventually reigned in, the medium in which a global consciousness may grow.

After nearly two decades of teaching courses on development issues, I began to sense that the hope that fuels the urge driving many of us to teach and practise development was waning. What was once a healthy and critical dialogue had turned into a perpetual chronicle of inadequacies that was devouring the subject. Students who came to the subject with a reformer's enthusiasm found themselves caught up in the critiques, became fluent in them, and soon convinced themselves that the subject was too flawed to hold their interest. I could hardly blame them when they turned away from development issues and issues of world poverty and focused their political energies on protesting against student fee hikes or people mowing their lawns.

Cynicism shrouds the very idea of development. Ironically, the most vocal cynics have often been those who, in a previous decade, were development's most ardent proponents. Robert Chambers (1983: 30) has rightly noted the inclination among academics to find fault, since they are more commonly rewarded for showing why projects fail to work than for showing why they do. Progressive academics who once demanded more international empathy from the Cold War bullies now make up a condemning chorus that finds in foreign aid a mechanism for marginalizing the weak and for imposing an unwarranted modernism on societies that ought better to articulate their own path of growth. The truth is that this chorus of critics includes, as ever, the noble reformers, and in dismantling what they often call the hegemony of development they are in search of more sympathetic alternatives. But all of the accounts that show how development programs targeted the wrong people or came at the wrong season or forgot one or another crucial features have amounted, in the end, to a radical dismembering of the concern for others which development originally embodied. Pulled here and there by progressive academics seeking profound explanations for why development ventures are failures or elitist or both, the entire enterprise has fallen into general disrepute.

The existing corpus of reading for students leads them to see in the development field only misguided activity. They are frequently presented with enticingly provocative critiques of the notion of progress which identify an intriguing connection between development and the concept of trusteeship or imperial ownership (Crush, 1995; Cowen and Shenton, 1996). Students enjoy reading these lively intellectual artisans who link development theory to a dynasty of now discredited ideas.

This persuasive corpus ends up, inadvertently perhaps, aligning with the conventional old-line isolationists who argue that welfare of any kind, national or international, amounts to little more than throwing hard-earned money at people who languish in the Dark Ages. The very notion of development has thus become ever more beleaguered. My discomfort has grown as I watch, year after year, the fresh idealism that students bring to the development courses turn to chagrin. It was time for a book that offered a hopeful prospect.

Hence the optimistic tenor of the present volume, which takes the side of development assistance. If this means defending or redefining aid, so be it. These essays and the experiments they describe are the raw material for the development imagination and the window through which the outlines of an international polity are barely visible.

To choose this path of guarded optimism is to assume a burden that others avoid and perhaps for good reason, for it carries the challenge of devising innovative strategies, of demonstrating not only the logic but a viable practice for keeping humanitarian aid alive. In some instances this involves showing how the increased level of global monetary flows can be pressed into the service of traditional aid schemes. Keith Griffin's chapter, as well as that of Roy Culpeper, outlines both the logic and viable strategies for such efforts. Others chapters, such as that of Ian Smillie, contribute a candid appraisal of how non-governmental organizations (NGOs) can participate in maintaining or even improving the efficacy of aid. By providing a lucid appraisal of the costs of surrounding aid with economic and political conditions, Gerry Helleiner justifies the doubts many of us have about using aid to meddle in local politics.

Each chapter inspects a dilemma or an anomaly within development's endeavours and, in lieu of charting how countervailing trends are pulling aid apart, casts about for ways of keeping it together. In lamenting the fate of compassion as a factor in formulating Canadian aid policy, Cranford Pratt appeals for a policy dialogue that will keep it alive. Similarly, Sue Horton and Ann Germain examine the declining reputation of food aid, and while appreciating the logic of food aid's detractors, convincingly prove its value. Norman Uphoff's account of how rethinking the sociology of watercourse committees did as much as physical structures in making water flow in Sri Lanka argues for the complementarity of hard and soft sciences. The mandate for each of the chapters has been to offer conceptual tools, step by step and subject by subject, for fitting development thinking more effectively to the tasks it must perform.

The chapters are arranged around seven themes which, although they may not exhaust every teacher's wish list of issues that courses should cover or every thinker's favourite topics, nonetheless cover a wide range.

The first section chronicles Canada's contributions to development assistance. All donors, and Canada is typical, straddle an ever-widening fault line between serving national interests of trade and security and preserving the aims of humane internationalism. The question is whether, in spite of the compromises made to strategically reconcile these countervailing mandates, Canada can preserve the humanitarian integrity of aid.

The second section addresses two issues raised by structural adjustment schemes. One is whether the reliance on international trade, which structural adjustment schemes promote, is capable of bringing benefits to all players. The other asks whether the political conditions that adjustment schemes impose are advisable and questions the extent to which aid ought to be used as an inducement for political change.

The third section scans the development assistance horizon for alternatives to state-based donor bureaucracies.

The fourth section asks whether private flows can serve the public spirit of foreign aid. As private flows of trade and investment increasingly overshadow the flows of public funds for development assistance, the question of whether they can deliver the kind of distributive justice aid aimed to provide inevitably arises.

The fifth section addresses a central question in development theory – whether social capital can have economic pay-offs – and in asking it, challenges development programs to pay attention to the reciprocal effects between distribution and growth, equity and affluence.

The sixth section offers a common-sense appraisal of the spectacular claims made for participatory approaches to development research.

The seventh and concluding section examines two sectors, commodity food aid and information technology, and shows why they have risen to such importance in the controversy over the future of foreign aid.

PART ONE

The Canadian Context

Chapters 1 and 2 examine development assistance policies in Canada. They appear at the beginning in part because Canadian aid is the turf from which many of the contributors are writing but also because the broad range of inconsistencies that makes the Canadian tradition one of the most perplexing also provides a fine mirror for the perplexities of aid globally. Canadian aid traditionally has sought, ever so characteristically, to be everything to everyone. Each donor can find a piece of its own tradition in the Canadian experience and every scholar's special insight can find confirmation in Canada's example.

David Morrison's chronicle of the history of foreign aid in Canada charts Canada's commitment over five decades, from its role as a founding member in the 1960s of what would eventually become the Development Assistance Committee (DAC) of the Organization for Economic Cooperation and Development (OECD), to the wave of support generated by Pierre Trudeau in the seventies, to the deep cuts behind the sophistry of Jean Chrétien's policy in the nineties. Above all, Morrison's chapter shows how difficult it is to characterize Canada's stance, falling as it does between the muscle of the United States and the conscience of the Scandinavians, between the World Bank's structural adjustment regimes and the non-governmental organization community's appeal for support to social welfare.

There are themes in this history nevertheless: a sluggish bureaucracy, the neglect of public opinion, and the ongoing tug between domestic politics and international pressures. Students of Canadian policy will find in Morrison's history of Canadian aid an ideal scaffolding for piecing together the fifty years of Canada's development agenda, with its high-minded ideals and contradictions.

One theme, in particular, resonates throughout: aid decisions, in Canada and elsewhere, are pinched between the self-serving program of promoting national interests and the charitable goal of making up for the gross differences in affluence throughout the world. The contradictory pull between the pursuit of national security and humane internationalism, can be detected in every development assistance decision. As Cranford Pratt demonstrates, aid is stuck between these two agendas, especially in Canada. The first asks aid to act as a cover for strategies to strengthen Canada's trade, to better position Canadian commercial interests and, to some extent, to strengthen national security. The second preserves the integrity of aid by committing resources to international concerns of poverty, literacy, gender equality, and care for the environment. Cranford Pratt reviews the arguments and charts the trajectory of foreign aid through these troubled waters over the last few years. His analysis has required a surgeon's care, for the space between the two arguments is constantly shifting and the shifts are themselves riddled with ambiguous pronouncements. Pratt's analysis guides us through a labyrinth of positions, warning of diversions whose claims may seduce the unwary. His own stance throughout is clear: the integrity of aid must be preserved, by keeping the aid agenda as committed as possible to compassionate humanitarian objectives.

1

Canadian Aid: A Mixed Record and an Uncertain Future

DAVID R. MORRISON

The transfer of capital and expertise from industrial country donors to developing country recipients through official development assistance (ODA) has been a noble but flawed means of promoting economic and social development and overcoming global poverty. The enterprise has had to contend with colossal human and biophysical challenges and vastly unequal relations of wealth and power. In addition, donor governments have undermined the effectiveness of their foreign aid by pursuing multiple and often conflicting objectives – political and commercial as well as humanitarian. Aid agencies have also been buffeted by internal conflicts and organizational constraints, as well as by pressures from elsewhere in government, from domestic business and other non-governmental interests, and from a shifting transnational discourse on development. As Jim Freedman observes in his introduction, the deficiencies of development assistance have led some to call for its demise. However, there have been successes as well as failures and, as Freedman and the others in this volume argue, there are still manifest needs for non-market resource transfers to support the development efforts of the world's poorest peoples and countries.

This chapter reviews Canada's mixed record in channelling ODA to developing countries – including a decline in the comparative generosity it once exhibited – and summarizes efforts to explain that performance.[1]

Five Decades of Canadian ODA: Growth and Decline

Prior to 1950 only a handful of Canadians had worked or travelled in what became known as the Third World – missionaries and their families and even smaller numbers of government, business, and military personnel. Not many more had even indirect contact with what were seen as distant and exotic lands. It was during the Liberal government of Louis St Laurent (1948–57) that Canada first became involved in what would become known as government-to-government or bilateral development assistance. Canadian officials (including Lester Pearson, who was then secretary of state for external affairs) attended the conference in 1950 that initiated the Colombo Plan for Cooperative Economic Development in South and Southeast Asia. The objectives of containing communism and transforming the British colonial empire into a multiracial Commonwealth of Nations, tempered by political caution and fiscal parsimony, resulted in modest capital and technical support for the new Commonwealth states of the Indian subcontinent. Canada's active involvement in UN agencies had already led to some multilateral assistance for refugee relief and training programs with even more constrained funding levels.

A variety of transitory arrangements were made for administering Canadian aid in the 1950s, when it was assumed that the activity would be as temporary as the Marshall Plan in post-war Europe. Total spending in 1955–6 on what was subsequently defined as ODA was $29.4 million. An application backwards to that year of the 1970 convention for measuring a donor country's aid effort – the percentage of its gross national product (GNP) expended on ODA – yields a figure of 0.10 per cent.

Canadian participation in aid efforts expanded slowly in the face of mounting pressure from the United States and the old colonial powers to assume a greater share of development assistance efforts. In 1960 Canada was a founding member of what became the Development Assistance Committee (DAC) of the Organization for Economic Cooperation and Development (OECD). That same year, the Canadian government set up a small External Aid Office attached to the Department of External Affairs. Supportive initially, Conservative Prime Minister John Diefenbaker (1957–63) resented insinuations that Canada was shouldering less than its fair share of international obligations. Aid reached $73.5 million in 1960–1 – 0.20 per cent of GNP – but then slipped to $57.7 million, or 0.13 per cent, in 1962–3. Meanwhile, after initially concentrating on Britain's ex-colonies in Asia, the program became more widely dispersed in the late 1950s among emerging Commonwealth countries in Africa and the Caribbean. In 1961, in response to French Canadian criticism of this Anglo bias, a modest technical assistance program was launched in francophone Africa. Elsewhere, the mainstays of the program were infrastructural projects in the fields of energy and transportation, food and commodity aid and (to a lesser extent) provision of technical expertise, education, and training.

After 1963 Prime Minister Lester Pearson's Liberal government responded to the challenge of international development more vigorously and growth was rapid. Popular support, largely on humanitarian grounds, was also rising. By 1966–7 ODA stood at $212.9 million (0.34 per cent of GNP). Bilateral aid was extended to more Commonwealth countries and the program in francophone Africa was expanded, first as an explicit component of the government's policy of biculturalism and bilingualism and then in the late 1960s, when the region became a major diplomatic battleground in the conflict between Ottawa and Quebec over the provincial government's ambitions for international recognition.[2]

From a cautious and tight-fisted participant in the 1950s, Canada emerged as an active supporter of multilateral assistance in the 1960s, as the federal government realized that multilateralism could be pursued in the sphere of aid as well as security. Ottawa became a key player in the International Development Association of the World Bank, regional development banks, and UN agencies. Canada went on to rank highly within DAC in the breadth of its institutional commitment and in the share of its ODA channelled multilaterally (typically between 30 and 40 per cent).

Pierre Trudeau, Pearson's successor as Liberal prime minister in 1968, made a number of stirring appeals for an enlightened response to the plight of the world's poor and disadvantaged. Shortly after his victory in the 1968 federal election, he proclaimed: 'Never before in history has the disparity between the rich and the poor, the comfortable and the starving, been so extreme; never before have mass communications so vividly informed the sufferers of the extent of their misery ... We are faced with an overwhelming challenge. In meeting it, the world must be our constituency.'[3]

One of Trudeau's early actions was to upgrade the External Aid Office into the Canadian International Development Agency (CIDA), which still reported to the secretary of state for external affairs but now through a president with the rank of deputy minister. With the formation of CIDA as a distinct entity came the desire to play a leading role in shaping all aspects of Canada's relations with developing countries, not simply aid policy. Although the agency repeatedly lost skirmishes to extend its influence beyond the realm of aid delivery and has always had to accommodate pressures from elsewhere in government, it did achieve considerable relative autonomy over programs within its own sphere of operations.

From 1968 to the mid-1970s CIDA oversaw a substantial increase in aid volume, expansion into Latin America, and dramatic growth in the number of countries receiving bilateral assistance in Africa, Asia, and the Caribbean. Several new initiatives were launched, including two that have been justly praised as distinctively Canadian contributions to aid programming: the International Development Research Centre, with its pioneering commitment to promote indigenous research capabilities within developing countries, and responsive funding mechanisms to tap the energy and experience and encourage the growth of non-governmental organizations (NGOs) committed to international development.[4] Within the bilateral sphere infrastructural projects still predominated, but more attention was being paid to agriculture and social problems. In 1970 Canada promised to make steady progress towards the target for donor countries endorsed by the UN General Assembly that year – 0.7 per cent of GNP. By 1975–6 total Canadian aid was $903.5 million, representing an ODA/GNP ratio of 0.53 per cent.

In the latter half of the 1970s Ottawa was preoccupied politically by the threat of Quebec's secession and economically by the 'stagflation' that gripped Western economies following dislocations in the postwar monetary system, the OPEC oil shock of 1973, and the challenge of newly industrializing countries in Asia and Latin America. Many developing countries suffered serious setbacks as well, and their collective efforts to achieve reforms in international trading and financial arrangements foundered amid an increasingly bitter 'North-South dialogue.'

Among donor countries of the North there was increasing scepticism about whether aid was contributing to economic growth and poverty reduction. Canada (where this concern was exacerbated by some bad press for CIDA)[5] joined other DAC members in cutting back development assistance and seeking from it more tangible economic and political returns for domestic interests. While aid discourse was now more focused on basic human needs and rural development, most bilateral programming was still channelled into major infrastructural projects. Canada's annual ODA spending amid rapid inflation rose above a billion dollars (reaching $1,282.5 million in 1979–80), but with a downward trend in the ODA/GNP ratio. After Trudeau's defeat in

1979, Joe Clark's short-lived Conservative government continued to project increases below the rate of inflation. Canadian ODA in 1980–1 was $1,308.1 million, which represented a fall to 0.43 per cent of GNP.

This trajectory was reversed when Trudeau returned to power in 1980. Although his government's domestic agenda was a weighty one (including the first Quebec referendum, patriation of the constitution, and the National Energy Program), he attempted to use Canada's seat in the G-7 to revive North-South negotiations. His efforts failed in the face of intransigent opposition from Margaret Thatcher and Ronald Reagan. To demonstrate the seriousness of Canada's commitment to international development, however, his government pledged to restore progress towards the UN target, to get back to 0.5 per cent by 1985, and to make best efforts to achieve 0.7 per cent by 1990. Despite cutbacks in the aid budget during the deep recession of 1982–3, Canada's ODA climbed above the $2 billion mark, reaching $2,104.6 million or 0.49 per cent of GNP in 1984–5. Meanwhile, though programming priorities continued to change more slowly than policy discourse, non-governmental organizations (NGOs) and institutions (NGIs) became more prominent in the delivery of projects oriented to basic human needs and human resource development.

Just before he retired in 1984 Trudeau promised that Canada would reach the 0.7 per cent threshold by 1990–1. When Brian Mulroney's Conservatives won the federal election later that year, both the new prime minister and Joe Clark, now secretary of state for external affairs, affirmed the commitment. It was almost immediately repudiated. Looking for ways of bringing down the federal deficit, the Tory government set back the date for achieving 0.7 to 1995, with an interim goal of 0.6 per cent in 1990. In 1986 each of these targets was deferred a further five years. At a time of public concern about deepening economic and social crisis in Africa and escalating debt in Latin America, however, Joe Clark fought successfully to keep funding pegged to the 0.5 per cent level during Mulroney's first term. As a result, aid spending rose to almost $3 billion in 1988–9 ($2,946.6 million) and the ratio kept pace with rising GNP (0.49 per cent).

Major infrastructural projects were now in disfavour, as Canada joined other donors in focusing more of its declining ODA budget on human resource development, capacity building, and support for the structural adjustment agendas of the World Bank and the International Monetary Fund. Women in Development and environmental sustainability also received considerable attention, and a 1987 review of Cana-

dian aid policy by a House of Commons committee chaired by William
Winegard pushed hard for a more focused emphasis on helping the
world's poorest countries and peoples. The government agreed with
the committee's call for an ODA Charter based on the principles of
putting poverty first, helping people to help themselves, and ensuring
that development priorities prevail.[6]

After the Tories' re-election in 1988 development assistance became a
prime target for spending cuts in the name of deficit reduction, and foreign aid was slashed more heavily than other federal program spending. An absolute decrease in 1989–90 was followed by sub-inflationary
increases in the two years that followed. Official development assistance reached a current dollar high of $3,182.5 million in 1991–2 before
the axe fell more heavily. Canada was now in a deep recession, public
opinion polls revealed growing support for cuts in government expenditures to bring down the federal deficit, and foreign aid ranked high
on the hit list. There were renewed efforts to make the aid program
serve commercial and foreign policy goals more fully, and the ODA
Charter became virtually a dead letter.[7] The final three years of spending plans developed by the Conservative government produced year-
over-year reductions. By 1992–3, ODA had fallen back to $2972.7 and a
ratio of 0.44 per cent of GNP.

By the early 1990s the end of the Cold War had changed the global
context of aid relations dramatically: with the geopolitical rationale
for ODA diminished, the relevance and efficacy of foreign aid were
increasingly questioned, and former Soviet bloc countries became competitors for scarce concessional capital. Politics emerged from the closet
as donors made more bilateral assistance conditional upon recipients'
performance in the spheres of human rights, democratization, and
'good governance' (often a surrogate for downsizing the state to make
way for market reform). Private sector development and, with a profu-
sion of contested meanings, 'sustainable development' also became
watchwords in the 1990s.

Elected in 1993, the Liberal government of Jean Chrétien authorized
much deeper cuts to the aid budget as part of its larger deficit-fighting
strategy. Nevertheless, it still proclaimed a commitment 'to making
progress towards the ODA target of 0.7% of GNP when Canada's fiscal
situation allows it.'[8] That bit of sophistry coincided with the February
1995 budget of Finance Minister Paul Martin Jr, which reduced international assistance by 20.5 per cent over three years (including an immediate cut of 15 per cent). A year later Martin's budget announced a

further massive reduction of $150 million in 1998–9 that would take ODA down below the $2 billion level.[9]

Following renewed growth in the Canadian economy and the Chrétien government's re-election in 1997 Martin's 1998 budget projected a zero deficit for the following year and the prospect of fiscal surpluses thereafter. Nonetheless, despite a slight reprieve in the severity of cuts scheduled for 1998–9 and thereafter, the ODA/GNP ratio – which had already tumbled to 0.30 per cent in 1997–8[10] – is projected to fall to 0.26 per cent in 1999–2000,[11] little more than half the level at the beginning of the 1990s and below that of any year since 1965–6. Deduction of various items not counted as ODA before 1980 yields an even more accurate figure for historical comparison – about 0.20 per cent, which would be the lowest since 1963–4.[12] Ironically, that was the year that Paul Martin's father, then secretary of state for external affairs, announced the Pearson government's commitment to a rapidly growing aid program.[13]

Jean-Philippe Thérien characterized Canada's 'singularity' among Western donors as arising 'from its lying between the G7 and the like-minded nations in its commitment to development co-operation.'[14] After 1975, however, its proportional effort had become more aligned to the G-7, which Canada joined on American prompting in 1976, than to 'like-minded' Denmark, Norway, Sweden, and the Netherlands. All of these countries went on to contribute more than 0.8 per cent of GNP to development assistance, sometimes reaching 1.0 per cent. Canada's ODA/GNP ratio of 0.53 per cent in 1975–6 was the highest ever attained.[15]

Throughout the 1980s, Canada was a middling to generous donor in comparison with other industrial countries. It was not alone in cutting back in the 1990s but, as Freedman notes, the free fall was staggering by comparison with other donors, except for the United States and Japan.[16] From a respectable fifth within the OECD in ODA volume in the mid-1980s, Canada dropped to ninth in 1996 before recovering to seventh in 1997, well behind the much smaller Netherlands and Sweden and barely ahead of Denmark. Comparative data for 1999 may reveal an even more dramatic collapse in proportional effort, from sixth among the twenty-one DAC members in ODA/GNP ratio as late as 1994 to perhaps eleventh or twelfth just five years later.[17] Canada's per capita ODA contribution of $US 64 in 1996–7 was less than one-quarter of the average of the Nordic countries, and a mere thirteenth among DAC donors.[18]

Mixed and Multiple Objectives

Successive Canadian governments have proclaimed the importance of humanitarianism as a foundation for Canadian aid. Most recently, *Canada in the World*, the Chrétien administration's 1995 policy statement, called international assistance 'one of the clearest international expressions of *Canadian values and culture* – of Canadians' desire to help the less fortunate and of their strong sense of social justice – and an effective means of sharing these values with the rest of the world.'[19] In common with previous official efforts to justify Canada's involvement in international development, however, the 1995 statement was made in the context of mixed humanitarian, political, and commercial rationales.

Some political objectives have already been mentioned: anti-communism, promotion of Commonwealth ties to supplant older colonial ones, and assertion of Ottawa's foreign policy supremacy over Quebec. Although successive Canadian governments have seldom used development assistance to secure international support for a specific foreign policy objective (the effort to court francophone African support for the federal government's constitutional agenda stands out as the major exception), they have pursued other, more general objectives, such as enhancing Canada's prestige and goodwill in both industrial and developing countries, augmenting its capacity and influence as an 'honest broker,' and promoting multilateralism. At various times (especially in Central America in the 1980s and in Cuba in the 1970s and 1990s), the aid program has been a vehicle for conveying a sense of difference from U.S. foreign policy.

Meanwhile, the justification of aid as a means of promoting international security, which had Cold War overtones until the collapse of communism, has been refashioned into the notion of 'common security.' In *Canada in the World*, the Chrétien government asserted that international assistance 'contributes to *global security* by tackling many key threats to human security, such as the abuse of human rights, disease, environmental degradation, population growth and the widening gap between rich and poor.'[20]

Seldom advanced as a primary rationale, the benefits of aid for the Canadian economy have always been strongly promoted by business and from within government, especially by trade ministers and officials. A paper prepared by the Department of Trade and Commerce in 1968 summarized what by then had become conventional wisdom. If aid succeeded, there would be long-term benefits for the Canadian economy: 'the Third World will be wealthier, will purchase more, and will offer a larger commercial market for Canadian exports.' Moreover, beyond short-term benefits for individual firms and sectors supplying goods and services for overseas projects, foreign assistance had the potential to stimulate the development of new products and skills, give Canadian enterprise international experience, smooth out 'the peaks and troughs in demand at home and abroad for particular goods and services,' and relieve depressed industries and regions.[21] Food aid was quite explicitly seen and defended as a mechanism for stimulating an ailing agricultural economy and disposing of mounting domestic surpluses, especially in the 1950s and 1960s.[22]

During the stagflation of the late 1970s, the government, with business support, increased pressure on the ODA program to deliver commercial returns, emphasizing stronger long-term 'mutually beneficial bilateral relationships between our developing partners and Canada.'[23] A persistent theme thereafter, it was pushed vigorously in recessionary periods, especially during Brian Mulroney's second Conservative administration from 1988 to 1993. In 1995, *Canada in the World* called development assistance 'an investment in *prosperity and employment*. It connects the Canadian economy to some of the world's fastest growing markets ... And, in the long run, development cooperation can help lift the developing countries out of poverty. This means that it contributes to a stronger global economy in which Canadian and other peoples can grow and prosper.'[24]

Terms and Conditions: Divergent Impulses

The contradictions of simultaneously pursuing humanitarian, political, and commercial objectives can be seen in the terms and conditions attached to Canadian bilateral assistance. Two important indicators of aid quality are its impact on long-term indebtedness and the extent to which ODA is tied to procurement of goods and services in the donor country. In Canada's case, generous, concessional terms of aid have been accompanied by stringency on procurement tying.

Prescient about the dangers of debt in the early years, Canadian policy makers extended most assistance in the form of grants. A loan program was added in the mid-1960s, but with very 'soft' terms – no interest, and repayment over fifty years with a ten-year grace period. Accounting for half of the bilateral program in 1969–70, lending gradually declined to under 10 per cent by the mid-1980s; even in 1970, the grant element of total Canadian aid was 94 per cent,[25] a level equalled or exceeded thereafter. ODA was put on an all-grants basis for least-developed countries in 1977 and all others in 1986. As debt strangulation deepened in the 1980s, the government took steps to forgive the aid-related debts of most African, Caribbean, and Latin American recipients. Unlike some other donors, Canada has always been in compliance with DAC-approved norms for concessionality.[26]

In response to criticisms that tied aid inflates costs for uncompetitive goods and services and skews development priorities by restricting projects to what donors are prepared to supply, politicians and senior bureaucrats have defended the practice as a means of securing domestic business support for ODA and demonstrating to the public that aid dollars create jobs in Canada.

In the early years, the program was completely tied to the purchase and use of Canadian goods and services, and recipient countries were even required to cover all shipping costs. Some flexibility was allowed on local and shipping costs in 1966. When aid was examined in the context of the Trudeau government's foreign policy review in 1969–70, academic experts urged greater latitude and the government agreed to cover shipping costs and untie up to 20 per cent of bilateral allocations. Subsequently, reflecting DAC and recipient country pressure, CIDA's *Strategy for International Development Co-operation, 1975–1980* promised to open up development loans to competition from developing country suppliers.[27] Intense business opposition soon scuttled that commitment.

A related issue came to the fore over the next few years, when Canadian firms exhorted the government to compete more forcefully with other Western countries that were blending concessional ODA with commercial export loans (*crédit mixte*) to secure major contracts in developing countries. After considerable energy was expended on this issue, plans to set up an 'aid-trade' mechanism within CIDA were abandoned when ODA growth was cut back in 1986. Concessional finance provided through the Export Development Corporation to ODA-eligible countries was subsequently counted as part of Canada's official development assistance, though amounts were modest amid a general scaling back of this sort of activity (which was opposed by the Unitd States as an inappropriate form of subsidization). Instead, increasing energy went into promotion of CIDA's Industrial Cooperation Program (INC) and other forms of support for Canadian firms seeking investment opportunities and private sector linkages in developing countries and contracts from the World Bank and other multilateral agencies. INC grew rapidly in the 1980s and was hit less by cutbacks than other programs in the 1990s.

Meanwhile, throughout the 1970s and 1980s Canada's posture on tied aid was criticized by parliamentarians, development specialists, non-governmental organizations, and DAC. While a generally poor record for supplying competitive inputs had improved, especially after a dwindling of efforts to use ODA for dumping surplus steel rails and railway equipment, extensive tying was seen as inappropriate at a time when CIDA, like other donor agencies, was being urged to devote more attention to meeting basic human needs and less to physical infrastructure. The searching review of the aid program by the Winegard committee urged relaxation of the 80 per cent rule to permit higher levels of local expenditure and developing country procurement. In response, the Conservative government agreed in 1988 to lower untying levels (though only for local purchases), especially for sub-Saharan Africa and least developed countries elsewhere. Recent comparative figures have pegged Canada somewhat closer to though still well short of the DAC average.[28]

CIDA avoided other forms of conditionality until the late 1980s, when it joined the donor community in supporting economic policy reforms advocated by the World Bank and the International Monetary Fund. Increasing proportions of bilateral aid to seriously indebted countries, especially in Africa, were made conditional upon acceptance and implementation of structural adjustment programs that pushed for open markets, less government, and 'getting the prices right.' This conversion to neo-liberal orthodoxy provoked intense criticism on both economic and social grounds, especially for the negative impact of adjustment on the poorest and most vulnerable. Many in the non-governmental development community in Canada were especially incensed.

The human rights performance of recipient governments became a concern among development activists in the 1970s. Three parliamentary committees between 1982 and 1987 challenged Canadian authorities to withdraw or curtail ODA allocations in cases of serious abuse and to use aid as a tool for human rights development. External Affairs and CIDA resisted explicit sanctions at first, fearing diplomatic and commercial repercussions and arguing that a loss of aid would hurt victims more than repressive governments. The Mulroney administration agreed, however, to set up the International Centre for Human Rights and Democratic Development as an arm's-length Crown corporation (it began operations in 1990) and to make human rights a 'top priority' of ODA policy. While human rights, democracy, and good governance became programming priorities for CIDA as well in the early 1990s, Canada's record on aid/human rights conditionality has remained uneven and controversial.[29]

Choice of Recipient Countries: A Global Reach[30]

Like terms and conditions, the choice of recipient countries is a crucial determinant of ODA effectiveness. Two issues are particularly important: first, though with no guarantee of success, potential impact is greater if resources are concentrated in selected countries rather than widely dispersed; second, the poorest countries with the weakest capacity to mobilize resources from internal and international markets are in greatest need of concessional transfers. In comparative terms, Canada has a weak record on concentration and a better-than-average one on assisting the poorest countries. Again, we see the historical interplay of political and commercial objectives mixed with humanitarian and developmental ones.

Rapid proliferation of assisted countries in the 1960s and early 1970s occurred through a combination of accident and design, the joint product of a growing aid budget, and an underlying political calculus – the Commonwealth-plus in Asia, a balance between Commonwealth and francophone states in Africa, and Commonwealth and broader responsibilities within the Americas. The use of ODA as a 'diplomatic calling-card'[31] to stake out a visible presence in a large number of countries was common enough among most donors. For Canada, however, this wide dispersal also meant a low degree of concentration on a designated group of priority recipients.[32]

From the mid-1970s onwards, repeated attempts to achieve greater concentration met resistance from politicians and diplomats who were worried about damaging existing relations and keen to take on new challenges. Moreover, as Martin Rudner noted, there were as well new pressures from 'influential domestic constituencies, ranging from export interests to immigrant communities and internationally-oriented associations and institutions, who tend to demand aid for countries of interest to themselves.'[33]

Even though the choice of recipients had little to do with levels of development, large initial allocations to the Indian subcontinent and subsequent expansion to former British and French colonies in sub-Saharan Africa tilted bilateral allocations towards low-income countries. When donors became increasingly accountable on these matters – because of the plight of the least developed and those most affected by the energy and food crises of the early 1970s – Canada was able to show that the bulk of its ODA went to the poorest countries.

Efforts by CIDA planners to entrench this as policy and to secure a more development-oriented eligibility framework were challenged by other bureaucrats who wanted aid programming to respond more fully to commercial and diplomatic priorities. The conflict yielded a compromise in the late 1970s – a two-track approach that maintained the commitment to the poorest countries but focused more energy on strengthening Canada's long-term economic relations with middle-income countries and other high-growth economies, especially in East and Southeast Asia. After a subsequent increase in the share of Canadian aid channelled to these better-off countries the distribution of bilateral aid by country income level remained fairly stable. However, cutbacks in the 1990s reduced total Canadian ODA to the world's least-developed countries from 0.15 per cent of GNP in the mid-1980s to a mere 0.08 per cent in 1997.[34]

Programming Priorities: Chasing Fashions

All public policy domains exhibit fads, fashions, and pendulum swings, and foreign aid, far from being an exception, has been especially prone to frequent twists and turns. To some extent, the changes have been driven by a well-meaning desire to find workable and relatively simple solutions for complex human, social, and material problems, and to do so in a hurry. Continually changing priorities have also reflected sweeping global changes, altered ideological assumptions, shifts in political and commercial objectives, and efforts to make development assistance more saleable to sceptical taxpayers. Often failing to stay the course as they have flitted about from one priority to another and taken on more and more responsibilities, aid agencies have undermined their own credibility and, more importantly, their professed efforts to achieve sustainable development.

Like other donors, but with more alacrity than most,[35] CIDA has associated itself with the new fashions and policy thrusts mentioned above: physical infrastructure, food and commodity aid, and technical assistance in the early years; agriculture and social development in the late 1960s; the poorest countries and basic human needs in the 1970s; human resource development, poverty alleviation, structural adjustment, women and development, and the environment in the 1980s; and sustainability, private sector development, and human rights/democracy/good governance in the 1990s.

Although Canada frequently experienced both time lags and marked discrepancies between policy declarations and the reality of project implementation, there have been exceptions. In both rhetoric and practice, CIDA has been a leader internationally in the development of responsive programming by non-governmental organizations and institutions and in the sphere of women in development and gender analysis. As one of two major food donors (along with the United States), Canada has also been at the forefront of efforts to develop, with varying success, an approach to food aid that contributes positively to development and food security rather than encouraging dependency. In addition, though many new priorities in the 1980s and 1990s led to a less-focused effort overall, programming in the field was substantially reoriented from conventional infrastructure projects to an emphasis on human resource development, capacity building, and poverty reduction.

Explaining Canadian ODA

Developmentalist critiques written from a policy-oriented perspective have tried to understand the uneven impact of Canadian ODA on the promotion of economic and social development in recipient countries. Much of the answer lies, of course, in unequal global relations of wealth and power, and all of the complex economic, political, social, and biophysical challenges in the developing countries themselves. Developmentalists claim, however, that the risks of development assistance – not least its inherent cultural arrogance – have been compounded by the many and often conflicting ambitions that Canada and other aid donors have sought to realize through their aid programs.[36]

The question of what drives multiple expectations and other aspects of ODA policy making in Canada has been the subject of considerable scholarly debate, chiefly between proponents of two schools of thought – statist and dominant class. The statist perspective argues that development policy tends to reflect the preferences of political leaders and senior bureaucrats rather than those of recipient countries or non-state domestic actors such as business and NGOs. A leading proponent of this view, Kim Richard Nossal, has contended that the aid program is shaped not by humanitarian, political, and commercial motives but rather by the pursuit of prestige, organizational maintenance, and the limitation of public expenditures.[37]

The dominant class approach, rooted in Marxist and neo-Marxist analysis, agrees that foreign aid has served many purposes and that state actors have dominated decision making. However, its advocates assert that ODA has been primarily an instrument for supporting the globalization of capitalist relations of production and entrenching the wealth, power, and privilege of dominant classes in both North and South. Cranford Pratt has been the most prolific analyst of Canadian ODA policy making over the past thirty years. Now professor emeritus of political science at the University of Toronto, he has been a persistent critic of the 'reluctance of the government of Canada, a comparatively liberal and humane country, to respond to ethical concerns as fully as public opinion would permit in its development assistance and other policies relating to global poverty.'[38] His position is well illustrated in Chapter 2, where he demonstrates the considerable role national security plays in the formulation of Canadian development policy. Though not a Marxist and receptive to some statist assumptions, Pratt has argued that the dominant class thesis offers the most convincing explanation of Canada's relations with developing countries.[39]

This author agrees that statist and dominant class perspectives have provided valuable insights, not least of which is their rejection of a pluralist model that views state officials as mere mediators among contending societal interests. Neither explanatory framework, however, is able to account for the complex history of Canadian foreign aid. Indeed, both fail to direct sufficient attention to the actual processes of political brokerage and interest mediation that have shaped multiple, often-conflicting objectives and policies and undermined the coherence of Canadian aid. These processes – state-societal, state-centred, and transnational – have in turn been mediated by organizational and managerial factors.

Domestic pressures from outside government have had more impact on the aid program than other aspects of foreign policy, or than Nossal and the statist perspective have recognized. State actors, as Pratt and others have argued, may in general defer to corporate hegemony but officials within CIDA have invested heavily in building up a strong voluntary sector that can provide political and programming support.

In the process they have become more responsive to lobbying by non-governmental organizations and institutions and have tried to balance demands from NGOs and NGIs with business interests, which have tended to focus more on obtaining funding and programming opportunities than on influencing policy (except where it directly affected their immediate interests, such as aid tying and *crédit mixte*).[40]

A focus on the black box of governmental politics is essential for understanding the history of Canadian aid policy making. Nossal's more general analysis of the interests of state actors, though consistent with an intrastate focus, yields little insight about the content of policies that reflect shifting patterns of conflict and cooperation within the bureaucracy, as well as occasional intervention from the political level. CIDA's junior position within the bureaucracy and a budget that makes it 'everybody's billion dollar baby'[41] have been key factors in muting developmental impulses within the agency, as aid officials have accommodated themselves to political and commercial objectives pursued by more powerful interests elsewhere in government.[42]

Writers employing 'regime analysis' have discussed the major impact upon DAC donors of an international aid regime whose 'principal teachers' have been the World Bank and USAID. In turn, DAC has provided bilateral donors with a locus for international networking, peer review, and collaborative policy making.[43] Consensus positions emerging from this constantly shifting, often contradictory, yet dominant transnational discourse have contributed to changing aid fashions and have also assisted aid agencies like CIDA to resist, to some degree, pressures to make ODA serve nondevelopmental objectives. For example, internationally developed principles and norms helped the agency move the policy for allocating food aid from surplus disposal to a more developmentally oriented strategy, and Canadians contributed to a DAC consensus on women in development that in turn energized work in that sphere within the agency.

Though with different nuances, the official donor consensus has coincided on certain aid priorities with what NGOs in Canada and elsewhere have seen as a progressive agenda for international development. Indeed, the transnational establishment has often been receptive to ideas and pressures from non-governmental activists. As a result, CIDA has been able to draw on both domestic and international support in promoting such priorities as poverty reduction, basic human needs, and women in development. In contrast, when World Bank/DAC and NGO perspectives became intensely polarized over structural adjustment and economic reform in the early 1990s, the agency lost voluntary sector support. Not coincidentally, though there were other reasons as well, CIDA became much more vulnerable in the early 1990s to domestic commercial and foreign policy pressures.[44]

Finally, aid policy cannot be explained simply by analysing political factors. Insights from organizational and managerial analysis remind us that constraints on developmental effectiveness imposed by multiple objectives, on top of the already formidable challenges of operating abroad in uncertain environments, have been compounded by organizational characteristics and dynamics. Inadequate clarity within the agency on what constitutes good development – together with an intensely individualistic institutional culture – have both reflected and reinforced a lack of organizational and programming coherence. Moreover, as Phillip Rawkins suggested, some academic criticisms of the gap between rhetoric and reality, or the time-lag between formulation and implementation of new donor orthodoxy, fail to appreciate that 'Development *theory* does not – except possibly at the macroeconomic level – translate readily into development assistance *policy,* let alone implementation of projects and programs ... [Implementation] is never a simple putting-into-practice of policy. It draws on the particular experiences, preferences and expertise, as well as the more immediate professional, bureaucratic and career concerns of those who will be responsible for programming.'[45]

At various times throughout CIDA's history disbursement pressures, regulatory controls emphasizing process over substance, overcentralization of decision making in Ottawa-Hull, the privatization of aid delivery, and inadequate evaluation have had a major impact on shaping the aid program and limiting its developmental effectiveness.[46]

Conclusion

All of these factors discussed above, together with severe budget cuts in recent years, help to explain why Canadian ODA, amid undoubted successes, has fallen short in helping the world's poorest people and countries. Nonetheless, while there is much to criticize about the historical record of development assistance, the need for ODA is as strong as ever, especially for countries and people who have limited access to other forms of capital. It is true that economic growth has been dramatic in parts of Asia and Latin America and that many developing countries have experienced remarkable improvements in health, life expectancy, and literacy. However, much of Africa remains desperately deprived, the gap between the world's richest and poorest people has widened alarmingly, and poverty and human insecurity – often amid abundance – are on the rise everywhere.

In 1970 the Trudeau government's white paper on development assistance proclaimed: 'a society concerned about poverty and development abroad will be concerned about poverty and development at home.' That statement was preceded by a corollary that, alas, appears more apt today: 'a society able to ignore poverty abroad will find it much easier to ignore it at home.'[47] As this author concluded in *Aid and Ebb Tide: A History of CIDA and Canadian Development Assistance*:

> Commitment to collective action ebbed with the end of the Cold War, the success of right-wing efforts to delegitimate the state as an instrument of human betterment, and the onset of a fiscal crisis that weakened the popular will to accept responsibility for the less fortunate at home and abroad. Now, as an obsession with deficit reduction gives way to the prospect of a fiscal surplus, there are strident calls for tax cuts, debt reduction, and reinvestment in domestic health care and education. Weaker voices remind us of the needs of the insecure and the disadvantaged in Canada and around the world, and of the commitment once made to channel a tiny but growing percentage of our national income to support people in developing countries in their efforts to achieve better lives for themselves and their children.[48]

Notes

1 The chapter draws heavily on David R. Morrison, *Aid and Ebb Tide: A History of CIDA and Canadian Development Assistance* (Waterloo: Wilfrid Laurier University Press in association with the North-South Institute, 1998), esp. the preface (xix), chap. 1 (1–26), and chap. 11 (425–52). Except where noted, the source for data on aid volume and ODA/GNP ratios is the Canadian International Development Agency (hereafter CIDA), Canadian Historical ODA System (data bank at CIDA headquarters in Hull).
2 For details, see Morrison, *Aid and Ebb Tide*, 75–9.
3 Notes for an Address by the Prime Minister to a Convocation Ceremony Marking the Diamond Jubilee of the University of Alberta, Edmonton, Alberta, 13 May 1968, 4.
4 See Morrison, *Aid and Ebb Tide*, 68–73.

5 See ibid., 135–41, 172–5.

6 CIDA, *Sharing Our Future* (Hull: Minister of Supply and Services, 1987), 23. *Sharing Our Future* was the government's strategy document framed in response to the recommendations of the Winegard committee's report: House of Commons, *For Whose Benefit? Report of the Standing Committee on External Affairs and International Trade on Canada's Official Development Assistance Policies and Programs* (Ottawa: Queen's Printer, 1987). See Morrison, *Aid and Ebb Tide*, chap. 8, for an account of the Winegard review and its aftermath.

7 For details, see Morrison, *Aid and Ebb Tide*, chap. 9, esp. 339–68 and Cranford Pratt, 'Humane Internationalism and Canadian Development Assistance Policies,' in Cranford Pratt, ed., *Canadian International Development Assistance Policies: An Appraisal* (Montreal and Kingston: McGill-Queen's University Press, 1994), 351–63.

8 Government of Canada, *Canada in the World* (Ottawa: Department of Foreign Affairs and International Trade, 1995), 43. For a detailed discussion of the Chrétien period from 1993 to 1998, including a parliamentary review of aid policy and the government's response, see Morrison, *Aid and Ebb Tide*, chap. 10.

9 Budget Speech of the Honourable Paul Martin, PC, MP, Minister of Finance, 6 March 1996, 31.

10 CIDA, *Statistical Report on Official Development Assistance, Fiscal Year 1997–98* (Hull: CIDA, 1998), 1.

11 See analysis in Brian Tomlinson and CCIC Policy Team, 'Canadian ODA Update: Analysis of CIDA 1999/2000 Estimates, Part III Report on Plans and Priorities' (Ottawa: Canadian Council for International Cooperation, April 1999), 1–2.

12 In 1996–7, reported ODA was $2,676.44 million. This included the following items not included in ODA before 1982 (in millions of dollars): EDC and Canadian Wheat Board debt relief, $164.34; administrative costs, $141.45; EDC Section 23, $12.34; imputed service and interest costs, $14.77; imputed student costs, $65.00; and estimated costs of first-year resettlement of refugees from ODA-eligible countries, $163.71. If these items are deducted (a total of $561.61 million), ODA falls to $2,114.83 million and the ratio in 1996–7 drops from 0.34 per cent to 0.27 per cent (calculations based on CIDA, *Statistical Report on Development Assistance, Fiscal Year 1996/97*, 2–4). An extrapolation to the estimated level for 1999–2000 yields a ratio in the 0.19 to 0.20 per cent range.

13 House of Commons, *Debates*, 14 November 1963: 4718. Paul Martin Jr alluded to the irony of cutting programs his father had helped to build up,

though with a quotation from Paul Sr about the necessity of governments not living in the past (see Budget Speech of the Honourable Paul Martin, PC, MP, Minister of Finance, 27 February 1995).

14 Jean-Philippe Thérien, 'Canadian Aid: A Comparative Analysis,' in Pratt, ed., *Canadian International Development Assistance Policies*, 327.

15 In Ottawa's federal fiscal year. In DAC data, which are recorded on a calendar-year basis, Canada's ODA reached 0.55 per cent in 1975 (OECD-DAC, *Development Co-operation: Efforts and Policies of the Members of the Development Assistance Committee 1977* (Paris: Organization for Economic Cooperation and Development, 1978), 170.

16 See Freedman, 'Introduction: Aid at the Forks,' in this volume at 3–11.

17 See OECD-DAC, *Development Co-operation 1998*, A11–A14.

18 Canada in 1996–7 stood thirteenth behind Denmark ($342), Norway ($308), Luxembourg ($226), the Netherlands ($212), Sweden ($222), Switzerland ($148), France ($125), Belgium ($88), Germany ($87), Finland ($81), Japan ($79), and Austria ($72). The figures are averages for these two calendar years (see data in OECD-DAC, *Development Co-operation*, A14).

19 Government of Canada, *Canada in the World*, 40 (emphasis in original).

20 Ibid., 40 (emphasis in original).

21 Department of Industry, Trade and Commerce, 'International Development and the Canadian Economy,' December 1968, 27–8.

22 See Mark Charlton, *The Making of Canadian Food Aid Policy* (Montreal and Kingston: McGill-Queen's University Press, 1992), 16–25.

23 CIDA, President's Office, 'Directions for the Agency,' 7 December 1977.

24 Government of Canada, *Canada in the World*, 40 (emphasis in original).

25 OECD-DAC, *Twenty-five Years of Development Co-operation* (Paris: Organization for Economic Development and Cooperation, 1985), 106.

26 See ibid., 106–10, and data in more recent DAC reports.

27 CIDA, *Strategy for International Development Co-operation, 1975–1980* (Ottawa: Information Canada, 1975), 32.

28 The most recent, though incomplete, data on untying suggest that Canada still falls well short of the DAC average (OECD-DAC, *Development Cooperation*, 1998, A50).

29 See T.A. Keenleyside, 'Aiding Rights: Canada and the Advancement of Human Dignity,' in Pratt, ed., *Canadian International Development Assistance Policies*, 240–67.

30 In addition to Morrison, *Aid and Ebb Tide*, see David R. Morrison, 'The Choice of Bilateral Aid Recipients,' in Pratt, ed., *Canadian International Development Assistance*, 123–55.

31 A term coined in Economic Council of Canada, *For a Common Future* (Hull: Minister of Supply and Services, 1978), 98.

32 Canada's bilateral program is the least concentrated in DAC if measured by the proportion of country-to-country aid channelled to a donor's top fifteen recipients. In 1996–7 the Canadian figure was 19.8 per cent, well below typical ranges of 30 to 60 per cent (see OECD–DAC, *Development Cooperation 1998*, A69–A82). Although CIDA restricts bilateral data to government-to-government aid, DAC comparative data use a broader definition of 'bilateral': one that is equivalent to CIDA's definition of 'country-to-country' aid, which subsumes the voluntary, business, and humanitarian channels as well as contributions from Crown agencies like IDRC. While the inclusion of these other elements produces a greater degree of dispersal than for government-to-government ODA alone (which is by far the largest component), the data are nonetheless comparable across all DAC donors.

33 Martin Rudner, 'Canada in the World: Development Assistance in Canada's New Foreign Policy Framework,' *Canadian Journal of Development Studies* 17, no. 2 (1996): 211.

34 OECD–DAC, *Development Cooperation 1998*, A66.

35 According to senior officials at DAC headquarters in Paris interviewed by the author in January 1989.

36 See Morrison, *Aid and Ebb Tide*, 428–30 for a discussion of authors who have written about Canadian aid from the perspective of trying to understand why it has fallen short in achieving developmental objectives. Much of the significant work of this sort has been undertaken by researchers associated with the North-South Institute in Ottawa.

37 See Kim Richard Nossal, 'Mixed Motives Revisited: Canada's Interest in Development Assistance,' *Canadian Journal of Political Science* 21, no. 1 (March 1988) and the summary of Nossal's arguments in Morrison, *Aid and Ebb Tide*, 431–3, 436–8.

38 Cranford Pratt, 'Ethics and Foreign Policy: The Case of Canada's Development Assistance,' *International Journal* 43, no. 2 (Spring 1988): 264.

39 See the discussion of Pratt's writings in Morrison, *Aid and Ebb Tide*, 428, 433–41. Also discussed are the more orthodox neo-Marxist writings of Linda Freeman (430–1) and recent contributions from discourse analysis (pp. 436–7).

40 See ibid., esp. 439–42. A high point for domestic interests was reached after the Winegard report in *Sharing Our Future*, CIDA's strategy for the 1990s, which was a remarkably populist document in its promises, material and symbolic, for all of CIDA's partners. It was followed by a souring of relations between the agency and NGOs, however, first as a result of CIDA's

championing of structural adjustment, and then when it became apparent that the Mulroney administration was backing away from commitments in the strategy and pushing for a greater commercialization of aid. While the Liberals had some success in rebuilding relations, these were severely strained in 1995 by drastic budget cuts, especially decisions to eliminate public funding for Canadian-based development education efforts and decentralized NGO coalitions.

41 Hugh Winsor, 'External Pressures Take Toll on CIDA,' *Globe and Mail*, 21 January 1994.

42 For a discussion of the literature on the impact of governmental politics on aid policy, see Morrison, *Aid and Ebb Tide*, 443–5.

43 For two quite different perspectives on the international aid regime, see the liberal, idealist analysis of David Lumsdaine, *Moral Wisdom in International Politics: The Foreign Aid Regime* (Princeton: Princeton University Press, 1993) and the neo-Marxist analysis of Robert E. Wood, *From Marshall Plan to Debt Crisis: Foreign Aid and Development Choices in the World Economy* (Berkeley: University of California Press, 1986).

44 See Morrison, *Aid and Ebb Tide*, esp. 445–8.

45 Phillip Rawkins, *Human Resource Development in the Aid Process: A Study in Organizational Learning and Change* (Ottawa: North-South Institute, 1993), 13 (emphasis in original).

46 See Morrison, *Aid and Ebb Tide*, 448–50.

47 Department of External Affairs, *Foreign Policy for Canadians: International Development* (Ottawa: Queen's Printer, 1970), 8–9.

48 Morrison, *Aid and Ebb Tide*, 452.

2

Alleviating Global Poverty or Enhancing Security: Competing Rationales for Canadian Development Assistance

CRANFORD PRATT

Two sharply different rationales for foreign aid currently coexist uneasily in the literature on Canadian development assistance: humane internationalism and international realism.[1] Humane internationalism argues from essentially ethical premises, beginning with an acceptance that we have obligations towards those beyond our borders who are severely oppressed or who live in conditions of gross and unremitting poverty. International realism, in contrast, highlights the contribution that foreign aid makes to global common security, which it suggests is the key to Canada's own security and prosperity.

The contradiction between these rationales should not be dismissed as a distracting debate between alternative rhetorics. They offer different foundations for Canadian development assistance and they also lead to rather different policy proposals. While the two rationales can and should be seen as mutually reinforcing, the ethical foundation provided by humane internationalism should take precedence as the central unifying principle on which to base Canadian development assistance.

The Two Approaches Examined

Two major, cabinet-endorsed policy statements on Canadian development assistance were issued between 1975 and 1993.[2] Each unequivocally defines the primary objective of the Canadian International Development Agency (CIDA) in humanitarian rather than commercial or political terms. Moreover, public opinion has always strongly endorsed the view that the primary purpose of the aid program should be humanitarian – to aid the development efforts of the poorest countries and peoples.[3] This was also the judgment of Canadian parliamentarians on the four important occasions between 1980 and 1994 when committees of Parliament gave detailed consideration to Canadian aid policies.[4]

Nevertheless, these several parliamentary reports, along with most observers of Canadian aid policies, have recognized that Canadian trade and investment interests as well as international and domestic political interests have greatly influenced Canadian development assistance policies.[5] Moreover, much has happened in recent years to complicate further the future of Canadian development assistance. Since 1989, Cold War considerations seemed to many realists no longer to provide foreign policy reasons to continue foreign aid. The government has been seized with the necessity of imposing severe cuts to government expenditures. There is greater scepticism about the efficacy of development assistance. And Canadian values and attitudes have shifted away from the socially responsible liberalism that for decades was their dominant characteristic. We have become less caring. Concern about the needs of the poorest in Canada has decreased and we have developed a remarkable confidence in the social and economic advantages of leaving unfettered the operation of the market, both nationally and internationally. All of these factors have contributed to a lessening of the government's responsiveness to the development needs of the world's poorest inhabitants and to its consequent imposition of severe and disproportionate cuts to Canadian development assistance since the late 1980s.[6]

Of the two rationales for foreign aid international realism is considerably more prominent than humane internationalism and has disproportionately shaped development policy. Many whose interests remain focused on the alleviation of global poverty have come to doubt that the government will be at all responsive to arguments that are primarily humanitarian and have begun instead to cast their arguments for development assistance in these newer international realist terms. Those who first developed such realist arguments were primarily concerned about Canada's changing security needs. They argued that the end of the Cold War called for a defence and foreign policy that recognized that a nuclear assault on North America was no longer the main threat to Canadian security. Central to their argument has been the view that Canada's national security can now best be advanced through the promotion of a common global security. Development assistance became one of the recommended ways to advance this common security.

The Alternative Rationales Examined

Humane internationalism argues that Canadian aid represents in significant part the projection of Canadian values into the international arena; in this way it is distinguished, and should continue to be distinguished, from most other components of Canadian foreign policy. In the 1960s increasing public policy responsiveness to domestic poverty was accompanied by a new sensitivity to the development needs of the world's poorest. Development assistance is a substantial reflection in Canadian foreign policy of a major shift in social values that simultaneously issued in extensive social welfare programs in Canada.[7]

Parallel to the emergence of a domestic, socially responsible liberalism as the dominant public philosophy in Canada,[8] many rich countries began to accept, after 1945, that they had obligations to protect and promote basic human rights beyond their borders and to aid the development of the world's poorest peoples and countries. By the mid-1960s Canada had begun to respond more than minimally to this new international obligation to aid the least-developed countries. The cosmopolitan dimension of our political culture has always been fragile. Nevertheless, the emergence of an international concern for basic human rights and for the development needs of the world's poorest has been, from a human perspective, as significant as the rise of the welfare state.

Those operating from a humane internationalist perspective recognized and indeed stressed the likelihood that development assistance would also be in Canada's long-term interest. Foreign aid can after all reasonably be expected to contribute to a healthy global economy and to a less strife-riven world, both clearly to Canada's advantage. Nevertheless the primary motive behind foreign aid should be humanitarian rather than the pursuit of national interests. Mitchell Sharp made the essential point over twenty-five years ago: 'There is one good and sufficient reason for international aid and that is that there are less fortunate people in the world who need our help ... [I]f the purpose of aid is to help ourselves rather than to help others, we shall probably receive in return what we deserve and a good deal less than we expect.'[9]

The newer international realist advocacy for development assistance was not in its origin narrowly focused on national security concerns. There had long been internationalists who argued that the sovereignty of any individual state would best be safeguarded by some form or other of collective security. However, until the end of the Cold War, the dominant view was that Canada's national security was integrally linked to the maintenance of the military dominance of the United States and its allies in NATO. For many, two initially unrelated developments dramatically challenged this assumption.

The first of these was the multifaceted international endeavour to shift the discourse on security away from its traditional focus on the military protection of national sovereignty from domestic and foreign threats and towards a recognition that the security of states was increasingly threatened by a wide range of non-military threats, which can only be met by common international action. Efforts to this end predated the end of the Cold War. For example, they were given powerful impetus by the Palme and Brundtland international commissions in the early 1980s.[10]

Ideas of this sort came to coalesce around the concept of common security. In Canada, as in many countries, an increasing number of nongovernmental organizations (NGOs) concerned with peace and development issues began to advocate that the government define its security interests primarily in terms of common security rather than military preparedness.[11] Common security was, for many, defined sufficiently widely to include the security to live in peace and to have basic human rights respected. Common security was thus solidly ethical in its motivation and distinctly international in its reach. It became another component, along with global poverty alleviation, of the emerging cosmopolitan ethic that is here labelled humane internationalism. Some, indeed, defined security even more broadly to include virtually the whole gamut of progressive social and international objectives.[12]

Students of Canada's defence and security policies also began to use the term common security.[13] These scholars included an important cluster who, after 1989, rejected the view then dominant within the government, that Canada still needed military forces capable of engaging in full-scale land, sea, and air operations. They stressed instead that the major threat to Canada's security since the collapse of the Soviet Union is no longer the possibility of global war: Canada's security in the future is more likely to be undermined by a range of interconnected threats that can only be contained through collective action. The litany of these threats is well known. It includes the international drug trade; the increasing prevalence of civil and interethnic wars; massive, uncontrollable movement of peoples in flight from poverty, oppression or civil strife; the spread of nuclear weapons; and mounting environmental degradation.

As they developed their ideas on common security many of these scholars came to include sustained international initiatives to alleviate poverty, oppression, and injustice among their policy recommendations. Without such initiatives, they suggested, world peace will be undermined and Canadian security threatened. Although they have tended to give much less emphasis to aid policies than to the implications of their common security perspective for foreign, defence, and environmental policies,[14] they have produced a rationale for development assistance that rests not on the ethical assumptions of humane internationalism but instead on the importance attached to the advancement of common security as essential for Canada's own security.

This alternative rationale for development assistance was embraced by the Liberal Party prior to the 1993 election. The 'Red Book,' which outlined its basic electoral program, cast its references to foreign aid in security terms. It promised that a Liberal government 'would adopt a broader definition of national security, encompassing such goals as sustainable development, a capable defence, and the eradication of poverty and social inequality.'[15] International realist arguments for development assistance thus by 1994 constituted an alternative to the ethically based arguments that had previously dominated among aid advocates.

The Government Chooses between These Alternative Rationales

THE ALTERNATIVES AS PRESENTED

That more is involved than rhetorical preference in the choice between these two different rationales for Canadian development assistance is clear from representations made to the 1994 Special Joint Committee Reviewing Canadian Foreign Policy. A humane internationalist position was solidly and fully developed before this committee by the Canadian Council for International Cooperation (CCIC).[16] Its brief to the committee built its recommendations around the concept of 'sustainable human development.' Summarizing a year-long process of consultation with its member NGOs, the CCIC proposed that 'sustainable human development form an integrated framework for *both* Canadian domestic and international policies ... By sustainable human development, we mean development that is based on justice, insists on popular participation in meeting basic human needs and other development goals, and is environmentally sound.'[17] CCIC noted that 'traditional forms of project aid and assistance, including those of the NGOs, are not sufficient to solve the problems of human development.'[18] Its recommendations, therefore, ranged very widely. They included proposals designed to ensure that Canadian development assistance was more single-mindedly focused on reaching and helping the poorest but they embraced as well radical proposals relating to peacekeeping, transnational corporations, trade and investment, and greater public participation in foreign policy decision making.

The CCIC even ventured into defence policy issues. In doing so, it endorsed the appropriateness of 'common security' as the primary objective to be served by Canada's armed forces. Nevertheless, common security was in no way the unifying idea around which it built the entirety of its recommendations. There is no suggestion that the primary argument for greater sensitivity to Third World needs was that Canadian security properly understood called for it. Rather 'Canadian values – social and economic justice, self-determination and democratic development, the pursuit of peace and respect for diversity' – led to its unifying central recommendation that 'the pivotal goal for Canadian policy be the promotion of global justice and sustainability.'[19]

In contrast to the CCIC brief, an international realist approach was taken by the Canada 21 Council,[20] the most powerful advocate before the Special Joint Committee of a common security perspective. This council had been created specifically to influence the parliamentary foreign policy review that was announced soon after the 1993 election. The self-selected council and its steering committee consisted almost entirely of Liberals and Conservatives who had been prominent in earlier decades, plus several media personalities, retired senior public servants, ex-officers from the armed forces, a few leading individuals from nationally important minorities, and very few academics, though Professor Janice Stein was its program director and one of its galvanizing prime movers.[21]

The Canada 21 Council was primarily concerned to integrate defence and foreign policies and thereby to secure a major redefinition of Canada's defence needs. To that end it stressed the need for coordinated decision making to accomplish integrated policies so that Canada's contribution to common security would be maximized. As part of that coordinated decision making, it wanted 'the management of Canada's policies towards the South (to be) integrated and coordinated with the broader set of political, financial and military instruments we use to build common security.'[22] Though sharply critical of CIDA's management of Canadian aid policies, Canada 21 did want a strong and effective development assistance program. However, it based this recommendation on security considerations, arguing that 'threats to common security will intensify unless a determined effort is made to deal with the underlying causes of poverty which will provoke increasingly violent conflict.'[23]

THE POSITION TAKEN BY THE 1994 SPECIAL JOINT COMMITTEE[24]
The Special Joint Committee (SJC) was heavily influenced by the arguments of the Liberal Party's 'Red Book' and the Canada 21 Council. It identified 'shared global security,' which it had clearly derived from 'common security,' as Canada's central security concern, indeed as its primary foreign policy concern. However, it did not subsume the objectives of foreign aid within a common security rationale. Instead, it discussed development assistance largely in humane internationalist terms. The committee declared:

> Help for those most in need expresses the basic moral vision of aid and corresponds closely to what the vast majority of Canadians think development assistance is all about.
>
> Accordingly ... the primary purpose of Canadian Official Development Assistance is to reduce poverty by helping the poorest people in the poorest countries that most need and can use our help.[25]

The committee was faithful to this rhetoric. The six priorities for CIDA which it recommended reflected this basic humanitarian purpose. It also recommended that 'essentially Canadian trade promotion activities should be transferred to the Department of Foreign Affairs and International Trade or the Export Development Corporation.' It wanted the government to commit itself to 'stabilize ODA at its present ratio of GNP.' It recognized the need to protect CIDA, to use its own endearing phrase, 'from random and wayward pressures' and therefore suggested a legislated mandate and an annual review of Canadian aid by a House of Commons committee.[26]

THE POSITION TAKEN BY THE GOVERNMENT IN 1995
Despite every effort to appear to accept this report, it is clear that the government was determined to give primary emphasis to Canadian trade objectives and to avoid any constraints upon its ability to deploy Canadian aid as it wished. By a most careful rewording it subverted the humane internationalist character of the primary objective of Canadian aid as it had been recommended by the parliamentary committee.

The government took the recommended central purpose of CIDA – 'to reduce poverty by providing effective assistance to the poorest people, in those countries that most need and can use our help' – and amended it to read 'to support sustainable development in developing countries in order to reduce poverty and to contribute to a more secure, equitable prosperous world.'[27] It thus removed any suggestion of a particular concentration on the poorest countries and, by giving equal billing to contributing to a more secure, equitable, prosperous world, it legitimated continued foreign aid to the richer less developed countries (LDCs).

A few months later, in *Canada in the World*, its official statement of Canadian foreign policy objectives, the government went one step further: 'International assistance is a vital instrument for the achievement of the three key objectives being pursued by the government. It is an investment in prosperity and employment ... It connects the Canadian economy to some of the fastest growing markets ... (I)t contributes to global security ... and is one of the clearest expressions of Canadian values ...'[28] Thus even in regard to foreign aid emphasis was first given to trade and security considerations. *Canada in the World* accepted none of the recommended safeguards designed to protect CIDA from those powerful forces outside and inside government that often divert CIDA expenditures to trade and foreign policy objectives. The government statement also recommitted CIDA to continuing its several programs that link aid spending to trade-promoting activities and it transferred to CIDA the administration of Canadian assistance to Eastern Europe and the former Soviet Union. As well, it rejected the suggestion that there should be a legislated charter for CIDA and it ignored the recommendations that Canadian aid be concentrated in the poorest countries and that trade-oriented activities be transferred out of CIDA. Finally, it announced that aid policies would be determined by an interdepartmental committee, chaired not by the president of CIDA but by the deputy minister of foreign affairs.

It would not be true to suggest that all signs of a continuing humanitarian responsibility were purged from the official policy statement. For example, five of the six program priorities for CIDA recommended by the committee were reaffirmed and the government committed itself to spend 25 per cent of CIDA's budget on basic human needs. Nevertheless, two generalizations about *Canada and the World* seem justified. First, primary emphasis was given to Canadian economic competitiveness in an increasingly open international economy; second, when defining the fundamental objectives of Canadian development assistance, the language of ethics and compassion was abandoned and replaced by the language of Canadian prosperity and security. With the appearance of *Canada in the World* Foreign Affairs[29] does seem to have decided that the language of national security rather than humanitarian obligations will be used to define the purpose of Canadian aid policies. André Ouellet, while secretary of state, favoured the term human security and employed it widely. More recently, Lloyd Axworthy first devised his own variant, 'sustainable human security,' but then settled on human security.[30]

It is difficult to distinguish between the motivations behind this sudden preference in 1994 for common security rather than humanitarian rhetoric and the political utility served by this shift. The minister and, no doubt, other officials within the Department of Foreign Affairs and International Trade, were genuinely committed to a strong and internationalist interpretation of common security. However, that the overwhelming central preoccupation of Canadian foreign policy was the advancement of Canadian international trade and political interests is undeniable.[31] At the least, it is legitimate to suggest that removing humane internationalist language from the consideration of foreign aid and locating that consideration firmly within a discourse of common security facilitated the accomplishment of what had in fact become the dominant preoccupation with Canadian foreign policy.

The extent to which Canadian internationalists outside of government have been converted to this basic orientation, or have at least come to accept that it is politic to cast their internationalism in such terms, became clear in November 1996 with the publication of the report of the International Development and Policy Task Force.[32] This task force had been created six months previously by three publicly financed agencies, the International Development Research Centre, the International Institute for Sustainable Development, and the North-South Institute. Its chair, Maurice Strong, and its other eight members[33] are in every instance highly knowledgeable and experienced in one or more of the areas of public policy, development, and research. They are also trusted internationalists, who might be expected to be close in spirit to older Canadian international traditions.

Despite the mandate implied by its title, the task force concentrated on a very narrowly focused argument. It accepted that there is to be no increase in Canadian development assistance; it addressed none of the major outstanding issues of North-South relations; it offered no critique of Canadian policies. Instead, it concentrated on arguing that 'a substantive policy research capacity on development issues in universities, independent research organizations, and government agencies' must receive a higher priority in the allocation of existing development assistance moneys and that leadership in these matters should be concentrated in the task force's three sponsoring organizations.

What is revealing for our purposes is how bereft the report is of any articulated ethical commitment or any closely argued linking of their specific recommendations to the alleviation of the gross poverty of the world's poorest. In introducing its specific proposals the task force stresses that 'the absolute numbers of those without the most basic necessities remained too high and continues to grow' and that 'international development will have to be dramatically transformed.' However, it deduced from this, not that we have an obligation as a rich country to do what we can to correct this deplorable situation, but rather that 'Canada's response to this challenge will determine our future position among the nations of the world and will be central to our own prosperity.'[34]

The report then immediately identifies 'three principal questions.' They are hardly reassuring to anyone expecting a considered view of Canada's role in regard to the world's poorest:

> How will the development of other countries affect Canada?
> What strategies will be most appropriate to the interests of Canada in the rapidly changing context for international development?
> More fundamentally, what are the interests of Canada in a world where the founding members of the United Nations are now in a minority and where the fastest growing economies are no longer in Europe and North America?[35]

In discussing development assistance the report is impatiently dismissive of 'altruism,'[36] concentrating instead on Canada's long-term self-interest in this assistance. Finally, when the report discusses how the need to increase Canadian research capacity should be explained to the Canadian public, its language is very close to that of *Canada in the World*. It argues that the need for this increased capacity 'must be related to the ultimate product; greater security for Canadians, the environment, and jobs.'[37] The decision of the committee to cast its recommendations so uncompromisingly within an international realist framework demonstrates how influential this perspective had become.

Assessing the Consequences of the New Canadian Internationalism

The approach and values of *Canada in the World* and the increasing deployment of an international realist rationale for development assistance more generally are more likely to contribute to the abandonment by the Canadian government of what remains of its humanitarian commitment to reach and help the world's poorest peoples and countries than to constrain it. Nevertheless, as many are persuaded that responsive policies towards the needs of the poorest countries should now be argued in international realist terms, this position needs first to be fairly considered.

The central argument for the deployment of an international realist rather than a humane internationalist rationale for development assistance suggests that the integration of development assistance fully into the nexus of Canadian foreign policy, plus the severe cuts in recent years to CIDA's budget, mean that the era in which poverty-oriented development assistance was an important component of Canadian foreign policy is effectively over. In this situation, it can plausibly be argued, proponents of greater Canadian responsiveness to the needs of the poorest countries should not look to an ever-weakening CIDA. They need instead to cultivate their contacts in Foreign Affairs and Finance and to develop their case in terms that are more likely to appeal to these departments than are arguments premised on humane internationalist values.

To that end, the argument continues, Canadian decision makers can be relied upon to be particularly responsive to arguments based on Canadian interests. Given as well the government's preoccupation with deficit reduction and the major shift in Canadian social values away from a responsiveness to the needs of Canada's own poor, humanitarian arguments for poverty-focused development assistance are less and less likely to influence government policy. International realist arguments that effective development assistance increases Canadian influence with Third World countries and lessens the threats to Canada's security from widespread anarchy, international terrorism, and uncontrollable mass migration, are more likely to prove persuasive to policy makers than arguments founded on considerations of ethics and human solidarity.

A second argument favouring a reliance on a security rationale for foreign aid is seen to follow from the fact that CIDA's responsibilities are no longer as discrete and separable from other components of Canadian foreign policy as they were in earlier decades. CIDA is now actively engaged, for example, in environmental projects, in peace-building activities, and in the promotion of human rights and democracy. 'Promoting common security,' or more recently human security it is suggested, is a better overall rubric to describe CIDA's activities than 'poverty eradication' or 'aiding the development of the poorest.'

Considerations such as these explain why some Canadian internationalists have abandoned ethical arguments in their discussion of the objectives of development assistance and are relying on arguments that stress that such assistance will bring long-term security and diplomatic and trade advantages to Canada. Understandable or not, this development is likely to affect adversely the responsiveness of Canadian aid policies to the development needs of the world's poorest people.

The Case against a Primary Reliance on a Security Rationale

Perhaps the most fundamental counter-argument to the new emphasis on security is that it shifts the primary focus of foreign aid discourse onto national self-interest. Since 1945, a cosmopolitan ethic has gradually emerged as a factor of international influence and importance, stressing greater sensitivity to international human rights and the development needs of the world's poorest. This emerging supranational ethic, though still fragile, has been from a humanitarian perspective a most significant development. To cease to champion the humane internationalist component would mark a significant erosion of our fundamental values.

There are also more immediate tactical reasons that tell against any major reliance on international realist argumentation. Fear of the poor is, in one guise or another, at the root of the security case for development assistance. However, fear is a vastly less reliable foundation on which to construct humanitarian policies than is empathy and compassion. Hostility and anger rather than generosity or solidarity are more frequently the by-products of fear. Exploiting fears of mass, uncontrolled migration, say, or of spreading anarchy, rather than sparking generous interventions is more likely to generate uncomprehending antipathy and a determination to build effective barriers. This is as true internationally as it is in our cities.

It is also probable that Canadian security is in fact not severely threatened by mounting poverty and increasing disorder in many parts of the world. When the recent task force argued that '[n]orthern prosperity cannot continue at the cost of growing poverty, disease, warfare and despair in the South,'[38] its intent can be applauded but the argument must be suspect. Canada is unlikely to be threatened physically by the present tragedies in Central Africa, the next famine in the horn of Africa, or the perpetuating poverty in Bangladesh. Similarly Canadian prosperity is unlikely to be adversely affected by continued gross poverty in the poorest countries nor is any assistance to them likely to 'pay off' economically. If we come to accept that the dominant motive for development assistance is and should be Canadian security and prosperity rather than compassion and solidarity, then it is more realistic to expect that Canada will be highly selective in its responses to Third World needs and will act but minimally in distant areas of little economic or geopolitical interest.

Even if the Canadian government were to be genuinely convinced by the argument that the prosperity and long-term security of the rich countries will be threatened if they pay little attention to global poverty, it is not reasonable to expect that this conviction would generate effective international action. There is a close and relevant parallel which is worth noting. In regard to effective international action on environmental issues, it is reasonable to fear that Canadian action to contain and reverse the degradation being inflicted on the global environment will be inadequate if it is founded primarily on the government's fear of the long-term impact of that degradation on the welfare of Canadians. Considerations of long-term interests alone are rarely sufficient to generate initiatives that would entail significant immediate sacrifice, especially if the long-term benefits anticipated require the active participation of most rich countries and cannot in any case be guaranteed.

International and Canadian action to lessen global poverty and to reverse the degradation of the global environment is therefore likely be inadequate unless there is a significant component in the first instance of ethically rooted concern for the welfare of those beyond our borders and in the second a 'green' passion for the preservation of the ecology of our globe.

Any high expectation that international realist arguments will inspire the Canadian government to initiate more responsive, poverty-oriented aid programs are flawed for a further very practical reason. Such expectations depend on the assumption that common security, or human, concerns are a central determinant of the objectives of Canadian foreign aid policies. Given that assumption, the tactically skilful might reasonably decide that poverty-focused development assistance is better championed in terms of its contribution to Canada's long-term security. But the impetus behind the determined effort of Foreign Affairs to integrate aid policies more fully into Canadian foreign policy has not primarily reflected a concern to advance shared global security. The Department of Foreign Affairs has for a number of years been motivated instead by a desire to deploy CIDA's resources in ways that would advance much more immediate and self-serving Canadian foreign policy objectives, the most prominent of which has been the promotion of the interests of Canadian exporters and investors in a world that has become increasingly interdependent.

This was made abundantly clear a few years ago in the international assistance policy update paper that launched the effort by the then Department of External Affairs to bring CIDA more closely under its policy direction.[39] That paper proposed 'an over-arching policy framework to provide coherence in objectives, strategies and funding in accordance with foreign policy priorities.' Major emphasis was then given ' to position the private sector for long-term market penetration' and to the creation of 'foreign policy thematic funds ... [that] would permit us to remain in countries of significant importance to Canada.' That the views expressed in the update paper were representative of the department's ambitions towards CIDA is confirmed by the central emphasis in *Canada in the World* on promoting Canadian economic interests and by the efforts of Foreign Affairs to bring CIDA policies more fully under its close direction.[40]

There is something artificial and unreal in discussing the rationale for Canadian aid as if the choice lies in fact between promoting humanitarian objectives or advancing common security. What has been far more at stake is the extent to which CIDA's humanitarian mandate will be further diluted by the government's near total absorption with Canada's international economic competitiveness, with CIDA becoming even more an agency whose primary purpose is to pursue Canadian economic and political interests internationally. Indeed, the final significance of the common security rationale may prove to be that it provides a more appealing public face for the efforts of Foreign Affairs to convert CIDA more fully into a policy-neutral agency implementing policies that reflecting the trade and political preoccupations of the Department of Foreign Affairs and International Trade.

A recent excellent CCIC Study[41] reveals evidence that the undermining of CIDA's putative primary focus on poverty alleviation continues. For example, Canadian aid to the poorest countries, that is, those with a per capita GNP of less than US$100, fell by over 33 per cent between 1992/3 and 1996/7 while foreign aid overall fell by only 21.2 per cent. Development assistance to sub-Saharan Africa was disproportionately cut by over 30 per cent during these years, even though 55 per cent of Canadian aid continued to go to middle-income Third World countries. Within CIDA's bilateral programs, special deference has continued to be shown to regions that are of special interest to Canadian exporters and investors. For example, during the same years in which Canadian aid to sub-Saharan Africa fell dramatically, aid to South Africa increased by nearly 36 per cent.

Nevertheless, the struggle over Canada's aid policies is surely not over yet. After years of preoccupation with the macroeconomic policies of the LDCs and the structural adjustment of their economies to accomplish their fuller integration with the international economy, a major resurgence of emphasis on the central importance of poverty alleviation and a heightened sophistication in the analysis of how this can best be accomplished are now evident. Not surprisingly, students of development who are close to the international NGO movement have been in the forefront of this revival,[42] but it has widened significantly and now influences many academic analysts as well.[43] It has even penetrated the World Bank and the Development Assistance Committee of the OECD, in each of which there has been a marked revival in the importance accorded to poverty alleviation.[44] In 1997 the member governments of the OECD, Canada included, endorsed as the shared target for their aid efforts a set of objectives, the first of which was that they would together by 2015 reduce by half the number of persons living in extreme poverty.[45]

These international developments have had Canadian counterparts. In 1996 the CCIC initiated a major public campaign, 'In Common,' whose central theme is that poverty eradication must remain the primary focus of Canadian development assistance. As part of that campaign it produced an agenda for international action against poverty.[46] It has also examined the adequacy of the poverty-focused activities of Canadian NGOs and has published a major study of how Canadian development assistance could more effectively contribute to the eradication of poverty.[47] Canadians have continued to contribute generously to the overseas work of Canadian NGOs[48] and CIDA has identified poverty alleviation as the overarching objective that integrates its six priorities. CIDA has developed a strategy related to this objective[49] and has appointed an experienced official to oversee its accomplishment. These efforts are neither exceptional nor untypical. Many within CIDA, within the NGO community, and elsewhere have continued to fight a rearguard action to protect and augment CIDA's poverty-focused development work. Had trade and security motivations entirely swamped humane internationalist considerations Bangladesh would not still be one of the largest recipients of Canadian bilateral aid, more than 40 per cent of Canada's total bilateral aid would not still be going to Africa, and emphasis would not still be placed on meeting basic human needs.

It is therefore reasonable to conclude that internationalists who are concerned to support a more generous, poverty-focused foreign aid program ought not to shift the basis of their advocacy to a rationale that primarily emphasizes the contribution of such a program to common security and therefore to Canadian security. The primary foundation for all that has been done within government and external to it to achieve a generous and effective development assistance program has been the humane internationalist dimension of the dominant liberal political culture in Canada. Those values admittedly have been seriously challenged in recent years. However, they are not yet vanquished. Without them a poverty-oriented aid program is surely doomed. The international dimension of our fundamental values must be reaffirmed as we enter the twenty-first century.

Since the writing of this chapter, Lloyd Axworthy, as minister of foreign affairs, has made 'human security' central to his many expositions of Canadian foreign policy. He stresses that the security of individual rather than state security should be the central preoccupation of Canadian foreign policy and indeed of the foreign policies of as many other states as he can influence. Axworthy's major contribution to the negotiation of an international treaty to ban anti-personnel landmines and his championing of international agreements to limit the proliferation of military small arms and light weapons, to eliminate child labour, and to create an international criminal court all demonstrate a genuine responsive to humanitarian concerns. His advocacy of human security cannot be represented as a subterfuge either for narrowly self-interested national preoccupations or for the special advocacy of international action on issues of particular importance to Canadian security.

It is legitimate therefore to ask whether the arguments of this chapter does not need to be re-examined. Surely abject poverty could be seen as a primary barrier to the global realization of human security. Does the fact that Canada now has a foreign affairs minister who vigorously affirms that Canadian foreign policy is founded on a central commitment to global human security suggest that the advocacy of poverty-focused development assistance should now be firmly cast within a human security discourse?

Two powerful reasons weigh against any such tactical decision to endorse human security as the appropriate conceptual framework within which to discuss Canada's foreign aid program. The bias of Foreign Affairs for many years has been that CIDA's resources should be deployed in ways that would advance immediate Canadian economic and political interests. Under any minister other than Lloyd Axworthy, it is reasonable to suspect that the department would return with relief to the emphasis on Canadian prosperity and Canadian security that is central to *Canada in the World*, the last cabinet-endorsed comprehensive foreign policy statement.[50]

The central difficulty is even more fundamental. Axworthy has repeatedly failed to acknowledge or to champion the ethically compelling case for generous, poverty-oriented Canadian development assistance policies and has consistently omitted from his essential components of global human security any mention of global poverty alleviation. This may reflect a tactical judgment on his part. Given the preoccupations of his cabinet colleagues with trade promotion and fiscal restraint, perhaps he judges that the best that he can accomplish are initiatives such as those he has taken, which share the characteristic that they do not require significant resources. This hardly suggests that the advocacy of generous and poverty-oriented development assistance would be advanced by shifting from an ethically founded emphasis on poverty reduction to an emphasis on security, common or human.

The argument of this chapter, despite Axworthy's innovations, does seem to remain sound. Development assistance should continue to be advocated primarily within an ethical and solidarity discourse that lays primary emphasis on poverty eradication.

Notes

The research for this chapter has been assisted by a much appreciated research grant from the Social Sciences and Humanities Research Council of Canada.

A 'comment and opinion' by the author presented, in abbreviated form, the argument of this chapter and carried a similar title. It was published in *International Journal* 54(2) (Spring 1999), 306–23.

1   The distinction between humane internationalism and international realism is developed more fully in my 'Humane Internationalism and Canadian Development Assistance,' in Cranford Pratt, ed., *Internationalism Under Strain: the North-South Policies of Canada, the Netherlands, Norway and Sweden* (Toronto: University of Toronto Press, 1989), esp. 13–22 and by Olav Stokke in 'Foreign Aid: What Now?' in Stokke, ed., *Foreign Aid towards the Year 2000: Experiences and Challenges* (London: Frank Cass, 1996), 20–9.
2   *Strategy for International Development Cooperation 1975–80* (Ottawa: CIDA, 1975) and *Sharing Our Future: Canada's International Development Assistance* (Ottawa: Supply and Services, 1987). This second policy statement, though carrying the date 1987, was not issued until 1988.
3   For discussion of public opinion on these issues from 1970 to the mid-1980s see Réal Lavergne, 'Determinants of Canadian Aid Policies,' in Olav Stokke, ed., *Western Middle Powers and Global Poverty: The Determinants of the Aid Policies of Canada, Denmark, the Netherlands, Norway and Sweden* (Uppsala: Scandinavian Institute of African Studies, 1989), 36–40. Evidence that public support in Canada for foreign aid continues primarily to reflect ethical values is provided in a recent detailed poll done for CIDA by Angus Reid Group published in September 1997.
4   That the primary purpose of development assistance should be to help the poorest was unanimously recommended in 1980 by the Parliamentary Task Force on North-South Relations in its Report to the House of Commons on the *Relations between Developed and Developing Countries* (Hull: Supply and Services, 1980); in 1986 by the Special Joint Committee on Canada's International Relations in its report *Independence and Internationalism* (Ottawa: Supply and Services, 1986); in 1987 in *For Whose Benefit? Report of the Standing Committee on External Affairs and International Trade on Canada's Official Development Assistance Policies and Program* (Ottawa: Supply and Services, 1987); and in 1994 by the Special Joint Committee of the Senate and the House of Commons in its *Canada's Foreign Policy: Principles and Priorities for the Future* (Ottawa: Parliamentary Publications Directorate, 1994). Each of these reports also specifically commented on and warned against the intrusion of commercial objectives into the aid program.
5   This was often conceded by the government. For example, in a publication intended to stimulate and guide public input into the 1986 parliamentary review of Canadian foreign policy, the Department of External Affairs

asked how rather than whether aid funds should be used to promote trade. Similarly, it did not question whether it was proper or wise to use Canadian aid to promote political and economic objectives; instead it asked what balance should be struck between 'our own economic and political well-being, our sense of moral responsibility and our overall foreign policy' *Competitiveness and Security: Directions for Canada's International Relations* (Ottawa: Supply and Services, 1985), 36. The title and dominant tone of that document make it clear that the department saw economic and political well-being as its most important concerns.

6 A recent CCIC publication reports that Canada's ratio of official development assistance (ODA) to GNP, which was an uninspiring 0.50 per cent in 1984/5, has fallen to an estimated .27 per cent in 1998. Brian Tomlinson, *A Call to End Global Poverty: Renewing Canadian Aid Policy and Practice* (Ottawa: CCIC, 1999), Appendix 6, 57.

7 Alain Noël and Jean-Philippe Thérien have thoroughly investigated this link in two important articles, 'Welfare Institutions and Foreign Aid: Domestic Foundations of Canadian Foreign Policy,' *Canadian Journal of Political Science* 27, no. 3 (September 1994) and 'From Domestic to International Justice: The Welfare State and Foreign Aid,' *International Organization* 49, no. 3 (Summer 1995). The link between domestic social values and foreign aid policies is also a major theme, though treated more discursively, in Pratt, ed., *Internationalism under Strain* and Stokke, ed., *Middle Powers and Global Poverty.*

8 For an authoritative discussion of liberalism as the dominant public philosophy in Canada, see Ronald Manser, *Public Policies and Political Development in Canada* (Toronto: University of Toronto Press, 1985). I draw heavily on Manser's analysis in my discussion of the links between Canadian attitudes towards foreign aid and Canadian domestic social values in 'Canada: An Eroding and Limited Internationalism,' in Pratt, ed., *Internationalism under Strain*, 49–51.

9 Mitchell Sharp, as quoted in Robert Carty and Virginia Smith, eds., *Perpetuating Poverty: The Political Economy of Canadian Foreign Aid* (Toronto: Between the Lines, 1981), 38–9.

10 Independent Commission on Disarmament and Security Issues under the chairmanship of Olav Palme, *Common Security* (London: Pan Books, 1982) and World Commission on Environment and Development under the chairmanship of Gro Harlem Brundtland, *Our Common Future* (Oxford: Oxford University Press, 1987).

11 For an outstanding example of this see The Citizens' Inquiry into Peace and Security, *Transforming Moment: A Canadian Vision of Common Security* (Tor-

onto: Project Ploughshares and Canadian Peace Alliance, 1992). In addition to the two organizations that published this report, fourteen other major citizen organizations were its co-sponsors. I am grateful to Professor Mark Neufeld for drawing my attention to the report and for allowing me to read his very clarifying chapter 'The Political Economy of Security Discourse: Reflections on Canada's 'Security with a Human Face,' in Ken Booth, ed., *Security, Community and Emancipation: Critical Security Studies and Global Politics* (Boulder, Col.: Lynne Rienner Press, forthcoming). Neufeld's political economy analysis of the changing discourse of security as influenced and structured by the government provides powerful evidence that the idea of common security has been captured by the government and is now used to present policies that are in fact substantially unchanged.

12 *Transforming Moment* is guilty of this excess. 'Common security looks at all security needs – from food, shelter, health care and education, to human rights, social harmony, a sustainable environment and peace ... [C]ommon security approaches security in terms of fundamental justice' (36).

13 For an interesting discussion of this literature see David Dewitt, 'Common, Comprehensive and Cooperative Security,' *Pacific Review* 7, no. 1 (1994).

14 For example, the chapter on development assistance in Canada 21 Council, *Canada 21: Canada and Common Security in the Twenty-first Century* (Toronto: Centre for International Studies, 1994) is far weaker than its sections on defence, peacekeeping and peacebuilding, the control of the spread of nuclear weapons, and the globalization of production. It is also noteworthy that development assistance policies are not dealt with in Janice Stein's interesting discussion of the effort of the Canada 21 Council to influence the way in which security issues are considered in Canada. Janice Stein, 'Ideas, Even Good Ideas are not Enough: Changing Canadian Foreign and Defence Policies,' *International Journal* 50, no. 1 (Winter 1994–5), 40–70.

15 As quoted in Bill Robinson and Ken Epp, 'Agenda for the Next Parliament,' *Ploughshares Monitor* 18, no. 2 (June 1997), 6.

16 The CCIC is the coalition of over 125 Canadian non-governmental organizations, including development organizations, churches, labour development and solidarity funds, and development education groups 'who are committed, through a wide range of programs, to achieving social justice and global development in a peaceful and healthy environment.' Canadian Council for International Cooperation, *Building and Sustaining Global Justice: Towards a New Canadian Foreign Policy* (Ottawa: CCIC, May 1994), 1.

17 *Building and Sustaining Global Justice*, ii. For a powerful and sustained advocacy of this perspective see Betty Plewes, Gauri Sreenivasan, and Tim

Draimin, 'Sustainable Human Development as a Global Framework,' *International Journal* 51, no. 2 (Spring 1996), 211–35.

18 Ibid., 3.

19 ibid., ii and 5.

20 Canada 21 Council, *Canada 21*.

21 The membership of the Canada 21 Council was determinedly centrist, with no NDP, Reform Party, or Bloc members. The council appears to have been moribund since it produced this publication and made its representation to the 1994 Special Joint Committee.

22 *Canada 21*, 40.

23 Ibid., 33.

24 For a fuller statement of the argument of this and the next section see my 'Development Assistance and Canadian Foreign Policy: Where We Now Are,' *Canadian Foreign Policy* 2, no. 3 (Winter 1994/5), 80–5.

25 Special Joint Committee Reviewing Canadian Foreign Policy, *Canada's Foreign Policy: Principles and Priorities for the Future* (Ottawa: Parliamentary Publications Directorate, 1994), 48.

26 Ibid., 51, 58.

27 *Government Response to the Recommendations of the Special Joint Parliamentary Committee Reviewing Canadian Foreign Policy* (Ottawa: Department of Foreign Affairs and International Trade, 1995), 58.

28 Canada, *Canada in the World: Government Statement 40*.

29 The new Liberal government changed the name of the Department of External Affairs and International Trade to the Department of Foreign Affairs and International Trade.

30 For his fullest statement of this see 'Notes for an Address by the Honourable Lloyd Axworthy Minister of Foreign Affairs to the 51st General Assembly of the United Nations.' Statement 96/37 (Ottawa: Department of Foreign Affairs and International Trade, 24 Sept. 1996). Axworthy later revised this text for his article 'Canada and Human Security: The Need for Leadership,' *International Journal* 52, no. 2 (Spring 1997), 183–96.

31 Jean-François Rioux and Robin Hay, in a recent interesting article, write that *Canada in the World* 'marked, if anything, a further withdrawal from the world or at least selective participation in it that is based almost entirely on economic and trade interests.' Rioux and Hay, 'Canadian Foreign Policy: From Internationalism to Isolationism?' *Norman Paterson School of International Affairs Occasional Paper 16*, (1997), 18.

32 International Development Research and Policy Task Force, *Connecting with the World: Priorities for Canadian Internationalism in the 21st Century* (November 1996; place of publication and publisher not given). This report was

sponsored by the International Development Research Centre, the International Institute for Sustainable Development, and the North-South Institute.

33 These other members were Jack Austin, Tim Brodhead, Margaret Cately-Carlson, John Evans, Yves Fortier, Gerald Helleiner, Pierre Marc Johnson, and Janice Stein.

34 For the several quotations in the above paragraph, see *Connecting with the World*, 15–16.

35 Ibid.

36 Ibid., 19.

37 Ibid., 22–3.

38 Ibid., 20.

39 This important paper was leaked to the NGO community in January 1993. The paper and the circumstances surrounding its production and its acquisition by interested parties outside of government are discussed in the final chapter of Pratt, ed., *Canadian International Development Assistance Policies: An Appraisal*, 2nd ed. (Montreal and Kingston: McGill-Queen's University Press, 1996), 357–63. The quotations from the policy update paper are from copies of that paper made available to the author by the CCIC and the North-South Institute.

40 These efforts to increase Foreign Affairs policy control of CIDA are examined in my 'DFAIT's Takeover Bid of CIDA: The Institutional Future of the Canadian International Development Agency,' *Canadian Foreign Policy* 5, no. 2 (Winter 1998), 1–14.

41 Tomlinson, *A Call to End Global Poverty*.

42 For excellent examples see *The Reality of Aid: An Independent Review of International Aid*, published annually since 1993 by ICVA, the International Council of Voluntary Agencies, and EUROSTEP, composed of over twenty European NGOs and *Social Watch*, since 1997 an annual publication of Institito dil Tercer Mundo, Montevideo. See also Adrian Cox and John Healey, *Poverty Reduction: A Review of Donor Strategies and Practices* (London: Overseas Development Institute, November 1997) and Roger Riddell, 'Trends in International Cooperation,' in David Gillies, ed., *Strategies of Public Engagement* (Montreal and Kingston: McGill-Queen's University Press, 1997), 19–62.

43 This is well illustrated in C. Gwin and J.M. Nelson, eds., *Perspectives on Aid and Development Policy Essay No 22* (Washington, D.C.: Overseas Council, 1997) and indeed in this volume itself.

44 See for example *Poverty: World Development Report 1990* (Oxford and New York: Oxford University Press, 1991), *Poverty Reduction and The World Bank: Progress and Challenge in the 1990s* (Washington: World Bank, 1996), and

Shaping the 21st Century: The Contribution of Development Cooperation (Paris: OECD, May 1996).

45 James Michel, *Development Cooperation 1997 Report* (Paris: OECD, 1998) 3.

46 *What We Can Do: A 10-Point Agenda for Global Action against Poverty* (Ottawa: CCIC, 1997).

47 Tomlinson, *A Call to End Global Poverty.*

48 The DAC reported that in 1996 the Canadian voluntary sector transferred almost US$ 312 million to developing countries, in addition to the CIDA funds. This was 6.2 per cent higher than the amount transferred in 1993. *Development Cooperation 1997*, Statistical Annex, Table 15.

49 CIDA, *Policy on Poverty Reduction* (Hull: CIDA, 1996).

50 It is indicative of the likely truth of this suggestion that in the one exposition of the new doctrine of human security by a senior Foreign Affairs official, human security becomes indistinguishable from common security as that term had been used by officials. Paul Heinbecker has recently suggested that the niches which are appropriate for Canadian human security issues are those such as 'drug-trafficking, organized crime, environmental pollution, terrorism and contagious diseases' are identical to those earlier labelled as common security concerns in which there is a clear and direct Canadian interest ('Human Security,' *Behind the Headlines* 56 (Winter 1999), 69. There is no mention of any humanitarian objective from which there would be no Canadian 'pay-off' and no emphasis is given to poverty as a key cause of human insecurity.

PART TWO

Conditionality and Freedom

S tructural adjustment schemes are the regimens of financial disci-
pline that donor countries require recipient countries to accept as a
condition of receiving assistance. The attention structural adjustment
schemes have received makes them seem complex, but they are not;
virtually all of the schemes employ the four Ds: devalue, decontrol,
deflate, and denationalize (Lipton and Toye, 1990: 101). In practice,
they amount to improving a government's resources through giving
up less to domestic programs and gaining more in international trade.
The logic, in most cases, has led recipient countries – those who have
been willing to meet the disciplinary conditions – to retool economies
for generating export earnings, in essence to seek their fortunes in the
international market place. It has been a risky game to say the least.
Just as economies were gearing up to enter the high stakes export
arena, the prices of primary products throughout the world began a
downward spiral. National current account deficits grew. Meanwhile,
aid institutions and banks which had provided loans to developing
countries joined arms in resolutely insisting that debtor nations continue to service their debts (Wood, 1996: 32–5). Not surprisingly, the
record of adjustment schemes has been mixed and controversial.

Some of the controversy concerns whether nudging emerging economies towards the international market place is really a good idea. The
risks were more obvious in 1998 than ever before, as the international
market place has begun to look more like a snake pit than the road to
economic salvation. One of the big questions is whether international
trade is capable of working to the advantage of all trading partners
and not just for those with the most clout in the market.

In the first of two articles on the subject Albert Berry asks whether international trade, if left to operate freely, can accomplish what aid never could in the community of nations: help every nation find a viable commercial niche in a neat international complementarity. In a post-aid world with a greater magnitude of trade, the notion of comparative advantage takes on a unique importance. If comparative advantage ensures that international trade can deliver the kind of distributive justice aid once pretended to provide, then aid borders on the obsolete. Berry follows the logic and the limitations of the theory of comparative advantage.

But there is another level to the controversy, a political one that goes beyond the compatibility of markets and distributive justice. Setting aside the theoretical question of whether the exposure to the market place that structural adjustment schemes promote can benefit all nations, there is a more practical question to be answered: should countries have the freedom to make that decision for themselves?

Many structural adjustment programs have had questionable records, and yet the logic that drove them has retained the ring of gospel. Even when structural adjustment schemes failed, that failure was not attributed to the schemes themselves; instead, it was argued that the corrupt governments of the recipient countries could not be trusted to carry out the programs reliably. There followed the controversial idea that donors should make aid disbursements conditional not just on economic reform but upon internal political reform as well.

In the second article in this section, Gerry Helleiner reviews the record of conditionality in the aid regime for both multilateral and national donors, addressing the thorniest of aid's present dilemmas. He questions the practice of imposing political conditions on aid where the developing country government does not accept the conditions, and in doing so Helleiner joins others (Cornia et al., 1987; Hyden and Karlstrom, 1993; Moore and Robinson, 1995: 287) in questioning the value of attaching political strings to the delivery of development assistance.

3

International Trade as the Answer to World Poverty: Is Foreign Aid Obsolete?

ALBERT BERRY

The Question

One of the ideas emerging from the great attention paid in recent years to globalization and the information revolution is that, in this new era of opportunity, poor countries will have an unparalleled opportunity to grow out of poverty through international trade and foreign investment. Not only will such trade and investment help the countries as a whole, it will also raise the incomes of their poorer members. Apart from providing the greatest chance yet for these countries and people, trade and investment also renders foreign aid unnecessary and obsolete. To quote John Stackhouse in the *Globe and Mail* (18 October 1997, D1): 'Throughout the Third World, foreign aid and assistance from wealthier countries has been replaced by a staggering amount of foreign investment. As a result, economies have started to boom.' Bangladesh, one of the world's poorest countries, is cited as a prime example of this phenomenon. It is also noted that Latin America has begun to emerge from the after-effects of the international debt crisis that afflicted it in the 1980s and that Africa's economy has started to grow at rates above those of its population for the first time since the 1970s. *The Economist* noted recently that if the World Bank did not exist, no one would think it necessary to create it now.

How well-founded is this confidence in the beauties of the new world order, in which the market plays the key role, the functions of the nation state shrink, and the giant multinationals become ever more dominant in both the world economy and the world polity? Of course, we do not know, and only the unfolding of events will tell us. Anyone who claims a high level of confidence in the way the world economy will develop under this new regime is likely to suffer either from the intellectual naiveté of thinking the issue is simpler than it is or the intellectual dishonesty of pushing a point of view while knowing that the evidence to support it is not really there. But the caution of the scientist need not and must not prevent careful thought about that future. This chapter attempts to lay out the evidence relevant to the question of whether foreign aid has in fact become obsolete in the context of a review of what economic research has told us about the benefits of international trade and investment.

There is wide disagreement as to what we have learned, as reflected in Canada during the debate on the North American Free Trade Agreement (NAFTA) during the 1980s. Some of the reasons for that disagreement become evident when the nature of the evidence used to reach conclusions on such an issue is examined.

The 'trade is better than aid' argument is not new. Developing countries have long pushed for greater access to the markets of industrial countries, noting that such access would in many cases be worth more to them than the aid they were receiving, the value of which was often lessened by its being 'tied' (i.e., the aid received had to be used to buy goods and services from the country providing it). This argument was undoubtedly valid; it did not, however, imply that aid was not useful, since the market access sought by the less developed countries (LDCs) was not forthcoming. The question more frequently asked about aid was whether it was useful per se, regardless of the level of trade. Here too there was little doubt that the outcome was less than one might have hoped. While some aid appears to have been productive, much has not and it is difficult to draw an overall balance. Some aid went to low pay-off uses, some disappeared into the wrong pockets, some was designed to avert looming crises and thus did not contribute to longer run growth. Proponents of the free market argue that much of the waste owes to the fact that aid was dispersed through governments. In determining whether trade and investment opportunities have rendered aid irrelevant it is necessary to consider the potential productivity of aid today, given the changed conditions from earlier decades and what has been learned over time about how to make it effective. But that is not our concern here.

The focus of this chapter is on changes in economic thinking with respect to the impact of trade and investment on developing countries, and especially on poor countries and their poorest inhabitants, and on the way in which the increasing resort to the market is likely to affect the disadvantaged peoples of the world. The central issue here, then, is not the overall advantages of more open international markets, but rather the implications for the poorer countries and people.

The Issues

Over the course of the last couple of decades a new 'conventional wisdom' has emerged within development economics on the merits of outward-orientation, the term used to summarize an economic policy that fosters international trade and capital flows by treating them on an equal footing with corresponding domestic flows. In accepting this position a country would give up the option of protecting its own firms through tariffs that raise the price of competing imports and of imposing conditions on foreign capital with the same objective – favouring its own firms. In a relatively short period of time the standard view shifted from an at least somewhat protectionist one to one that prefers near total freedom of trade and capital movements. What we may call the 'optimistic view' of the role of foreign trade and investment came into vogue as part of the neo-liberal or pro-market revolution in economics.

In the evolution of the central ideas of Western economic thought from the time of Adam Smith a little over two hundred years ago a continued emphasis has been placed on the importance of trade in general and international trade in particular. How international trade ought to be managed has been a frequent source of disagreement, both within countries and among them, partly because trade affects different members of a community or country in different ways, leading them to adopt different stances on the issue. But some of the important ideas are also difficult and counter-intuitive, making consensus unlikely and discussion in the more democratic polities a delicate matter at best.

Two general points should be made at the outset. First, there is considerable agreement about some of the benefits of trade. Just as it seems obvious that the doctor and the carpenter should specialize in the provision of their particular services and buy them from each other in the domestic market, so it is obvious that the tropical country should produce fruits and rice for buyers of temperate climates and the latter in turn should produce surpluses of wheat and temperate fruits for sale in the former. No one believes that such trade should be drastically limited. Hence the debate is about the optimal level of restrictions to trade and foreign investment, within the range from none to medium. Second, in much of the public discourse on matters of trade and even in the professional discourse there has always been a striking element of dogmatism and preformed views. Much public discourse occurs at what might be called a primary school level of analysis.

The process whereby the new view has gained ascendancy shows many of the features of the 'paradigm shift' described by Kuhn (1962). It involved a generally valid attack on some of the foundations of the previous pro-protection paradigm, including considerable evidence of incompetent and corrupt management and rent-seeking practices in its application. From an analytical point of view the substantial support for the new position is not surprising. The empirical evidence seems at first glance rather persuasive, and it is in accord with the simplest trade theory, to which many participants in the debates have been exposed. Ideological perspectives on the role of markets in general and of freedom of trade in particular tend to predominate and many participants on both sides of the debate have little detailed familiarly with the empirical evidence.

There are some very strong predispositions. Vested interests are at work; it was to be expected that Northern corporations aspiring to more open access to Third World economies would put their weight behind the shift, as would those Southern interests expecting to benefit. Intellectual followers have hastened to get on the right side of the arguments and thereby position themselves for jobs and favours, while resisters lose influence. In the World Bank, for example, a certain amount of 'intellectual cleansing' occurred during the transition of views on this issue. The shift of views on trade and foreign investment was facilitated by its being in tune with the broader ideological shift – in society and in the economics profession – towards markets as the best way to organize the production and distribution of nearly all goods and services. Finally, the shift of views has been hastened by the fact that policy cannot wait for all the evidence to come in; it must be formulated on the basis of best guesses. The policy shift was also accelerated (perhaps permitted in the first place) by the crisis brought on by the debt situation and the heavily indebted countries' resulting loss of bargaining power, and by the dearth of kindness or concern displayed by the industrial world at the time.

The most extreme claim made in favour of complete market openness is that it is significantly better than partial openness for all developing countries, regardless of their economic structure or context.

Opponents mount a range of criticisms, from the argument that elements of import substitution strategy remain valid to the proposition that fostering exports in the same product category (whether primary or light manufacture) in many large LDCs will eventually redound to the damage of everyone through trade effects (falling prices) or (partly the same idea) that it will flood industrial country markets to the point of raising protectionist pressures in those countries, thereby narrowing market opportunities. It is clear that the statistical base for many of the positive claims and many of the criticisms remains fragile; only time will tell whose views are closer to the truth.

The free trade debate in developed countries has in many ways paralleled the debate in the Third World. In both cases an interesting disjuncture has arisen between frontier economic theorizing and the practical views of applied economists and policy makers. In the last few decades increasing emphasis has been placed within international trade theory and the related area of industrial organization on situations of imperfect competition. This implies the decreasing direct relevance of the perfectly competitive model that tended to underlie many of the positive theoretical proofs with respect to the likely performance of free markets. Just at the time that the street-level debate has swung in the direction of markets the theory has moved, if not the other way, at least into a grey area where clear predictions are few and far between. Paul Krugman, a leading international trade economist, notes that the relative merits of more open or closed trade regimes for a country like the United States cannot be nailed down on the basis of either theory or easily interpretable empirical evidence; one must make a best guess. His own inclination is to lean towards the free trade end of the spectrum (Krugman, 1987), but he admits that it is a judgment call rather than a black-and-white matter. What is good for the United States may of course not be optimal for developing countries.

A somewhat separate debate in both the industrial and the developing countries concerns the internal distribution/employment effects of more open trade. Employment is the variable on which much of the political discourse focuses, since it is the most concrete and the most emotive; campaign rhetoric always focuses on the creation of jobs. However, since imports displace workers while exports create jobs, it is not immediately clear in which direction a more open trade regime (i.e., higher levels of imports and exports) would affect the level of employment. In fact, few industrial country economists believe that the level of trade has much net impact in the medium or long run on levels of employment or unemployment. It may, however, affect the aggregate demand for labour to some degree, and through that variable the level of wages. It can certainly affect the demand for specific types of labour and hence the distribution of earnings and of income. The industrial country advocates of free trade thus have a conceptually harder case to make than those from low-income, labour abundant countries, since simple theory suggests that freeing trade between these two groups would lower wages and increase income inequality in industrial countries while having the opposite effect in labour abundant countries (as argued by Krueger, 1988). In the industrial countries and especially in the United States the former view has been the object of a major wrangle (Wood, 1994, 1995; Katz and Murphy, 1992; Bound and Johnson, 1992). For the developing countries the theory was reassuring, since it suggested an increase in wages, but events have tended to contradict it. A major reconsideration of whether and how globalization is contributing to the widespread observed increases in inequality in the Third World is now ongoing, with particular fervour in Latin America (Berry, 1997; Bulmer-Thomas, 1996; Altimir, 1994).

The central conclusion of the traditional argument for free trade was that through international trade each country could specialize in what it did best, thereby improving its income and standard of living. The current argument in favour of the vigorous pursuit of international competitiveness, via productivity increases, industrial and labour flexibility, and so forth, represents a quite different strand of thinking, one which is often paired with the argument that withdrawal from the international economy is too costly an alternative to even contemplate. The current wave of globalization has nearly all countries scurrying for possible sources of competitive advantage. Michael Porter's much publicized writings (Porter, 1990) and frequent consulting forays into countries other than the United States have contributed to and symbolized this mode of thought. Fiscal prudence and keeping costs competitive have become buzzwords. It is widely accepted that some of what a society might otherwise have opted for (strong social security network, high social expenditures, high minimum wages, job security, etc.) may have to be sacrificed in order to attain the needed level of competition. These are clearly persuasive arguments at some level, judged by the fact that many people and countries have taken them seriously. But they are much less persuasive at the level of professional economics, for two main reasons.

First, the idea that a country's international competitiveness is based on its cost level is wrong. It denies and defies the most basic theorem of international trade, the law of comparative advantage, which says that all countries have a comparative advantage in exporting something even if they do not have an absolute cost or productivity advantage in anything. This comparative advantage will be manifest in export performance as long as they do not overvalue their currency, which is in any case hard to do continuously since it leads to a balance of payments deficit. Although a country can be productive in everything it does it cannot be internationally competitive in everything, in the sense of being a net exporter. The error rests on an extrapolation made from the fact that cost competitiveness determines a firm's success in international (and domestic) trade to reach the erroneous conclusion that the same holds true for a country as a whole. Such a conclusion neglects the fact that the basic determinant and regulator of export performance is the exchange rate.

Under certain conditions and in certain ways the idea of competition among nations is of course relevant and useful. A country that obtains the lead in producing and exporting a good the presence of which generates many positive externalities (say in research and development) may certainly benefit from 'getting there first.' And a given country can have a basically competitive relationship with other individual countries, though not with all other countries taken together. A country's relationship with the rest of the world is mainly complementary rather than competitive.

A second questionable idea prevalent in the recent debate on openness is that countries, either individually or collectively, have little chance of avoiding the collective loss of some social 'goods' at the altar of international competitiveness. For individual countries, and depending on their particular links with other countries, such loss may indeed be very hard to avoid, as was often said of Canada during the debates leading up to the Canada–United States Free Trade Agreement. We may be so closely linked to the U.S. economy and Canadian firms may be so willing to gravitate towards the larger neighbour that high taxes designed to pay for social services will backfire in weaker economic performance. But for the G-7 or OECD countries as a group such an argument cannot be made. Per capita income continues to rise in these countries. Though the range of selection of social strategies has narrowed in certain ways (associated with the degree to which it is possible for the present generation to borrow from future ones via fiscal deficits) and appears to be diminishing in others (e.g., in the area of medical care, as costs rise), it is not plausible to argue that international competition automatically reduces the range of social options for the world as a whole (or for the industrial countries as a whole) as long as incomes continue to rise. It does frequently reduce the options of individual countries, and this may make some reorganization of government and society necessary if earlier preferred options are to be retained. If Canadians can collectively agree to pay for a publicly funded medical system through higher personal income taxes than their counterparts in the United States, no one is going to stop them. It might be true that the system would be rendered expensive if many people tried to 'cheat' by going to the United States in the best earning and low medical cost years of their lives and then returning to Canada when their medical costs become higher, or if people particularly important to the functioning of the Canadian economy (e.g., certain classes of entrepreneurs) were to prefer the American option and emigrate. But only if a case can be made for such specific situations does the argument that freer trade necessarily narrows the options for social policy hold water. It still may, de facto, have that effect, depending on how the political process works. If the typical voter believes that Canadian social policy could not diverge much from the American pattern without some dire consequence, that belief might be self-fulfilling. Alternatively, the coalition of voters that led to the social policy choices in the past might be eroded in such a way that even though most people preferred the traditional outcome it would no longer be chosen. The relationship between social preferences in a population and the directions public policy takes can be very complicated and only when those complications are well understood in a given context can one predict how a change like freer trade will feed into policy choice. Often the 'loss of options' argument is used at the convenience of those who prefer in any case to move away from previous social sector patterns by persuading people that they are no longer affordable.

Globalization and the associated liberalization of trade and international investment do however lessen the policy space of national governments in certain ways. Is such loss good or bad? Those who feel the national state is the organ whereby nations define and implement their collective will in positive ways tend to decry the loss of independence. Where national governments misbehave, either in the extreme form of Nazi Germany or in the less drastic version of the incompetent administrations of a number of countries in recent times, the opposite conclusion is more natural. Much of the politics of Europe in the early post-war period involved an attempt to reduce Germany's economic independence to the point where its freedom to embark on military aggression was enfeebled. In any event, mutual dependence among countries may be expected to do more to curtail independence for some countries and less for others.

Trade theory implies that small countries on average gain more from trade than large ones, since they typically have within their own borders a narrower range of raw materials, skills, and so forth. But they are also more vulnerable. This will always be the case, unless the world moves to a genuinely rules-based system in which, despite having little role in creating the rules, small states are nonetheless relatively well protected by them. Much of the Canadian worry about free trade with the United States has its roots in this fear of being assimilated, forced, induced, or quietly sucked out of their own ways of doing things and into conformity with the American way, as U.S. cultural industries push for greater access to the Canadian market. If Canada, with its high levels of income and political participation, feels near defenceless in the face of the American juggernaut it is not hard to believe that other countries, even if better protected by distance, language, and cultural differences, would have comparable fears.

Then there is the even more acute vulnerability of the benighted populations of Zaire and Nigeria, who have seen the mineral wealth of their countries split between foreign investors extracting resources and corrupt governments sending any remaining profits to bank accounts in Europe. Nations that have reached a level of economic and political maturity are more able to defend themselves against both local and foreign exploiters; in that situation the power to intervene in the free flow of trade and investment may be wisely used, as it has generally been in Japan and other countries of East Asia.

A study of history and a look at the structure of world power both suggest that it would be naive to confidently expect an increasing level of trade and developing country integration into the world economy to provide a quick fix for world poverty. A prominent pattern, frequently repeated over the last century or two, is that in which, when lucrative export opportunities arise, the rich are quick to appropriate the natural resources involved and hence the benefits from the exports. Where lower-income people held the resources before this appropriation, it is likely to make them worse off. Such was the experience of the indigenous groups who farmed land that became commercially valuable as the countries of Central America shifted to coffee exports in the nineteenth century and to cotton and cattle exports in this century (Berry, 1988a). To understand how general this pattern may be, one must understand the politics surrounding the control of natural resources. At the world level, it would be similarly naive to believe that the rich industrial powers would create a world economic system the first priority of which was not their own economic interest. The tiny level of influence that the developing countries have recently had in the design of changes in world economic institutions underscores this concern.

Smaller states and developing country governments can lose power relative either to other countries or to the private sector, and this latter concern is important in much recent thinking. Given the lack of a world government with real capacity to act, does internationalization leave governments in general on the sidelines? One of the difficulties in predicting the full implications of increasing free trade and investment lies in the fact that such political effects are harder to predict than the economic ones. Will globalization leave national governments with so little decision-making autonomy that they become marginal actors? Or will the state 'come back in' and preserve its authority, as some globalizers claim it will? Before attempting to answer these questions let us first take a look at the historical evolution of ideas on the freedom of trade and at the arguments pro and con, ranging from the simplistic to the sophisticated.

The Smithian et al. Attacks on Impediments to Trade

Adam Smith's powerful statement on the value of letting markets determine who produces what and who sells to whom involved a critique of other arrangements, such as government planning and regulation, and of the limits to competition imposed by occupational cartels and by the European nation states. It involved an attack on the rent-seekers who were in a position to charge people for the right to trade with each other (e.g., those who controlled access to rivers or to a country's markets). A clear theoretical case can be made that such actions usually lower the total income of all those affected, that is, they hurt the losers more than they benefit the gainers. Smith's argument also involved the proposition that because of specialization and economies of scale, the opportunity to trade could raise productivity in many industries. These were powerful arguments and no reasonable person would now deny them. In fact, since the breakdown of the U.S.S.R. and the market-ward drift in China, it is generally recognized that markets are likely to be an important component of any optimal system for the production and distribution of goods and services. As suggested above, however, relative superiority does not necessarily imply a high absolute performance level.

Smith's ideas on the potential of markets were extended and elaborated by the great British classical economists of the nineteenth and early twentieth centuries. John Stuart Mill's (1848) classic argument for free trade was politically convenient for Britain at the time, since the country was by then the world's economic leader. Not surprisingly, other countries following in England's wake found Mill's arguments less persuasive, as reflected in the protectionist writings and/or actions of Friedrich List (1827, 1841) in Germany and Alexander Hamilton (see Taussig, 1893) in the United States. The simple static theory in which all countries gain from free trade (unless they happen to have some degree of monopoly or monopsony power in the markets in which they sell or buy) continued to dominate the textbooks but never the policy actions, although it no doubt had some influence on them. Thus the LDCs of the twentieth century followed the lead of their earlier counterparts in opting for protection. Dyed in the wool free traders (such as Bauer, 1976) viewed this as a case of policy being hijacked by vested interests in the protected sectors confounded by those who simply did not understand international trade theory. Writers such as Prebisch (1950) and Singer (1950) emphasized the barriers to Latin American access to U.S. markets and the declining international terms of trade between the primary products that they exported and the manufactured goods they imported as a strong reason to develop their industrial sectors, behind protection if necessary (and they assumed it would be necessary). True free traders did not oppose development of such industries, but argued that the process would be most efficient if it followed the dictates of the market, thus concluding that where such industrialization would benefit the country it would occur on its own without protection. Meanwhile, writers in the Marxist stream (Lenin, 1966; Frank, 1969) and later those of the dependency school in Latin America (Sunkel, 1969, 1973) and elsewhere argued that international economic interaction between the centre countries and those on the periphery was designed to benefit the former at the expense of the latter, an argument most pertinent under colonialism but relevant under post-colonial conditions as well.

The great wave of globalization that characterized the late nineteenth and early twentieth centuries brought many developing countries into closer contact and involvement in world markets than had been the case before. The Nobel Prize winning economist W. Arthur Lewis (1978) concluded that this involvement was the definitive turning point that set many countries on a path of growth and development. It also, however, coincided with and by some estimates contributed to a widening of income gaps both between countries (see Bairoch, 1975) and within the richer countries. Williamson (1996) argues that the worsening of the gap in the rich countries was accompanied by a decrease in inequality within the poorer ones.

The First World War and the Great Depression

The expansion of world markets and the world economy over the previous half-century failed to lay the groundwork either for political peace or sustained economic advance and was instead followed by the Great War, the Communist Revolution in Russia, and the Great Depression. The Russian Revolution eventually put into play a non-market system that constituted the main visible alternative form of economic organization. The Great Depression, in turn, constituted the major internal challenge to the effective functioning of markets since the dawn of the modern capitalist era. The enemies of that system believed it to be on its deathbed and not a few friends feared the same outcome. Under the pressure to save national economies, reasonably free trade with other countries came universally to be viewed as a cost too heavy to be borne. The idea that the import of goods that could have been produced at home led to a 'loss' in terms of employment and output seemed to be 'common sense.' Believers in the merits of trade wrung their hands at the downward spiral both in the level of trade and international investment and in the intellectual support for it. The new Keynesian economics, developed to help explain and formulate policy under the conditions of the Great Depression, gave little emphasis to the mechanisms that, according to classical economics, bring gains from trade, from specialization, and from efficient allocation of resources. On the contrary, it focused on mechanisms that emphasized its possible costs. Williamson (1996) argues that the inequality trends that globalization produced prior to the First World War were also at least partially responsible for the inter-war retreat from it.

The Post-War Drift from Keynesian Economics back to Neoclassical Economics and the Primacy of the Market

In the immediate aftermath of the Second World War a major objective of market supporters was to defend an institution under attack, both from its weak performance during the Depression and from the competition of a fast-growing centrally planned economy (the U.S.S.R.). It was recognized that competitive devaluation and protectionism had contributed to the spread and severity of the depression and that an institutional structure was needed to discourage a repetition of these circumstances. The result was the creation of the Bretton-Woods institutions, the World Bank, the International Monetary Fund (IMF), and the General Agreement on Tariffs and Trade (GATT). Whatever the components of the recipe were which made the difference, post-war growth and development in the Western industrialized countries surpassed most expectations, both in the rate of growth and in the relative stability of the world economy. Recessions came and went but none remotely approached the dimensions of the Great Depression. Japan emerged from the ashes of the war to record never-before-witnessed growth rates and quickly established itself as the first non-Western country to achieve true 'developed' status. Although the Keynesian model remained important in the economist's tool kit for several decades, the concern with inadequate aggregate demand gradually waned and was replaced by the fear of excess demand and inflation and a focus on efficiency of resource allocation, coupled with a growing fear of excessive and ineffective government.

The developing countries were systematically protectionist and interventionist in their economic policies in the early post-war decades. The thinking of Prebisch, carried into action through the Economic Commission for Latin America, was influential in that part of the world. In East Asia, Japan was determined to protect its own industries and to eschew the use of foreign investment from other, then-richer countries, while organizing a strong public-private collaboration designed to capture foreign markets. The East Asian followers also protected their markets and encouraged exports, while taking a variety of different stances on the question of foreign investment. Virtually all countries accepted the importance of the state as investor in infrastructure, given the relative lack thereof, and the importance of protection for infant industry; many assigned it a role at the 'commanding heights' of the economy, essential for keeping those key industries out of private and/or foreign hands. There was much suspicion of colonialism, especially in the recently independent countries whose leaders had grown up on a diet of anticolonialist ideas.

A widespread recognition that market size could matter (given the prevalence of economies of scale in parts of manufacturing and other activities) placed some limits on the scope for protectionism and suggested that local industry might only be feasible in some sectors and that there might be grounds for regional protectionism through trading arrangements.

Fear of the power of foreign states was accompanied by a fear of foreign multinational corporations, which came to be viewed as a threat to national sovereignty because of their size, their independence from political authorities, and their unusual capacity to extract rents from poor countries. In some circles they were demonized; in others their economic clout and technological level led to their being seen as the stars of the future, to which all reasonable countries would need to hitch their waggons.

Throughout this period there were, of course, stalwarts of the free trade persuasion, among whom Harry Johnson (1967) and Little et al. (1970) were prominent. On the other side of the fence, Emmanuel (1972) popularized the term 'unequal exchange' to describe what he considered to be a world trading system in which the rich countries exploited the poorer ones. The literature is striking for the scarcity of balanced observers who tried to understand the arguments on both sides and who could have been swayed in either direction according to the empirical evidence available. Many presented and defended only the arguments in favour of or against freer trade. The protectionists' lack of concern about the capacity of governments to implement coherent policies in this area was in many parts of the world an unforgivable naiveté. Neither side had much quantitative evidence at hand. No doubt some economists and perhaps some of the important decision makers had a better feel for the various sides of the issue than is evident from the literature; but one is pushed towards the conclusion that the level of professionalism among the writers at this time was generally low.

The post-war decades were economically successful ones, both in the industrialized countries and in the developing ones. Many economists have argued that much of the developing countries' success was due to that of the former. International trade rose faster than output, in part a simple recovery from the low levels of the Great Depression and the war. Several countries of East Asia followed Japan in establishing new growth performance records, vigorously pursuing foreign markets and upping their export/GDP ratios while, like Japan, using protection of their domestic markets to foster new industries. Brazil's economy grew very quickly, though not because of a high level of trade or increasing openness. By the end of the 1970s, however, a cross-country statistical association between fast export growth and fast overall growth had been clearly established (see Tyler, 1981; Feder, 1982) and a new 'conventional wisdom' emerged on the merits of outward-orientation, the term used to summarize a policy structure that favoured trade and other economic dealings with the rest of the world.

A Current Appraisal of the Free Trade and Investment Debate: Between Naiveté, Mystification, and Sophistication

How should the current understanding of the relative merits of free versus somewhat controlled movements of goods and capital between countries be described? And what are the implications of this understanding for the future of foreign aid? Do foreign aid flows become more critical because of the inequities caused by trade, or do they become redundant? Can trade take up where aid leaves off? In Chapter 7 Roy Culpeper suggests that as trade grows, the moral responsibility of the trading countries should similarly increase. But this may or may not happen. Determining whether a country will gain or lose from opening up trade involves weighing the gains of some against the losses of others. Not only are the relative merits and liabilities of freer trade difficult to measure, they vary depending on whose interests are at stake. This makes the question of freer versus controlled flows of international debate on trade and capital an ideal culture for breeding contesting ideologies, with all of the attendant mystification. It leaves the critical question of whether freer trade can replace aid in reducing economic misery a ready victim for ideologies.

Politicians may phrase the question in nationalist, common-sense terms: does a more outward orientation increase employment and reduce equity, or does it take away jobs and aggravate poverty? A more sophisticated version might enquire more directly about the international distribution of wealth: does freer trade lead to benefits for all participant countries or is there a tendency towards an 'unequal exchange' that favours the more powerful, industrial centre countries and handicaps those less powerful participant countries? Economists, however, may eschew any interest in what is good for a country or a portion of the globe in favour of an interest in 'world efficiency': does freer trade raise the growth rate by lowering the relative price of capital goods and making new technology more available? Or does it throw fledgling and 'infant' industries into the dog-eat-dog world of the international market and contribute to the stagnation of growing economies by killing off new ventures and encouraging a specialization in the risky world of primary products?

To answer these questions one has to know whether markets will in fact work as they should, that is, allow all participants to play the game. And if some governments decide they will not, then how effective are they in protecting their own industries? Markets certainly have their costs: they may underutilize resources, fall prey to monopoly domination, suppress new products, allow consumer preferences to be so influenced that consumers behave wastefully – the list goes on. The social damage of incessant competition may in fact undermine whatever gains accrue in the market place from getting the best performance out of participants. But if one decides the economic and social costs are too high, then the only recourse is to ask public bodies to regulate them, and rent seeking in inefficient governance is too common to lead one to expect that government action will compensate for the dereliction of the market place. The quandary only deepens.

A final answer to the questions posed above is, more than anything, an exercise in demystification. Within another decade or two, it is likely that a new near-consensus on the role and impacts of trade and foreign investment will take shape. It may not be too different from the present one (which favours the free movement of goods and capital, or something close to it), although serious empirical support for this paradigm is modest at present. However, the modest support for freeing trade may become stronger over time. And some of the negative effects that have been laid at the door of increased trade, such as increased inequality, may turn out to be transitory or the result of unrelated phenomena. In any event, opinions are likely to be better informed, given the advantage of hindsight. And aid's niche in the rising tide of international exchanges may be better defined.

Outlines of the Next Consensus

The next near-consensus will probably differ somewhat from the present one. My guess is that it will involve the following views.

Over the years the importance of trade and international interaction have frequently been exaggerated by both supporters and critics; these variables are in fact less central than both have tended to believe. The small estimates of loss from trade restrictions suggest that, unless economies of scale or dynamic arguments are important, a country's openness to international trade may be only a minor variable in explaining either rates of growth or levels of income. The importance of international trade (usually measured by its value in relation to national income) tends to be higher for small countries; the other side of this coin is that most of the world's population lives in countries with low international trading ratios and hence in situations where trade is less likely to be an important determinant of welfare. The very fact that trade theory is one of the more elaborated components of economic theory has focused a high level of attention on trade variables in interpretations of economic performance (Ranis, 1987). The current focus on human capital formation and institutions may eventually take some of this rather accidental prominence away from trade-related aspects.

Economic theory does not suggest that the optimal trade policy would be laissez-faire (no intervention). In many situations intervention could in principle make a positive contribution, so the laissez-faire option makes sense mainly when government is incapable of intervening efficiently. This issue is part and parcel of the more general question of industrial policy, and whether it is helpful for the state to point directions. If it is, then one of the logical instruments with which to point is protection. The debate, currently seen in part as a conflict between the 'American' view that governments cannot pick winners effectively and hence should not try, and the 'Japanese' view that they can and should, has surfaced in the World Bank and many other places. It has at times had an air of unreality, given the vast difference in performance over the last thirty years between the two countries, though with Japan now slowing to the pace of the other rich countries this contrast may be less telling. The next couple of decades will help to clarify in what degree Japan's past outperforming of the U.S. economy was due to its being in 'catch-up' mode, to its very high savings rates, or to its active industrial policy. It may well be that government intervention, in some form, is optimal for catching up countries though not for leaders.

The optimal policy on international trade and investment will vary greatly from country to country. A relatively high level of openness may be optimal in some countries, for reasons of small size, already mature economic structure, or government incompetence, while it may not be desirable for those with the opposite characteristics.

In the future it appears that the range of policy options open to most developing countries will narrow. This will affect these countries' potential and actual gains from trade and foreign investment, and it will also shift the focus of policy discussion to those instruments still under country control – things like anti-dumping strategy, free trade areas, and a tax system that is supportive of trade goals, capital controls, and human resource policy.

The above considerations, taken together, suggest the need for a new and more effective set of international institutions to protect the interests of the more vulnerable developing countries by giving them some influence in how their economies are affected by the rest of the world. Their policy freedom will diminish as the price of continued participation in the world economy; they will not receive the same foreign assistance nor will they have a seat at the table where the rules governing the international economy are established. The optimists who believe that free world markets will benefit all countries in adequate degree see no need for them to have such a seat. If the benefits of freer trade fail to compensate for the costs they incur or the reduction in foreign assistance, institutional reform will be called for. Such change will occur only when the present optimism is shown to be inappropriately naive.

In the interim, as countries wait to see whether trade will bring large benefits even to the poor, they will have to face the challenge of designing good social policies with limited resources. Trade reform greatly cuts the tax revenues from imports, and fiscal constraint curtails spending potential in general. There are in fact many ways in which social expenditures can be made more effective without additional resources; in most countries far too much is spent on costly curative medicine and far too little on effective preventive interventions. Though there are now many voices pushing for improvements in such directions (including frequently the World Bank) it remains to be seen whether the weight of inertia and the dominant position of the rich and powerful will permit significant improvements. Targeting of various expenditures towards the poor has been widely touted as an effective way to achieve more poverty alleviation from fewer resources, but it remains to be seen where it will work well on a sustainable basis (Berry, 1988b).

Any future consensus, however partial, will more than likely ignore whether the emerging global economy does or does not contribute to societal welfare in the developing countries, where welfare is defined broadly enough to include not just national income and its distribution but also those other determinants affected by the way an economy is structured – the psychological effects of the act of competing, crime and violence, the sense of belonging, and so forth. Economists are neither very adept at measuring or taking account of such factors nor particularly willing to confess to the possibility that they may be important. Others better equipped to understand them are often leery of measuring such subtle aspects of welfare and hence are unlikely to enter into a dialogue with economists. Some brave souls will probably launch into this area nonetheless, and it is to be hoped that their insights and conclusions will enrich the thinking around these issues.

4

External Conditionality, Local Ownership, and Development

GERRY HELLEINER

Introduction

Any reasonable definition of development incorporates more than sheer improvement in per capita gross national product (GNP). In the United Nations Development Programme (UNDP), emphasis is placed upon direct measures of human welfare such as infant mortality, literacy, and life expectancy. In earlier discussions of the meaning of development the focus was on employment, poverty alleviation, and equity in income distribution, with attention in some instances directed to 'independence' and/or the degree to which 'dependence' was being reduced. Dependence/independence relates to national (or individual) freedom of choice and the self-respect and dignity associated with having it. In more recent discussions, these considerations merge into discussions of participation and/or 'ownership.'

The weights to be assigned to different dimensions of development have always been a matter of dispute among statisticians and analysts of development phenomena. Increasingly, however, the prior view that there may be trade-offs among some of the most important ones, like equity in distribution and GNP growth, or participation/democracy and/or growth, has been displaced by an optimistic consensus, at least with respect to some of them. In particular, there seems to be general agreement that ownership of programs, policies, and projects is likely to bring economic success.

Yet the poorer of the developing countries see increasing intrusions from external sources upon the independent formulation of their own policies and rising conditionality associated with external assistance. Policy-based lending on the part of the International Monetary Fund

(IMF), the World Bank, and donors of official development assistance has increased dramatically during the past fifteen years or so. A high proportion of donor assistance to the poorest countries is now conditional upon an IMF 'seal of approval.' At the same time, in the policies of countries to which it lends the IMF has extended its range of interests to the composition of government expenditure, the environmental consequences of policy, the efficacy of domestic governance, and other such microlevel spheres. The World Bank, always more inclined to meddle in domestic policy formation, albeit mainly at the project level in its earlier years, has likewise extended its range of conditions upon its program lending to an enormous range of policy areas. The degree of detail in recent World Bank conditionality has at times reached ludicrous levels, such as its insistence upon the privatization of the dog-sniffing service at the airport in Jamaica (Kapur, 1997).

Externally financed projects and programs in the poor countries of sub-Saharan Africa continue to be overwhelmingly donor-driven. This is evident both in multilateral deliberations in the IMF and World Bank (within which recipients have marginal individual or collective influence), the Special Program of Assistance for Africa (SPA) (donors only), the Consultative Groups (CGs) (World Bank in the chair) and, of course, in bilateral donor–recipient relationships.

Is it any wonder that local governments and citizenry frequently find difficulty in feeling much sense of ownership of their policies, programs, or projects? When economic events are going badly, local political leaders, who find it convenient to blame external forces for their problems, may also contribute to this local sense of powerlessness and dependence. Perhaps it cannot be otherwise. Donors are donors. Particularly when funds are becoming scarcer, suppliers of funds are prone to the imposition of more controls, greater selectivity, and the provision – in substitution for money – of more (often unsolicited) advice.

This increasing intrusion upon domestic sovereignty and increasing effort to lever external finance into domestic policy change has, somewhat oddly, been accompanied by firm declarations on the part of the donors of the need for national ownership of programs and policy. The principles of effective aid, as enunciated by the Organization for Economic Cooperation and Development (OECD) Development Assistance Committee (DAC), go so far as to say: 'Developing countries themselves are responsible for determining and implementing their programmes and policies. This principle applies with particular force to programme assistance, which is often related to important policy reform measures and has broad-based impacts upon the economy. In particular, developing countries must "own" their own structural adjustment programmes. This implies that the basis for coordinated international action must be the policy and programme statements and actions of the developing country itself, which must also, to the largest extent possible, be in charge of international aid coordination arrangements' (OECD, 1992, para. 248).

Excellent principles for aid coordination were also agreed by DAC donors in 1986. They begin: 'Central responsibility for aid coordination lies with each recipient' (quoted in World Bank, 1995b: 121).

Technical assistance has been one of the most difficult and divisive areas of donor intrusion. A high proportion of the technical assistance provided to low-income developing countries has not been requested by them. Rather, its provision is a condition associated with the provision of finance and other forms of assistance, and frequently seems to have become little more than a device for the monitoring and enforcement of external conditions and/or the creation of employment for the nationals and firms of donor countries. Typically such assistance has carried enormous costs not only in terms of the opportunity cost of the donor funds but also in local costs associated with 'servicing' inexperienced and expensive foreigners. Independent analyses of the benefits and costs of technical cooperation in sub-Saharan Africa have uncovered a pretty sorry record (e.g., Berg, 1993).

Technical assistance provided as a condition of financial aid has been singularly ineffective in the creation and development of indigenous capacity. Moreover, such support for capacity building as has been attempted by donors has often been frustrated by other elements of their own policies. For example, donors and international financial and aid institutions are among the main employers of those whose skills have been upgraded via local or foreign training programs. One study noted that over half of the Kenyan government economists seconded for MA training in the late 1980s subsequently left for such better-paid jobs (World Bank, 1995b: 36).

Again, the Development Assistance Committee of the OECD has adopted impressive principles for 'new orientations in technical cooperation' that stress the 'strategic objectives of ... long-term capacity building ... rather than immediate short-term performance improvement'; 'the central role of developing countries in the planning, design and management of technical cooperation'; 'ownership, i.e. responsibility and control of technical cooperation programmes and projects at all stages by the intended beneficiaries ...'; 'greater use of local expertise and existing structures'; 'objectives in terms of outcomes to be achieved rather than inputs to be provided'; and 'greater attention to the costs and cost effectiveness of technical cooperation activities' (OECD, 1994: 21). Yet there has been little sign of change in donor approaches. In one recent instance (Tanzania, January 1997), only minutes after donors had committed themselves, in a donor–recipient meeting, to a new 'development partnership' incorporating such principles, some of them were again emphasizing the need for their continuing control of selection processes and the utilization of their own nationals in technical assistance.

The Meaning of 'Ownership'

The World Bank has summarized its consensus on ownership issues as follows: 'Typically, assistance programmes that the recipient country perceives as being imposed end in failure or have only a small development impact. Governments and beneficiaries do not feel they have a stake when they have not contributed to the development of a programme. Furthermore, "home-grown" programmes may be more effective in incorporating institutional capacity, reflecting the needs of different domestic constituencies, and addressing constraints' (World Bank, 1995b: 6).

How can this increasing rhetorical emphasis on the importance of local ownership be reconciled with the increasing intrusiveness of external conditionality?

One obvious potential source of the apparent paradox is the extreme fuzziness that frequently surrounds the concept of ownership. In a recent study of relationships between an African country and its aid donors in which I was involved (Helleiner et al., 1995) representatives of donor agencies were asked about their understanding of ownership issues. This elicited some remarkable responses, some of which, although not reported in the published study, deserve quotation verbatim here:

- 'Ownership exists when they do what we want them to do but they do so voluntarily.'
- 'We want them to take ownership. Of course, they must do what we want. If not, they should get their money elsewhere.'

- 'We have to pressure the local government to take ownership.'
- 'We have to be realistic. Our taxpayers want to be sure their money is being used well. They want to know there's someone they can trust, a national of their own country, in charge.'
- 'I routinely instruct my staff to draft terms of reference for technical cooperation projects and then spend half an hour with a local government official on it.'

In the hands of determined and powerful aid bureaucracies the need for local ownership can become the basis for yet more conditions on donor assistance. However much it may have conceded as to the pace, sequencing, and details of adjustment programs, the World Bank, which has been the de facto intellectual leader of the aid agencies in the 1980s and 1990s, has not significantly altered its basic recipe for development-oriented reform. But it now wants local policy makers not simply to do what it recommends but also to believe in it.

The Bank evidently has no intention of allowing recipients of its loans to develop their own programs if it has the power to prescribe them itself. Having observed the correlation between ownership and success, the World Bank's operations evaluators now urge staff to rate borrowers on such indicators of the 'intensity' of ownership as: the locus of initiative for the program, the level of local intellectual conviction, expressions of 'political will' on the part of political leaders, and local efforts towards consensus-building among relevant constituencies (Johnson and Wasty, 1993; Jayarajah and Branson, 1995: 234–41). Unfortunately, as a recent World Bank summary of aid issues laconically observes, 'One of the difficulties with ownership ... is that it is much easier to recognize with hindsight than in advance'! (World Bank, 1995b: 6). This new emphasis on the need for local commitment and ownership of Bank-prescribed programs is a far cry from World Bank (or donor) support of genuinely local approaches, complete with their unapproved (by donors or World Bank staff) components, some of which may be quite 'heterodox.'

This discussion of qualitative donor assessment of ownership obviously overlaps that of even more controversial new donor assessments of the quality of local governance (Kapur, 1997). Indeed the World Bank is now frequently explicit in linking ownership, governance, and participation in its assessments of recipient country commitment to change (e.g., World Bank, 1995b: 5–7).

Of course, countries with significant alternative sources of finance and/or greater political and economic clout do not allow their policies and programs to be unduly influenced by the World Bank or any other external actor. The Bank has thus been peculiarly aggressive and intrusive in the smaller and lowest-income countries, notably those of sub-Saharan Africa, where its relative power is greatest. Commenting on the enormous variation in the salience of governance issues in Bank Board, CG, and other country-focused discussion, Kapur notes that: 'Financial dependence on official external finance and economic outcomes have been at least as important as the intrinsic objective reality of "governance" related issues, in the degree of pressure brought to bear on individual countries' (Kapur, 1997: 137; see also Mohammed, 1997). To the recipients' irritation with the donors' conditionality is consequently added their resentment over the non-uniformity of donor relationships with different recipient countries.

Donor Needs and Ownership

National ownership of programs is lost not only because of the pushing of external agendas but also via the more pragmatic considerations and approaches of donors. A remarkably high percentage of bilateral development assistance to low-income Africa goes directly to overseas contractors and foreign technical personnel, or to local suppliers, non-governmental organizations (NGOs), or even local government officials (topping up their inadequate salaries), without going through any local governmental budgetary system. The local governments frequently have no information on these flows or on the projects they support. Indeed, most donors cannot or will not supply information on these flows to the local governments even when asked to do so. Externally supported projects frequently exist as 'islands' within the local economy and society, supplying certain services to a select few but otherwise unconnected in any way to indigenous development processes.

How can such practices be explained? In part, they are the result of faulty domestic policies and approaches. In significant part, however, they are the result of aid donor practices. Aid donor agencies typically develop medium-term country strategies or country programs that enunciate their own priorities for the recipient country and are used in domestic parliamentary and public discussions within their own political systems. Donor aid strategies may encompass cross-country priority issues of their own that bear no relationship to the priorities of local governments. Moreover, the timetables and administrative requirements associated with these country-level aid programs may not coincide either with those of the recipient country or with those of other aid donors.

Our earlier study of aid relationships addressed these issues as follows:

> The forces pushing bilateral donor agencies in directions which undermine [local] ownership are varied and deep-seated. Each donor has its own aid policies and 'agenda,' and is anxious to pursue its own objectives even when these are not shared by the government. Constitutional, parliamentary and accounting requirements, aimed at ensuring proper accountability for the use of taxpayers' money, may also increase donor intrusiveness, a tendency that can only be enhanced by the perception ... that corruption is a large and growing problem ... It is also likely that agency staff will be under pressure to ensure that they spend their budgets, even if it requires a degree of bulldozing to achieve this result, and they may well see it as in their own career interests to secure a high level of aid giving or lending. They are also under pressure to show quick results and short-term efficiency. There are few rewards for those who are prepared to sacrifice short-term performance for the sake of slower but more sustainable progress. (Helleiner et al., 1995: 15)

Needless to say, the degree of control and/or intrusion by the International Monetary Fund and the World Bank, about which much has recently been written, is no less than that of bilateral donors and quite possibly considerably more – both at the level of overall country policy formation and at the project level.

A recent report, in which (unusually) significant African inputs were included (World Bank, 1996a), assesses the performance of donors, the World Bank, and governments in Africa in devastating terms:

- 'The World Bank and other donors may actually have made matters worse on the capacity building front because they have tended to "exacerbate Africa's capacity problems through approaches that have been supply driven and geared to satisfying internal institutional demands rather than the capacity building needs of the countries".'
- 'The donors' flawed approach in Africa is in part attributable to host governments' failure to develop a coherent vision of capacity building, leaving the field open for donors to impose their own ideas.'
- 'Despite their stated intentions to promote sustainable development

and local capacity, donors have often behaved in a way that has either had no impact on local capacity or, worse, has eroded it. Donors have been too quick to seize the initiative for policymaking and project and program preparation from local agencies. This has often been met by complacency on the country side; the result has been to reduce demand for local capacity development and to atrophy existing capacity. A closely related point is that national authorities have rarely been strongly "committed to" or had "ownership of" capacity building efforts. Most, instead, have been driven by external donors.'

Aid donors can and do rationalize their high degree of intrusion and conditionality. They can frequently point to government ineffectiveness or corruption or repression. They can assert the need to 'get on with' the pressing needs of poverty alleviation and development in the face of enormous local constraints. Their recent emphasis on the liberalization of markets and the need for local participatory political processes can provide them, at least in their own eyes, with the moral authority of the (self-appointed) role of initiator and protector of liberal values. Sometimes donors argue that they are bolstering reformist groups within the local government or society in their struggles against interest groups that oppose developmental change.

Non-governmental organizations are as frequently involved in such rationales for their behaviour as are donor governments. Northern NGOs are perceived by many developing country policy makers as seeking 'to superimpose their own cultural values on societies subscribing to different ethical and spiritual values' (Mohammed, 1997). They promote their own ideological or cultural preferences in a new manifestation of 'rich-country paternalism' (ibid.).

Conditionality and Its Problems

The evidence as to the limited efficacy of external conditions and the importance of local ownership is by now fairly extensive. The foremost independent analyst of IMF activities in developing countries summarizes the evidence as follows: 'the high-conditionality adjustment programmes of the IMF and World Bank have only rather weak revealed ability to achieve their own objectives' (Killick, forthcoming). Killick, like many others, notes that reforms are undertaken and sustained only when governments have themselves decided to enact them, and for such decisions to be made external conditionality is neither necessary nor sufficient.

Conditionality is obviously most powerful when it is collectively imposed by all or most of the external financiers upon which a low-income country is dependent. In recent years, individual bilateral donors have ceded much of their decision-making power, in respect of their program assistance to the lowest-income countries, to the IMF. (They are less inclined to reduce their powerful roles in project finance and technical cooperation, but in those spheres as well they have been influenced by IMF decisions.)

The IMF 'certifies' that macroeconomic management of a country is sound and that it is 'deserving' of support. The IMF's monitoring and signalling activity has been the basis for many donors' actions in the poorest countries over the last fifteen years or so: aid flows to these countries have been significantly correlated with IMF agreements.

Bilateral official development assistance provides much larger sums to the poorest countries than do the international financial institutions. Much of it is in the particularly valuable form of balance of payments finance, which is relatively fast disbursing, once conditions are agreed, and provides desirable financial flexibility for the recipient. Such program finance is an essential element in longer-term development financing, not least when a country is undertaking major policy reforms involving significant short-term social costs. When provided by the IMF (or International Development Association (IDA)) this finance is provided as a loan rather than in the (more valuable) grant form which many aid donors provide.

The IMF's current role in the provision of such finance to the poorest countries is only that of a 'bit player.' Yet IMF influence seems great. Since this point is often misunderstood, it is worth elaborating in some detail.

Because its loans must be serviced and repaid, the IMF has generally registered net transfers from the poorest countries over the period of the late 1980s and the 1990s. In 1996, IMF net transfers were negative in respect of the low-income countries as a whole, the severely indebted low-income countries (SILICs), and sub-Saharan Africa. IMF net transfers to sub-Saharan Africa were positive only in 1994 and 1995, with a maximum of $450 million in 1994. IMF net transfers to SILICs were positive only in 1994 – $270 million. IMF net transfers to the low-income countries as a group were positive only in 1991 and 1992, with a maximum of one billion dollars in 1992.

These numbers can be compared with those of the IDA, which, like the IMF, offers low-interest loans rather than grants. IDA net transfers have been positive throughout: in 1994, $2.6 billion to sub-Saharan Africa; $2.6 billion to the SILICs; and $5.1 billion to the low-income countries as a whole. Of these IDA transfers, perhaps 10 to 15 per cent are now made available on a general (multisectoral) basis, and further sectoral loans are effectively also program finance. The IDA is clearly a significantly more important source of balance of payments finance to the poorest countries than the IMF.

Much bigger still, however, is the role of bilateral aid donors. Excluding technical cooperation agreements, their finance, in the form of grants, totalled, in 1995, $12.7 billion to sub-Saharan Africa, $13.2 billion to the SILICs, and $19.8 billion to the low-income countries as a whole. The proportions made available in balance of payments forms vary enormously but probably are, on average, similar to those in IDA funding. (All of these numbers are taken from the World Bank's *World Debt Tables, External Finance for Developing Countries*, 1995.)

To the degree that aid donors rely on the IMF for their decisions as to commitments and/or disbursements, either for balance of payments finance or for development finance more generally, the IMF plays a major role as a 'gatekeeper' for such funding. The IMF performs a similar signalling role for the Paris Club of official creditors. Bilateral debt relief in the Paris Club is contingent upon the IMF seal of approval.

This key signalling role is performed whether or not the IMF itself supplies finance, which, as has been seen, it has not (in net terms) recently been providing. Indeed the IMF would undoubtedly continue to perform this role, through its Article IV consultations, standby agreements, and 'shadow programs,' if its own Enhanced Structural Adjustment Facility (ESAF) no longer existed. The provision of IMF finance on a concessional basis through ESAF is irrelevant to the IMF's performance of its enormously important role – as long as the aid donors and official creditors continue to rely upon the IMF's signals in making their own decisions as to bilateral financing and debt relief.

Through the application of its conditionality and the leverage it has over debt relief and other funding, the IMF is believed by many to have a major effect upon the design of macroeconomic policy in the poorest countries. There remains considerable doubt, however, as has been seen, as to the effectiveness of any such conditions in circumstances where the developing country government does not itself

believe in the policies it is implementing. Without indigenous ownership, at least at the level of the government and quite possibly at the
level of the entire society, policies are unlikely to be sustainable and
externally imposed conditions will not work.

There are also, of course, continuing controversies as to the appropriateness of the programs in which the IMF is involved. Among the
informed, such controversies do not relate to the overall need for effective macroeconomic management – the maintenance of both internal
and external macroeconomic balance. Developing country policy makers' (and others') important disagreements with the IMF relate to such
matters as the pace of change, the sequencing of policy reforms, the
degree of reliance upon the market, the distributional impact of
changes, and political feasibility and not to the need for effective
macroeconomic management, in particular via prudence in the government budget and maintenance of a realistic exchange rate. (Less
informed criticism, much of it from the NGO community, has blamed
the IMF for the effects of exogenous shocks or mismanagement, or for
policies that were responses, often not very effective ones, to such
shocks and/or prior mismanagement.) The high mortality rate and
limited apparent effectiveness of IMF-related programs in the poorest
countries (and, of course, the continued or increased poverty associated with them) are the product of a complex mixture of difficult initial
conditions, exogenous shocks, slippage in necessary policy changes,
policy misjudgments (including those of IMF advisers), political influences, and genuine technical or political ignorance as to what may
work. In many of the poorest countries, in recent years, this list of negative influences must also include the limited degree of local ownership of many programs, the blame for which has to be shared with
other donors, not least the World Bank.

It is therefore extremely difficult to assess the effect of IMF pressure
upon outcomes in the poorest developing countries. In general, the
IMF probably tips the balance of political and/or technocratic forces
within the poorest countries towards the central bank and the ministry
of finance. How much it does so and whether the effects are beneficial
clearly depends upon the country. In cases where there is corruption,
mismanagement, incompetence, or political pressure for unsustainable
macroeconomic policies, the effect of its external pressure may be beneficial. But where there is a competent and accountable administration
the IMF's inherent conservatism may generate less desirable outcomes.
A critical question with respect to both the makeup of local policies

and their eventual effects is, in any case, the degree of local ownership of policies and programs.

Bilateral donors should be encouraged to base their finance to individual countries much less on IMF decisions and much more on the basis of longer term and more developmental criteria than those of the IMF, with their relatively erratic 'stop and go' consequences. But such longer term signalling and monitoring should not simply be left by donors to the World Bank, for the Bank has often been more intrusive, demanding, and doctrinaire in the poorest countries than the IMF.

The difficulties with IMF gatekeeping derive not merely from the specific content of its approaches but also, and even more, from the de facto monopoly power awarded by the international community to a single agency, and a relatively secretive one at that. Bilateral donors, while trying to improve their coordination, should be able to rely on a variety of independent sources for analysis, including the UN and independent analysts. Having selected particular countries for support, donors should insist on continuing local ownership of programs and make long-term commitments or contracts with them, including contingency provisions that provide for the unexpected.

Current Perspectives and Possibilities

In 1995, bilateral donors of the OECD adopted a new and widely heralded statement on 'development partnerships' which they published in the 1996 annual report of their Development Assistance Committee. In it, donors sharpened their emphasis upon 'participation, good governance and accountability, the protection of human rights and the rule of law' (OECD, 1996a, 6). In commenting upon it, the DAC chairman noted: 'If donors believe in local ownership and participation, then they must seek to use channels and methods of co-operation that do not undermine those values. External support must avoid stifling or attempting to substitute for local initiative ... The principles of self reliance, local ownership and participation which underlie the partnership approach are inconsistent with the idea of conditions imposed by donors to coerce poor countries to do things they don't want to do in order to obtain resources they need. That view of conditionality was always of dubious value. Treating development co-operation as a partnership makes clear that it is obsolete' (OECD, 7).

If only matters were so easy! Old-fashioned conditionality may be obsolete in the partnership rhetoric of aid diplomats, but the reality of aid relationships is quite another matter. It is worth recalling that partnership was also the theme of the Pearson Commission Report of 1969! The commission was appointed to conduct a 'grand assize' of the record of development assistance in response to the perceived disillusion and crisis in foreign aid of the late 1960s. Its comments on the development relationship and its recognition of the needs of both partners could easily have come from last year's DAC Report (e.g., Pearson et al., 1969: 6; OECD, 1996a: 7). And I.G. Patel's response to the report to the effect that '... the concept of a genuine partnership in development ... lacks credibility' (Patel, 1971: 305) is still apposite. His penetrating analysis of the aid relationship and his heartfelt plea for a quieter style therein – a 'long-term trust' approach – could have been written yesterday. Very little has changed, except that aid levels are now more firmly projected to decline.

There does seem, however, to be greater emphasis in some circles of the OECD (1996a: 7–8) and in the World Bank on capacity building and the need for longer time horizons. Reviewing the lessons of recent experience for donors, the Bank now explicitly acknowledges that 'in the short-term donors' desire to speed implementation and disbursement may conflict with ownership, institutional development and capacity building goals' (World Bank, 1995b: 3). The latter goals are now seen (at least in this source) as deserving of priority.

This new thrust may elicit a whole new barrage of World Bank study teams and research missions, which have in the past frequently been neither requested nor wanted and are too often of dubious social productivity. The World Bank's active pushing of requests for technical assistance and further studies is well known.

One route forward may be to rework the application of conditionality. Policy conditionality is typically now deployed via a set of targets for performance or action, compliance with which is in principle required to trigger the release of the next tranche of funding. In some cases, where the targets are multidimensional (with lack of clarity as to the weights to be assigned to each) and/or where the donors have other dominant objectives, the missing of such targets may not result in a reduction of funding. In other cases, rigid adherence to the original targets can impart an undesirable 'stop/go' character to the development program. In general, this short leash and intrusive approach creates irritation surrounding the negotiation and subsequent interpretation of the targets, incentives to 'fudge' numbers and facts, uncertainty about funding prospects, and hence unduly short-term perspectives on the part of both private and public investors and decision makers.

Many of these problems could be reduced by shifting to a longer leash approach, in which donors would undertake to make steadier and longer term commitments after a donor–recipient dialogue had established agreement as to the general nature of the requirements for development and the government's credibility with respect to their pursuit. Conditionality could thus take more the form of an ex post reward for appropriate approaches rather than an ex ante lever against future change. To be more effective, such donor commitments could include pre-agreed financial supplements and/or waivers to prevent shortfalls emanating from (foreseeable) adverse contingencies. Recipient governments would thereby be enabled to develop their own programs with less uncertainty about their funding.

But how much commitment is enough? And commitment to what? Donors and the World Bank still seem to assume that the required policies are agreed and obvious and that the only question that arises is therefore the degree of commitment on the part of the locals to what everyone agrees is necessary. If there is dispute, external advice is generally more sound and should prevail over the views of those locals (national governments) with whom they engage in 'consultation.' But that can only be true, if true at all, of a few of the key program issues. Beyond the basics of fiscal and exchange rate management, to what must a government be committed? There are bound to be differences of opinion and different degrees of commitment to a wide variety of other policy issues – and the differences are not purely a matter of pace or sequence. Breaking up the program into a series of smaller, focused elements has been suggested and may help to prevent inappropriate holdup of some program finance. But differences of opinion and differences in the degree of commitment in these separate areas will remain and what, then, can be meant by the degree of commitment to the overall program?

At present, donors and the International Finance Institutions (IFIs) seem to want recipient governments to commit to whatever it is that they prescribe. And the IFI record, not to speak of the many other donors with their own prescriptions, is not without blemishes, particularly in Africa. Consultation can be a fig leaf for continued aggressive donor behaviour. The number of spheres in which the IFIs and donors may be within their rights to continue to bulldoze are relatively few.

Yet their propensity to try to push in a variety of spheres shows no sign of declining.

Conclusions

Are the policy conditions attached to the supply of external finance by international financial institutions and aid donors generally such as to improve the prospects of its effective use and to contribute to long-run development in the recipient country? As long as they relate to the need for prudent macroeconomic management, the answer may generally be 'yes,' but, even so, the bluntness and pacing of required policy reforms may be harmful to development prospects. The developmental effects of premature or weakly designed reforms in such spheres as trade and financial liberalization, privatization, and civil service 'reform' have sometimes been dubious. Many observers believe that external conditions have often reflected too doctrinaire and rigid a view of development's requirements.

Does the application of such external conditionality work, in the sense of promoting sustainable change towards policies that promote development? There is growing consensus that the answer to this question is typically 'no.' Rather, it breeds a reduced sense of local responsibility for and ownership of national programs.

Finally, are such external conditions applied uniformly and fairly to all prospective recipients of external finance from official sources? Absolutely not. They are applied most stringently to the smallest, poorest, and most aid-dependent countries.

What is to be done? Ultimately, the responsibility for taking control at the local level must rest with the locals. Marie France Labrecque, in Chapter 14, has shown the benefits of taking control over development planning at the community level, but the principle holds for regional and national levels as well. It is possible, in most circumstances, for potential recipients to reduce the donor-driven character of external assistance by 'just saying no.' In the present environment, this may involve significant short-term costs and risks. There is nevertheless no substitute for developing one's own planning, budgets, and policies.

In the vast majority of low-income countries, those characterized by roughly 'normal' standards of governmental probity and politics, the realism and pragmatism that aid donors proclaim as their basis for intrusion is in actual fact extreme myopia. Long-run development can come only with locally owned efforts and indigenous capacity. Sustainable change is likely to take place relatively slowly and cannot be unduly pushed from above or from outside. As far as national-level developmental programs and policies are concerned, there is no substitute for an effective local state. This implies that donors must back off from intrusion and conditionality if they truly seek to promote development.

Ultimately, the choice before the donors lies between two kinds of potential error: the first involves failures and mistakes that might have been prevented through greater conditionality; the second involves the suppression of indigenous capacity building because of an over-eager imposition of external conditions. Tightened conditionality, it has here been argued, typically has minimal developmental effect. The appropriate choice therefore seems clear: donors should take more chances on local decision making.

When conditionality is eased and the leash upon external funding is lengthened there are bound to be some failures and disappointments. Where there is local ownership, however, at least some indigenous learning will ensue from failure. Effective learning processes typically involve a degree of trial and error. Such learning is a critical element in indigenous capacity building.

What should the donors do? Ideally, the answers are fairly obvious – and they are implied in the rhetoric of the World Bank and the donors. Suppliers of aid should adopt longer time horizons in their approaches to developing countries, emphasize capacity building and institutional strengthening, reduce significantly their degree of intrusion into domestic policy making, encourage genuine policy dialogue, and adopt a more supportive rather than substitutive stance. Incentives within donor agencies will have to change substantially if such aspirations for change in their practices are to have any hope of serious implementation.

Donors may prove incapable, despite their rhetoric, of such major change. Recipient governments may have to face up to the fact that 'soft' money will only henceforth be forthcoming 'with more and more strings attached' (Kapur, 1997). It will then be for them alone to decide whether the funds are worth the conditions. In such circumstances, it should come as no surprise if increasing numbers of recipients think not, that aid relationships remain difficult, or that ODA continues to decline.

PART THREE

Beyond Donor Agencies

State-based donor bureaucracies are too entangled in the vines of national interests to give much support to the creation of a different institutional vehicle, be it a supranational body or a version of a non-governmental organization (NGO), to coordinate the international development mission. But this is what must be done if development assistance is to survive. The present national agencies are too sluggish with the fatigue of fifty years and the welter of expectations they now shoulder to think beyond the current institutional vehicles of development assistance. Each of the following two chapters considers alternatives to the national bureaucracies that now administer assistance. They are, in each case, products of authors who have challenged aid's mandarins for years and with such flair that the mandarins now look to them to divine what new institution will emerge from the aged remains of Bretton Woods.

The background for both of these chapters is a dramatic turn of events in the composition of global flows of wealth. While development assistance from the twenty-one member countries of OECD's Development Assistance Committee dropped by 4 per cent between 1995 and 1996, private flows increased by 40 per cent. Private commercial flows are approaching $300 billion per year, while development assistance flows are in the neighbourhood of $45 billion. These figures mark a dramatic change in the complexion of global capital flows since, prior to 1990, public development assistance flows exceeded private ones. Public flows of aid are now so outflanked by private flows that development assistance from national donor agencies may appear to border on the obsolete. As much as anything, this reversal ushers in a changed global era in which private market flows predominate. The question then becomes what this shift means for the aid regime.

This section offers two very different answers. Keith Griffin traces the rapid decrease of aid and the equally rapid increase in private flows and concludes that aid's rapid decline and the international market's supremacy presages a post-aid era. The fact of aid's declining quantities is matched by its ineffectiveness, and this sets the stage for asking what will take aid's place. More to the point, who will represent the interests of the powerless in this busy global bazaar? Griffin's proposal is to establish an international mechanism with the power to advocate social justice and to reduce poverty and inequalities. The future global commons, when it comes, will rely on a supranational body with the power to redress the inequities that are inevitable in this global bazaar.

Ian Smillie considers the role of the NGO in the transformation of aid. Neither public nor private, profit nor non-profit, non-governmental organizations bubble directly out of citizens' concern. They have come to the world stage relatively free of the institutional baggage of market firms and government bureaucracies, driven for the most part by a vision of a more humane world. The classic NGO is the cottage industry office staffed by volunteers and good neighbours who believe that even a small organization can diminish the world's grief in some way. But Ian Smillie, once the director of a large Canadian NGO and an articulate spokesperson for NGOs poses the compelling question: if companies can globalize why should not NGOs do the same? The answer is that they can, and a half of dozen now do, like World Vision, supporting large offices in New York and London. These few NGOs have risen to uncommon influence in the last few decades as service providers and contractors to large donor agencies. They are curious hybrids, free of the irreconcilable mandates of national and international agencies and yet large enough to provide a viable mechanism for advocating global justice.

5

The Death and Rebirth of International Economic Cooperation

KEITH GRIFFIN

Foreign aid as we have known it for fifty years is in rapid and probably terminal decline. Aid programs limped along for decades with donors reaching about half of the United Nations' target of 0.7 per cent of gross national product (GNP), but with the end of the Cold War the political incentive for rich countries to assist the poor became much weaker and the frailty of the economic arguments justifying foreign aid became more widely acknowledged.[1] The combination of weak political incentives and unpersuasive economic arguments is likely to prove fatal.

Indeed, starting in 1993, foreign aid programs have been sharply reduced. This initial fall may have been due in part to economic difficulties experienced in major donor countries, but I believe there has been a fundamental change in outlook and that the decline will be irreversible. Between 1992 and 1995 official development assistance (ODA) fell from 0.33 to 0.27 per cent of the GNP of donor countries.[2] That is, the aid ratio fell by 18.2 per cent in just three years. Moreover, between 1991 (the peak year) and 1995 the absolute amount of aid also fell in real terms by US$8.5 billion and the proportion of aid that had to be devoted to emergency relief rose (from 2 per cent to 10 per cent).[3] In other words, the amount of aid in real terms available for long-term development assistance is falling precipitously.[4]

The fall has been led by the United States but the cuts in aid programs are widespread. In 1990 the aid ratio (ODA/GNP) in the United States was 0.21. Five years later it was 0.10, a fall of more than 50 per cent. Canada, one of the more generous donors, saw its aid ratio slip during the same period from 0.44 to 0.38. The fall was even greater in the Netherlands, a country long known for its strong commitment to international economic cooperation: the aid ratio in that country fell from 0.92 in 1990 to 0.81 in 1995. Perhaps most telling of all is the decline of aid in Scandinavia. The three major Nordic countries (Sweden, Denmark, and Norway) have been generous both to the poor at home (through their advanced welfare state) and to the poor abroad (through their foreign aid programs). These three countries, in fact, have been the most generous donors, allocating more than 1 per cent of their GNP to foreign aid. This exemplary record, however, is under pressure. The aid ratio has fallen to 0.87 per cent of GNP in Norway, to 0.96 in Denmark, and to 0.77 in Sweden. Moreover, the Swedes have announced plans to reduce their aid ratio to 0.70 in 1997, which implies a fall of 32 per cent since 1992. This is a harbinger of the future of foreign aid.

Does Aid Matter?

Aid is of declining significance from the perspective of the donors, but what about the recipients? Does aid matter to them? One way to address this question is to compare flows of aid to other flows of resources received by developing countries. In order to make this comparison the developing countries have been divided into three groups:

1 *Poor countries* are those with a real per capita income in 1993 in purchasing power parity terms of less than US$2,200. There are fifty-eight poor countries ranging from Ethiopia ($420) to Azerbaijan ($2,190).
2 *Lower middle countries* have a real per capita income between US$2,200 and US$5,000. There are fifty-two lower middle income countries ranging from Cameroon ($2,220) to the Seychelles ($4,960).
3 *Upper middle countries* have a real income per capita between US$5,000 and US$10,000. There are twenty-eight upper middle income countries ranging from Latvia ($5,010) to Saudi Arabia ($9,880).

In Table 5.1 I include data for 1993 on official development assistance (ODA), foreign direct investment (FDI), net transfers of commercial loans (NL), and workers' remittances (WR), all expressed as a percentage of real gross domestic product (GDP). As can been seen in the table, foreign aid varies inversely with real income per head, that is, on average the poorest developing countries receive proportionately more

TABLE 5.1
Resource flows to developing countries, 1993 (Percentage of real
gross domestic product)

Country group	ODA	FDI	NL	WR
Poor countries	0.96	0.11	−0.04	0.23
Lower middle countries	0.31	0.62	0.12	0.34
Upper middle countries	0.06	0.54	0.06	−0.10

Source: Keith Griffin and Terry McKinley, *New Approaches to Development Cooperation*, UNDP, Office of Development Studies, Discussion Paper Series, No. 7, 1996, Tables 4.2, 4.3, 4.5, and 4.8.

aid than the less poor countries. Even in the poor countries, however, the average amount of aid received is slightly less than 1 per cent of the recipient country's GDP. This inflow is clearly too small to make much difference to the long-term development prospects of the poor countries. In the case of the lower middle and upper middle income countries, foreign aid is of very little significance.

Foreign direct investment is twice as large as foreign aid in the lower middle income countries and nine times as large in the upper middle income countries. It is relatively unimportant in the poor countries, however, reflecting the fact that capital is not necessarily attracted to countries where it is scarce but rather to countries (such as China) that are growing rapidly. The same, perhaps surprisingly, is true of net lending. Commercial loans to the poor countries are negative, that is, interest payments exceed new loans minus repayment of principal. In the two groups of middle income countries, in contrast, net lending is positive and in the case of the upper middle income countries, commercial lending is as important as foreign aid. In other words, movements of private foreign capital are quantitatively much more important than foreign aid in the eighty middle income countries whereas foreign aid is much more important than flows of private foreign capital in the fifty-eight poor countries.

Consider next workers' remittances. Despite considerable restrictions almost everywhere on the free mobility internationally of labour, workers' remittances are quantitatively significant in the two lowest income groups. Poor countries receive on average remittances equivalent to 0.23 per cent of their GDP. Lower middle income countries receive half as much again relative to their income, and more than they receive in the form of foreign aid. The upper middle income countries, on the other hand, are net importers of labour and hence experience an outflow of remittances equivalent to 0.1 per cent of their real GDP. It is reasonable to assume from these figures that if global labour markets were liberalized, the developing countries as a whole, and especially the poorest developing countries, would benefit considerably.

Foreign direct investment, commercial lending, and workers' remittances are market driven: these flows are largely determined by considerations of material self-interest on the part of transnational corporations, international banks, and overseas workers. Foreign aid, in contrast, is driven by politics. Flows of aid are largely determined by political interests, including of course humanitarian concerns, as reflected in national legislative bodies. The relative importance of the two types of flows in our three groups of countries can be assessed by considering the ratio of market-driven to politically driven resource flows: (FDI + NL + WR)/ODA.

In the poor countries the ratio is 0.31. The three types of market-driven flows combined are only 31 per cent as large as official development assistance. The poor countries, in effect, are 'de-linked' from the world economy or, more accurately, they are integrated into the world economy in such a way that they receive relatively little benefit from international factor movements. There is consequently a strong *prima facie* case for continued use of politically driven flows to compensate for the weakness of market-driven flows.

The same argument does not apply to the middle income developing countries. In the case of the lower middle countries the ratio is 3.48, that is, market-driven resource flows are nearly three and a half times larger than aid flows. And in the case of the upper middle countries the ratio of market-driven to politically driven resources flows is even larger: 8.33. These middle income countries can manage, indeed are managing, without reliance on foreign assistance. The significance of this point will become more apparent later.

Meanwhile, let us return to the question of whether aid matters. The answer is, not much. Its quantitative importance is low: even in the poor countries aid accounts for less than 1 per cent of total income and in the middle income countries it is even less important. Moreover, compared to private capital flows and workers' remittances foreign assistance is unimportant in the middle income countries, whereas in the poor countries, where market-driven resource flows are negligible, foreign aid is still relatively important.

Does Aid Work?[5]

There has been a long-standing debate in the professional literature and serious press about the effectiveness of foreign aid in promoting long-term development. That debate is now coming to an end, along with the demise of conventional foreign aid programs. The proponents of aid have not declared victory and gone home; on the contrary, they continue to advocate an indefinite prolongation of the aid effort.[6] But in spite of ardent appeals, such as that made by Cranford Pratt in Chapter 2, their pleas are increasingly falling on deaf ears. Public support for foreign aid has declined, the political incentive for governments of donor countries to provide aid has declined and, as we have seen, the amount of aid actually provided has declined. The critics of aid have won the debate, at least in the arena of public opinion.

There is no need to rehash the arguments of aid critics here. Perhaps it will suffice merely to list the items on the charge sheet. First, it is impossible to demonstrate that foreign aid has increased the rate of growth in the recipient countries. In fact, it is evident that aid is neither necessary nor sufficient to accelerate growth. Second, because external resources are partial substitutes for domestic resources, it is impossible to ensure, even in the case of 'tied' aid, that an inflow of foreign aid increases expenditure on development-promoting activities such as investment in physical and human capital. We know that in practice foreign aid has been used to raise private and public consumption, to cut taxes, to finance increased military expenditure, to facilitate capital flight, and so forth, as well as to finance increased investment. Third, there is no evidence that aid has contributed to a more equal distribution of income and wealth. On the contrary, aid has tended to strengthen the status quo, to reduce the incentive to implement redistributive reforms, and to perpetuate in power authoritarian regimes and military dictatorships. Finally, there is no evidence that foreign aid in general has been able to reduce world poverty. Most of the benefits of aid seem to have been captured by the economic and political elites and the middle class. Few benefits have trickled down to the poor.

Most donors claim that one of their objectives is to reduce poverty. The United Nations Development Programme, for instance, says, 'the most important "customer" is the neediest person in the neediest country the UN serves.'[7] This is an admirable statement of intention, but as a matter of fact, very few foreign aid programs are able to reach the poor, let alone the poorest person in the poorest country. Almost

all ODA is channelled to governments, not directly to poor people,
and whatever impact it has on levels of poverty depends largely on
the government's general economic policies, not on the intentions of
donors or the characteristics of aid-financed projects and programs.
In practice, half a century of foreign aid appears to have done relatively little to reduce poverty in places such as South Asia and sub-
Saharan Africa, where most of the world's poor are located. The disappointing record of foreign aid is one reason for growing scepticism
and declining support even among humanitarians with an international perspective.

Globalization and the Rules of the Game

There has been a shift of emphasis from international transfer payments, that is, foreign aid in its many forms, to international economic
cooperation within a liberal, market-oriented framework. Mutual self-
interest as reflected in unimpeded market transactions has replaced
humanitarian considerations as the basis for interaction at the global
(and indeed country) level. The new rules of the game are intended in
principle to permit the unrestricted flow worldwide of goods and services, technology, capital, and labour. Departures from this liberal
regime may sometimes be justified, but they should not be arbitrary
and no country should be allowed to ignore the rules with impunity.
The new regime that is gradually emerging can be understood as a
shift from global anarchy in which 'might makes right' to a regime of
rule of (commercial) law. Such a rule-based system of economic cooperation requires an enforcement mechanism in order to prevent the
re-emergence of global anarchy.

The ideological justification for a shift towards a rule-based system
is that a liberal global economy would make it possible for everyone to
share in global opportunities. Market transactions, freely entered into,
are a positive sum game in which everyone benefits. The implication is
that under a liberal regime commodity markets, capital markets, and
labour markets should be allowed to operate freely.

It is a standard proposition in economics – reviewed by Albert Berry
in Chapter 3 – that in all but exceptional circumstances both parties to
a transaction benefit. The benefits may not be distributed equally, that
is, the distribution of the relative gains may be unequal, but both parties are better off in absolute terms. In the market for goods and services, both the buyer and seller gain. In the credit market, both the

borrower and the lender expect to profit. In the labour market, both those hiring workers and those seeking employment benefit when job vacancies are filled. A refusal by one party to engage in a potentially beneficial transaction with another thus harms both parties.

Within individual countries there are often rules intended to prevent one agent from harming another. In many countries discrimination against workers on the basis of race, ethnicity, gender, or religion is illegal. Similarly, discrimination against particular groups of borrowers or businesses owned or managed by particular groups of people is illegal. The injured party may take the offender to court and claim substantial damages in compensation. This same principle now must be applied systematically at the international level. A body of international law is needed to stop discriminatory behaviour by one country against another and to compensate the victims when discrimination occurs. The rule of law requires an enforcement mechanism, internationally just as much as nationally, and countries that inflict injury on others – by restricting free trade, by obstructing the free movement of capital, or by erecting barriers against the freedom of migration of labour – should be required to pay compensation.[8] The slogan 'trade not aid' is in many ways commendable, but only if all international transactions are free of arbitrary restrictions and the new rules of the game of a global economy are truly liberal.

Market Failure and Mutual Interests

My concern in the previous section was to identify ways of preventing arbitrary interference in market processes within a global liberal framework. This does not imply that all markets function perfectly and that there is never a case for policy intervention. On the contrary, there are numerous instances at the global level of market failure and of missing markets. These failures point to a need for a mechanism to facilitate bargaining over potentially mutually beneficial exchanges and to effect side payments.

Examples of potentially mutually beneficial bargains include the following:

- Environmental programs in developing countries that also benefit industrial countries.
- Programs to phase out nuclear power stations and thereby reduce risks of radiation to countries downwind of nuclear facilities.

- Programs to destroy nuclear weapons and thereby reduce the risk of nuclear war and nuclear terrorism.
- Programs to convert armaments factories to civilian purposes as a way of reducing military exports and contributing to global peace.
- Public health measures in developing countries designed to prevent the spread of AIDS and other communicable diseases.
- Measures to improve the health and economic and social position of women as a way to slow the growth of the world's population.
- Programs to control transnational crime and international terrorism.
- Joint financing and management of natural resources that cross international boundaries, such as coastal fisheries and river systems.
- Management of the global commons (Antarctica, the oceans, outer space).

If the industrial countries wish the remaining tropical forests to be preserved in order to prevent global warming and maintain biodiversity, for example, it is reasonable that they should bear part of the costs of preservation. Their portion of the costs should reflect the portion of the benefits that accrue to them. Similarly, if the industrial countries wish to discourage the use of chlorofluorocarbons (CFCs) in developing countries in order to stop or at least slow the depletion of the ozone layer, they should compensate the developing countries for the net social benefits foregone by making cash payments, by providing substitute technology, or by helping to finance the development of alternative technologies.

'Externalities' and 'free rider' problems are becoming global in nature. At present no one has a strong incentive to contribute to the solution, even though it is in the interests of all of us that a solution be devised. Establishing a mechanism to arrange mutually beneficial transactions, to facilitate the transfer of funds, and to monitor results would solve this problem. Payments under such a scheme should not be regarded as foreign aid but as payments for services rendered and disbursements should be linked to fulfilment of an internationally agreed contract.

Participation in the scheme would be open to all countries. The scheme would involve creating an international facility to identify mutually beneficial transactions, quantify benefits and costs, assign benefits to the countries concerned, negotiate an agreement among the relevant countries, handle payments, and monitor compliance with the agreement. By acting as a disinterested intermediary, the international facility would also help to ensure that no one party to a negotiation could excessively exploit its bargaining power to the relative disadvantage of its partners. A mechanism for international economic cooperation in this field is becoming increasingly necessary because of globalization. Growing global interdependence is increasing the number of potentially beneficial transactions that do not take place because there is neither a market mechanism to allocate benefits and costs nor a government with a global jurisdiction and powers to tax and spend that can 'internalize' externalities and provide public goods.

Helping Poor Countries

A new framework for international economic cooperation should rest on three pillars. First, the rule of law should be extended and a mechanism created to prevent discrimination and to enforce the rules of a global liberal regime. Countries that are harmed when others adopt illiberal practices should be eligible for compensation. Second, a mechanism should be established to facilitate mutually beneficial transactions when global markets fail and to effect side payments for services rendered. Third, a mechanism should be created to assist the poorest countries through direct transfers. This mechanism would replace existing foreign aid programs and extend to the international arena notions of solidarity and social justice that underpin national programs to reduce poverty and inequality. The first two pillars have been discussed briefly. Let us turn now to the third pillar.

The United Nations aid target of 0.7 per cent of the donor countries' GNP is unrealistic and ought to be abandoned. As we have seen, in 1995 ODA was only 0.27 per cent of the GNP of donor countries. The scheme proposed below would generate revenues equivalent to 0.37 per cent of the donors' GNP in 1993, or slightly more than half the UN target.

A central question is how to generate revenue that is adequate in volume, predictable, obligatory on donors, and equitable in the sense that the 'burden' of assistance is distributed progressively. The answer involves some sort of global taxation. Numerous proposals have been advanced, ranging from taxes or surcharges (on national income, international financial transactions, foreign trade, oil exports, arms shipments) to exploitation of untapped global resources (royalties from mining in international waters, charges for fishing in international waters or for use of the electromagnetic spectrum) to various gimmicks (an international lottery or sale of part of the IMF gold stock).[9]

TABLE 5.2
Rates and contributors for a progressive international tax

Real GDP per capita, 1993 (US$ in purchasing power parity)	Tax rate (percentage of GDP)	Number of countries
$10,000–11,999	0.200	4
12,000–15,999	0.250	6
16,000 and above	0.375	26

TABLE 5.3
Disbursements of tax revenues assuming two groups of recipients

Real GDP per capita, 1993 (US$ in purchasing power parity)	Transfer payment (US$ per capita)	Number of countries
less than $1,100	$50	31
1,100–2,200	30	27

The most straightforward solution would be to introduce a progressive international tax on the GDPs of rich countries. This could be done very easily if there were a modicum of good will. A simple scheme with only three (very low) tax rates is illustrated in Table 5.2. Under this scheme countries with a per capita income of less than US$10,000 (in purchasing power parity terms) would be exempt from international taxation. Only the thirty-six richest countries in the world would be liable. These thirty-six countries would collectively finance an assistance fund, which (in 1993) would be equivalent to US$68.7 billion. Disbursements from the assistance fund should be large enough to make a significant impact on the development prospects of the recipient countries, the criteria for eligibility for assistance should be transparent, and the allocations should be equitable.

One possibility which commends itself would be to limit assistance to the poor countries, fifty-eight developing countries with a per capita income of US$2,200 or less. Assistance to these eligible countries would be made in the form of grants. The transfers would be automatic and allocated in such a way that the poorer a country is, the larger the transfer relative to its per capita GDP would be. Such a negative international income tax could be very simple. A scheme with only two groups of eligible recipients is outlined in Table 5.3.

Under this negative international income tax scheme, countries containing more than 1.8 billion people would be assisted and the amount of assistance per capita would be sufficiently large in principle to significantly raise the well-being of the population. For example, the poorest country among those eligible for grants, Ethiopia, would receive an annual transfer equivalent to 11.9 per cent of its real GDP and the richest, Azerbaijan, would receive a transfer equivalent to 1.4 per cent of its real GDP. These figures can be compared with those in Table 5.1, where it will be seen that on average the poor countries received combined resource flows from the four sources listed equivalent to only 1.19 per cent of their real GDP. That is, the foreign assistance scheme proposed here would be far more effective in reducing world poverty and inequality than the present system of ODA supplemented by foreign direct investment, commercial lending, and workers' remittances. And of course foreign direct investment in poor countries and commercial lending to them would probably increase considerably if the proposed aid scheme were implemented, because the economies of poor countries would become stronger and the rate of growth would accelerate.

Conclusion

The old system of international economic cooperation has died. That system, created after the Second World War, entered into irreversible decline after the end of the Cold War. The task now before us is not to revive the dead but to assist in the birth of a new system, one that reflects contemporary concerns, is less arbitrary and more equitable.

The rules of the game have changed. The new system of international economic cooperation that is emerging is based on the principles of a market economy. Planning, widespread market interventions, and national autarky have been superseded by liberal ideas of multilateralism, free trade, and the free movement of capital. But the rules are not always followed; some countries ignore multilateral arrangements to pursue national advantage through unilateral actions, and liberal ideas are applied only selectively. The free movement of labour in particular encounters numerous obstacles. There is much scope to extend the rule of law to international intercourse, to devise enforcement mechanisms, and to require those who break the rules to compensate the victims for damages.

Liberal principles do not imply *laissez-faire* and it has become apparent that in a globalizing economy markets have their limits. Missing markets, externalities, and free rider problems abound. There are many opportunities for mutually advantageous bargains to be negotiated outside the market mechanism or as a supplement to it. A global facility to take the initiative in encouraging multilateral negotiations, assess the distribution of benefits and costs across countries, arrange side payments and compensation for services rendered where these are appropriate, and monitor compliance with the terms of internationally agreed contracts would allow these bargains to be made.

Efficient global markets and mutually beneficial negotiations are not enough. There will still be a need for redistributive transfers from rich countries to poor ones to help reduce world poverty and redress global inequalities in the distribution of real income. A progressive international tax on the GDPs of rich countries combined with a negative international income tax for the poorest countries is the best way to accomplish this goal. Such a tax and transfer system would be inexpensive to administer, transparent in its operation, and equitable for both donors and eligible recipients. It would be much more effective in achieving development objectives than the present system of foreign aid.

The three pillars combined – a genuinely liberal global economy, a mechanism to handle cases of global market failure, and a tax and transfer program to temper poverty and inequality – constitute a framework for a new system of international economic cooperation that is worthy of support by those who believe that we do indeed live in a global village.

Notes

This paper is based upon Keith Griffin and Terry McKinley, *New Approaches to Development Cooperation*, (UNDP, Office of Development Studies, Discussion Paper Series, No. 7, 1996).

1 See Keith Griffin, 'Foreign Aid after the Cold War,' *Development and Change* 22 (October 1991).
2 OECD, *Development Cooperation*, the 1996 Report of the Development Assistance Committee (Paris: OECD, 1997).
3 Ibid., Table III-1, 64.
4 The Development Assistance Committee of the OECD notes that 'Aggregate donor expenditure on the humanitarian emergencies of recent years has

been substantial. It averages over $3 billion in bilateral aid, over $2 billion in multilateral aid, and over $3 billion in military costs annually. This $8–$10 billion of annual expenditure is aimed at mitigating suffering and privation, not at long-term improvements in economic and social welfare.' Ibid. 98.

5 The reference is to Robert Cassen et al., *Does Aid Work?* (Oxford: Clarendon Press, 1986) who argue, with qualifications, that it does.
6 See, for example, Roger Ridell, *Aid in the 21st Century: Towards a Research Agenda to Strengthen the Case for Aid* (UNDP, Office of Development Studies, Discussion Paper Series, No. 6, 1996).
7 UNDP, *Beyond Aid: Questions and Answers for a Post-Cold-War World* (Division of Public Affairs, November 1995), 9.
8 In Griffin and McKinley, *New Approaches to Development Cooperation* 32–40, we discuss how a system of compensation might actually work in the cases of trade restrictions, brain drain, and restrictions on immigration.
9 For a list and discussion of proposals see Overseas Development Institute, 'New Sources of Finance for Development,' *Briefing Paper* No. 1 (February 1996).

6

NGOs: Crisis and Opportunity in the New World Order

IAN SMILLIE

The non-governmental organization (NGO) chapter in a wide-ranging book on development assistance traditionally begins with a lengthy definition of NGOs and then talks about numbers: 10,000 or possibly 12,000 Northern NGOs working in developing countries. From the South come travellers' tales of vast numbers of community-based organizations and informal village associations, with many hundreds of a more modern type of NGO springing up everywhere. The standard discussion might then slide sideways into consideration of whether the negative – 'non' (as in non-governmental) – is appropriate, testing one or two of the dozens of alternative names that have been floated over the years. Some of the discussion is likely to ponder whether, in consideration of the fact that so many NGOs now receive hefty government subsidies, the label 'non-governmental' is appropriate. Sooner or later, the discussion will turn to management and professionalism, so that even the word 'organization' may be called into question as (possibly) being something of an exaggeration. This chapter assumes that the reader has been through much of this before and that this paragraph can be taken as a proxy for what might otherwise consume a dozen pages.

Briefly then, 'NGO' will be taken to mean that broad set of organizations, large and small, government supported or not, that makes a reasonable showing in five categories identified by the Johns Hopkins Comparative Nonprofit Sector Project: the organization should be 'formal' – institutionalized to some extent. It should be private and institutionally separate from government. It should be non-profit and self-governing, equipped to control its own activities. And it should involve some meaningful degree of voluntary participation.[1]

The chapter will discuss briefly where NGOs come from and then move on to consider three of their major functions: NGOs as service providers; NGOs as civil society; and NGOs as balm for the troubled conscience. These functions will be placed within the historically evolving context of official development assistance (ODA), divided for convenience into three 'eras': an era of tolerant government support for 'happy amateurs' from the mid-1960s to the early 1980s; an era of partnership based on comparative need and advantage from the early 1980s to the early 1990s; and an era of confusion and rivalry, beginning in the early 1990s and extending into an uncertain future.

Where Do NGOs Come From?

The tradition of forming associations is omnipresent and as old as civilization. The most basic motivation is simple altruism, deeply rooted in every organized religion and in most caring societies. The most remote village in Mongolia or Zaire or Australia will find some way to care for the sick, the elderly, and the homeless. The response may be temporary or it may become institutionalized over time. It may even form a basis for the creation of a new religion or a new social or political movement. In some cases, the motivation is self-interest: in medieval Europe, for example, it was eventually deemed preferable and more cost-effective to help rather than to fight the poor and to form organizations to this end. Tocqueville noticed the organizational phenomenon as a distinctive feature of youthful American democracy in the 1830s: 'Americans of all ages, all stations in life, and all types of disposition are forever forming associations. They are not only commercial and industrial associations in which all take part, but others of a thousand different types – religious, moral, serious, futile, very general and very limited, immensely large and very minute. Americans combine to give fêtes, found seminaries, build churches, distribute books, and send missionaries to the antipodes. Hospitals, prisons and schools take shape in that way.[2] Sometimes the motivation for organization or for giving to charity is guilt. 'One has only to remember some of our wolfish financiers,' Steinbeck wrote, 'who spend two thirds of their lives clawing fortunes out of the guts of society, and the latter third pushing it back.'[3] And sometimes the motivation is anger. 'I felt impelled to do it out of a sense of rage and shame,' Bob Geldoff said of his fund-raising efforts for Ethiopia in the mid-1980s. 'Shame was the overriding thing. I felt ashamed that we allowed these things to happen to others.'[4]

This idea of helping others beyond one's own community is also an old one. Tocqueville noticed it in 1831 America, but European churches had already been sending missionaries to 'the antipodes' for three hundred years. Much of this effort had a religious purpose, but schools, hospitals, social and economic upliftment, however well- or ill-conceived, were always an important part of it. It was the twentieth century that spawned the more secular, modern type of Northern NGO, usually during or after a war: Save the Children in 1919, Foster Parents Plan during the Spanish Civil War, Oxfam and CARE emerging from the Second World War, and World Vision from Korea. Their immediate purpose in each case was emergency assistance, to relieve suffering. But these organizations and the thousands of others that have sprung up in the past three or four decades – in the North and the South – soon realized (as in medieval Europe) that an ounce of prevention was worth a pound of cure; that if you can get ahead of disasters and work on development, emergency assistance may not be so badly needed.

NGOs as Service Providers

The backdrop for one of the primary roles of the NGO is thus service provision. Churches and later, NGOs, began the North-to-South tradition of service provision before the borders of the modern nation state were drawn in Asia, Africa, and Latin America. Today, supplemented and sometimes replaced by local NGOs, they provide a third or more of the clinical health care in Cameroon, Ghana, Malawi, Uganda, and Zambia. They provide more than 10 per cent in Indonesia and India, and they own a quarter of the health facilities in Bolivia's three largest cities. In Brazil, one NGO alone has more than 47,000 community health workers providing health care and training in nutrition, prenatal care, breast-feeding, immunization, and the management of diarrhea. Where efficiency is concerned, NGOs often get more mileage from their investments than governments. A doctor in a Ugandan mission hospital treats five times more patients in a day than one working in a government hospital, and mission hospital nurses handle twice as many patients.[5] In most cases these services are supported financially by government. In Zimbabwe, for example, government subventions to mission hospitals grew by more than 500 per cent between 1981 and 1991, representing almost 10 per cent of the budget of the Ministry of Health.[6] Similar sorts of statistics could be cited in the provision of education and welfare services. And NGOs have moved into other forms of service, doing, for example, what the formal banking system could not do in many countries, reaching the poor with sustainable financial services and assisting legions of the poor out of penury.

Numbers give a sense of the scope and magnitude of the Bangladeshi NGO, Bangladesh Rural Advancement Committee (BRAC). In 1997 the organization had almost 18,000 staff. There were 1.8 million members in almost 54,000 village organizations, most of them women. Collectively they had saved over one billion taka – about US$30 million. And in 1996 they borrowed over five billion taka (US$128m) for productive enterprises, repaying virtually all of it on time. A million women were actively involved in poultry projects and 25 million mulberry trees had been planted to support a sericulture enterprise, which produced 43.5 metric tonnes of silk between 1992 and 1995, half the entire national production. Twelve million notebooks, twenty-one million textbooks and readers, and more than three million pencils were purchased in 1996 for BRAC's 34,400 nonformal primary education schools. Every three years, these schools convert over a million dropouts into literate children ready to re-enter the formal education system. In 1996, BRAC purchased 42 tons of corn seed, 200 tons of corrugated iron sheet, and 120 motorcycles. Every month, BRAC buys one million day-old chicks. An estimated 12 million people are covered by BRAC's health and population programs.[7]

BRAC is large, efficient, and effective. But like almost every NGO in the North or the South, it began small, with little more than an idea, some commitment, and the willingness of its people to work under difficult and sometimes demeaning circumstances. Demonstrating what can be done in twenty-five years, BRAC serves as an example and as a model for hundreds of smaller but no less important organizations emerging throughout the developing world.

NGOs as Civil Society

'Civil society,' a somewhat dormant concept after Hegel, Gramsci, and others had a go at it, began to take on new life towards the end of the 1980s, thanks in part to ferment on the subject in both Eastern Europe and Latin America. By the end of the twentieth century, civil society discourse had mushroomed into a voluminous library of books, papers, monographs, and conference proceedings. Like the definition of an NGO, the definition of 'civil society' can occupy chapters and even entire books, at the end of which the average reader, especially one hoping to locate NGOs somewhere in the morass, is often none the wiser. Charles Bahmeuller's definition is as good as most: 'The term, 'civil society' refers to voluntary social activity, activity not compelled by the state. Civil society is the whole web of spontaneous social relationships that lie outside the institutions of the political order and legal duty.'[8]

This obviously includes NGOs. When the new civil society discourse began, however, it was thought – at least in some quarters – that NGOs were the predominant exemplar of civil society. This idea coincided with two major changes in the way ODA had been conceived. One of these changes was heralded by the collapse of the Berlin Wall, after which many donor governments felt less constrained to support corrupt and undemocratic regimes on the basis of how, for example, they might vote at the UN. 'Good governance,' a new canon in the early 1980s, could now take on even greater prominence. In the search for alternative delivery mechanisms in countries where 'governance' was not so good, donors began to recognize the usefulness of NGOs. It was possible to reduce or even cancel bilateral assistance to countries like pre-Aristide Haiti or post-Nawar Sharif Pakistan, for example, but through NGOs, emergency assistance and support to the most vulnerable could continue with political impunity.

The search for good governance, however, was in some ways less important for NGOs than the enthusiasm for structural adjustment that began sweeping through the corridors of international financial institutions at the beginning of the 1980s. Among the primary tenets of structural adjustment was the notion of a smaller state, less government, and reduced spending on, among other things, social services. Here again, NGOs (or civil society, call it what you will in this scenario) came to the fore. NGOs could pick up the slack, fill gaps, rally communities, and build social capital. It all fit together quite nicely: less government, better 'governance,' the opportunity to reduce aid to bad regimes (and then simply to reduce aid altogether). American management guru Peter Drucker turned his attention to the voluntary sector and 'community.' Long-time 'communitarian' Amitai Etzioni enjoyed new prominence. Robert Putnam's book about democracy in Italy, an unlikely source of inspiration, proved to be an all-time best seller among academic publishers, inspiring a whole new level of interest in civil society and 'social capital.' Putnam was helpful because, unlike most writers on the subject, his work was based on empirical evidence over time, and he demonstrated that – at least in Italy – there really is some connection between democracy and civil society.

The upshot of the debates on civil society, structural adjustment, and good governance was not negative for NGOs. In the heady rush to find civil society 'actors,' or gap fillers, or whatever was required to fit the bill, NGOs often came up trumps. Northern NGOs could assist with a range of democracy-type programs, from election monitoring to reconciliation work in an emergency situation. In helping to form and support local institutions, they could strengthen community efforts, build new civil society organizations, provide new welfare services, and so on. During the mid- to late 1980s some bilateral donors began to fund Southern NGOs directly, in the belief that the Northern intermediary offered little in the way of added value, and might actually get in the way of the kind of institution, or service, or concept they had in mind. So Southern NGOs too, came up trumps.

The ink was barely dry on the first generation of civil society tracts, however, when it became fashionable to criticize NGOs as non-exemplars of civil society. Civil society, the argument went, was much more than NGOs. It included the arts, sports, religious groups, political and labour associations, organizations of journalists, academics, women, the aged, youth. Non-governmental organizations, it turned out, were only a small part of civil society. It is difficult now to find a paper on development assistance and civil society that does not take a swipe at NGOs for being something akin to impostors in this great panoply of democratic and societal glue.

Where NGOs are concerned, two points can be made about all this intellectual onanism. First, NGOs did not invent or even re-invent the expression 'civil society.' Few of them have ever claimed that they were in the vanguard of civil society; most do not use the expression at all. It was donors in search of a new label, one that would kill many birds with one stone, who first applied it to NGOs. And it was donors (ably assisted by academics), entering the period of confusion and rivalry with NGOs that will be described below, who began to decry as illegitimate any NGO claim to a position in civil society.

The second point is that regardless of whether or not NGOs are a large or even a small part of civil society, the funding they receive through official development channels has never been greater. Support to NGOs from some governments (Spain, Italy, France) remains relatively low, but for others it represents more than 10 per cent of overall

ODA (Canada, Australia), while in some countries the percentages are much higher: Denmark over 16 per cent, the United States (over 20 per cent), Austria (more than 50 per cent). The World Food Program (WFP) channels half a billion dollars worth of food aid through NGOs, and one third of the United Nations High Commission for Refugees (UNHCR)'s activity – more than $300 million worth in 1996 – was carried out through NGOs.[9]

NGOs as Balm for the Troubled Conscience

Northern NGOs have struggled for thirty years with the trade-offs between their dual role as service providers and agents of change. Most accept their role as change agent where projects, skills, and technology are concerned, but many have difficulty with change at a broader level. Most Northern NGOs recognize the difficulty of advocating macrolevel change overseas. First, it may be inappropriate for outsiders to delve deeply into the domestic policy of another country. Second, an attempt to do so may be costly: going against strongly held beliefs or customs, no matter how wrong-headed they may be, could result in program closure and expulsion. International NGOs working on the basic human rights of women and children, for example, face opprobrium and censure when they get too close to cherished beliefs and vested interests. And although clearly a part of international civil society, foreign NGOs that intervene in a country's struggle for democracy may find their own rights constrained.

Oddly enough, the problem is even more complex at home. Oxfam's critique of British government aid policies has more than once become a subject of interest for and censure by the Charity Commissioners for England and Wales. The Canadian International Church Fund for International Development (ICFID) had its CIDA funding severely reduced after it publicly criticized the agency's policies on structural adjustment. 'A coincidence,' said CIDA. 'Cause and effect,' said ICFID.

This is not to suggest that the democratic rights of NGOs in the North are being widely or systematically curtailed by governments. But no government relishes criticism and most will take measures to reduce it. Altering levels of funding is one means available to a government to express its confidence or displeasure in an NGO. Many recognize this, and – striving to make the most of the connection between what they say about and receive from government – minimize or eschew criticism of aid and foreign policy. 'We are not political,' many

NGOs argue, conveniently forgetting that to say nothing is as much a political act as to say something.

Avoiding complex political and economic debate at home also pays off where the individual donor is concerned. Greenpeace, one of the most political of environmental NGOs, has found that as long as it sticks to emotive issues – whales, seals, nuclear testing – it can retain its donors. But when it strays into the economic sphere, for example recommending the cancellation of Third World debt, its donations plummet.[10] Some international NGOs, of course, have taken high-profile, principled positions on issues that are neither popular nor well understood at home: the campaigns against baby food, structural adjustment, or workers' rights are good examples. More recently, even less political NGOs have taken up safer political issues such as child labour and the campaign against landmines.

But most of the biggest Northern NGOs are not selling ideas, change, or reform to their donors. They are not building consensus around the social, political, and economic changes that inevitably pre-cede genuine and broadly based development. They are selling salve for the troubled conscience, small feel-good opportunities for busy people living in a crass, materialistic world. The best example of this is child sponsorship which, almost unnoticed among the wider develop-ment set, has become not only the most successful fund-raising tool in the North, but the pre-eminent lens through which a very large and growing number of Northern citizens view the South.

In 1982, World Vision, Foster Parents Plan, and Christian Children's Fund had a combined total of 701,000 children under sponsorship. By 1996, this number had grown by a factor of more than six, to 4,479,000 child sponsorships.[11] At least another half-million children are spon-sored through ActionAid, Save the Children (US), Compassion Inter-national, Children International, and a dozen smaller organizations.

Child sponsorship worked when Foster Parents Plan offered a first small victim of the Spanish Civil War for 'adoption.' It continues to work, regardless of the community spin that is now placed on it, because it dramatically reduces the distance between the giver and the receiver. People admire the Salvation Army at home because its efforts are visible. They give to cancer and heart research because the threat of cancer and heart disease is real, and it is close. But giving for causes overseas requires a leap of faith and understanding. Charges that 'it never gets there' and tales of corruption and mismanagement must be surmounted. Alan Fowler has explained how child sponsorship gets around all this. NGOs that can 'shorten the perceptual distance between the giver and beneficiary are more likely to touch [a] sense of distant moral obligation ... Identification with an individual in the South is one way of making a distant obligation more immediate. Child sponsorship organizations ... have a natural advantage in this regard.'[12]

In 1982, *The New Internationalist* produced an exposé on child sponsorship: 'Please Do Not Support This Child' ran its headline, arguing that child sponsorship was costly and actually created more problems than it solved, singling one child out for special attention over others.[13] That issue of *The New Internationalist* was something of a watershed for child sponsorship. One or two agencies agreed with the magazine and in a principled move abandoned sponsorship. Canadian Save the Children was one of them. Changing their name to Cansave, they suddenly saw their fund raising patron – pop singer Anne Murray – take off in a flurry of negative publicity for more heart-warming pastures, followed in quick succession by most of their donors. This was perhaps a lesson *pour encourager les autres*, for few followed suit. Instead, most took the basic criticism of child sponsorship to heart, and began to develop community programs from which the sponsored child and many others could benefit. Most child sponsorship advertising today spells this out: support for a child benefits the whole community.

But for the $29-a-month donor, very little has really changed. S/he is still 'adopting' a child somewhere. S/he still writes letters to the child; still gets letters and pictures back. It is still costly. And it still encourages a literally paternalistic attitude on the part of hundreds of thousands of well-intentioned donors who are rarely made to understand that if each one wrote a single letter to their prime minister about, say, tied aid, it might have a more positive impact than all the child sponsorship combined. Most are not made to understand that 'their' child needs help because its parents do not have an adequate livelihood; they are not made to understand that the child is the symptom of a problem, rather than the problem. Nor do they understand that by treating the symptom they fail to address what the more activist NGOs like to call 'the root causes' of poverty.

But even the most activist NGOs are cautious in their fund-raising and their advocacy. Many have curtailed development education work in recent years, in part because governments in some countries – the United States, Britain, Canada, and Australia – have cut back support for it, and in part because political and economic messages seem to drive all but the most committed donors into the arms of feel-better NGOs.[14]

The problem is not unique to Northern NGOs. Addressing the venerable All Pakistan Women's Association, the even more venerable and much respected development guru, Akhtar Hameed Khan, had this to say: 'APWA ladies, the challenge before you is much bigger than you think. It is not simply a question of improving or uplifting rural women or children by opening industrial homes, or mother- and child-care centres. Those are laudable activities, but they scarcely touch the fringe of the problems. Your challenge is to see clearly the fetters, the old customary practices which are holding back our women and, consequently our men, and ultimately our whole nation. Your challenge is to break these fetters and change these customs ... You must strive for the emancipation of all women, to put an end to their illiteracy, disease and oppression, to make them equal partners in national progress.'[15]

Government Relations: The Era of Tolerant Support Gives Way to Partnership

In the beginning, Northern governments supported NGOs in their overseas development efforts because they were doing good work and because taxpayers were supporting this good work over and above the taxes used for ODA. Germany was the first to develop a matching grant scheme in the early 1960s, but by the end of the decade similar approaches had been adopted by most OECD-member countries. If there are 'good old days' for NGOs, these simpler times qualify. Government guidelines were minimalist in nature and most of the priorities were set by the NGOs. Although larger organizations such as CARE, Oxfam, and Foster Parents Plan hardly needed government support, the extra could always be put to good use. Other organizations, however, might never have survived without it. The volunteer-sending organizations – VSO, CUSO, Australian Volunteers Abroad, and others – struck a chord among Northern youth and met a human resource need in the South that could never have been filled by highly paid experts. Initiated on a shoestring, these volunteer-sending organizations went on to become very large, world-class organizations courtesy of government funding.

These golden years leading up to the mid-1980s can be seen as a period of tolerant support by governments for NGOs. Official development assistance was growing and NGOs were often seen as another way of expressing donor goodwill. Non-governmental organizations could reach areas and people that bilateral agencies could not. And NGOs could show the flag in countries of relatively low political priority. In the 1960s and 1970s, Canada, for example, had no aid program worthy of the name in countries such as Sierra Leone, Nepal, Papua New Guinea, or Bolivia. But NGO activities and dozens of Canadian volunteers helped to make Canada at least visible, if not prominent. It was a time of political maturation for some NGOs as well. The Biafran War, the Bangladesh war of independence, the wars of liberation from Portuguese colonialism, and the Vietnam War each raised questions for NGOs about how and whether to act, how and whether to speak out. For those who did act and those who did speak out there were sometimes penalties, confrontation, and reductions in donor support. By and large, however, NGOs emerged from the 1970s stronger and wiser for the battles and for the government support that they had received.

The 1980s can be seen as a period of 'partnership' between governments and NGOs for various reasons. First, NGOs were no longer seen as happy amateurs. Some had become impressive development organizations with large numbers of donors who also happened to be voters. By the mid-1980s, it was more clear than ever that the trickle-down approach to development was not working, or at least it was not working as fast as it was supposed to. Bilateral and multilateral aid agencies seeking to reach areas that governments could not began to see NGOs as an effective and inexpensive delivery mechanism. This coincided with the greater welfare needs arising in many countries from structural adjustment programs. And as the idea of 'civil society' gained momentum, NGOs once again fit the bill.

Over time, it is possible to trace the evolution of government support for NGOs through a number of iterations. In the beginning, there were very few strings attached and very few forms to fill out. Then came the more formalized matching grant programs. While program or project design lay with the NGO, the organization had at least to fulfil a few basic government requirements. These may have excluded work with Southern African liberation movements or programming in, say, Cuba. But generally the conditions were not onerous. Then, when governments began to appreciate what NGOs could do, they encouraged them to work in additional areas. Special funds were developed for areas of special need: Mozambique at the end of the war; the Philippines after Marcos. Thematic funds were also established: for gender programming, the environment, for work in areas of democratic training and peace building. These special funds, often developed in consultation with NGOs, always came with better matching arrangements. Instead of one-to-one or two-to-one funding, governments would offer as much as 90 per cent or even 100 per cent of the costs. This 'needs-based' approach meant that an NGO could leverage its private donor income even further and it would have been an imperceptive NGO manager who did not notice the opportunity for institutional growth in these funds. The problem was subtle compared to what would come later. But subtle or not, it did mean that governments were beginning to set more of the parameters for where and how NGOs would work, albeit using carrots rather than sticks. By the end of the 1980s, special funds had come to dominate government support mechanisms in many countries. In an extreme case, by 1990, the matching grant program represented only 17 per cent of AusAid's support to Australian NGOs. The rest were carrots, aimed at persuading NGOs to work on governmental priorities.

Beyond the matching grant arrangements, there was a significant shift towards NGOs in the way governments viewed emergency assistance. By the early 1990s, 75 per cent of British food aid was being channelled through NGOs. Forty per cent of Swedish spending on emergencies and refugees was going through Swedish NGOs, and in 1991 the European Commission spent three times more on food and emergency assistance through NGOs than it did on development spending.[16] Between 1992 and 1997, approximately 65 per cent of USAID's budget for disasters, not counting food aid, was programmed through NGOs. During the heady days of these partnerships, several governments began to offer NGOs contracts for the management of bilateral programs and projects. The practice had been common in the United States for years, but Switzerland, Canada, and other countries were not far behind.

The trend would continue, but only at a price, part of which was the evolution of a new sort of relationship, one marked by rivalry and confusion. The start of the rivalry can be seen in the Swedish experience. In 1991 there was a change of government and a more conservative administration took office. That administration reduced ODA but required the Swedish International Development Authority (SIDA) to increase its allocation to NGOs. Until then, there had been no serious evaluation of Swedish NGOs apart from standard monitoring and reporting. It had always been assumed that NGOs did good work, but that in any case, the primary purpose in supporting them had been to build domestic support for the overall development assistance effort. The new competition changed all that and evaluation became the order of the day. Evaluation, to put it bluntly, was aimed as much at putting NGOs on a level playing field with SIDA as anything else.

Sweden was not unique. Between 1991 and 1995, large-scale donor evaluations of NGOs' work were carried out – often for the first time – by Australia, Canada, Denmark, the European Union, Finland, the Netherlands, Norway, Sweden, and the United Kingdom. While the general results were positive, listen to how the Overseas Development Institute summarizes the finer points: 'A high proportion of NGO projects aimed broadly at the poor were found not to be based on any community-based poverty assessments, and many of these failed to reach some of the poorest ... It is rare to find an NGO that does not express its commitment to gender issues. However, the impact assessments indicate that a wide range of NGO projects remain "gender blind," and fail to conduct a gender analysis or fail to address prevailing patterns of discrimination ... The small scale of most NGO projects means that they have very little capacity to influence the natural environment either positively or negatively ... The impact studies reveal a high proportion of projects that are financially unsustainable.'[17] And so on.

A more exhaustive review of NGO evaluation, co-sponsored by the Finish International Development Agency (FINNIDA) and the DAC Expert Group on Evaluation in 1997, reviewed evaluative material from seven industrialized countries, the European Community, and five developing countries. Many months and a couple of hundred pages later, the summary comment was 'There is still a lack of firm and reliable evidence on the impact of NGO development projects and programmes.'[18]

In a time of dwindling resources, conclusions like these are music to the ears of those who were offended or in some way reduced by the rise of NGOs through the 1980s. While such findings did not show that NGOs were ineffective, inefficient, or bad, they demonstrated that the basic tenets of the NGO faith were 'not proven.' This 'finding' coincided with another change in the way some governments were doing business: demanding proof of results. The DAC chairman's report for 1994 referred to a 'growing demand by parliaments, media and the public for the demonstration of tangible *results* from aid.'[19] A 1995 United Nations Development Programme report said that 'the climate of doubt and lack of confidence about the role and *results* of international assistance ... directly challenges the function of evaluation to contribute to the formulation of responses to fundamental questions.'[20] In their trend-setting (and trendy) book, *Reinventing Government*, Osborne and Gaebler devote an entire chapter to 'results-oriented government,' arguing that 'if you don't measure results, you can't tell success from failure.'[21]

In the United States, one of the Clinton administration's first efforts was to establish a national performance review, which led to the passage by Congress in 1993 of a far-reaching Government Performance and Results Act (GPRA). USAID planners appear to have read both *Reinventing Government* and the GPRA: a 1994 paper reported that USAID 'is now fully committed to reinventing itself as a more efficient, effective and *results*-oriented organization.'[22]

It was a short step from governments reinventing themselves to a demand that NGOs do likewise. In a results-oriented climate, the way to do this was clear: to insist that NGOs become much more results focused. Not in itself a bad thing, the forced march from inputs and outputs to results has been accompanied so far (in Canada, the United States, New Zealand, and Australia) by much confusion and anguish. Part of the problem has been the difficulty governments have in explaining what they actually mean by results. Where the object of an exercise is a long-term impact, there is an even greater problem. The impact may not occur during either the funding period or during the life of the project. Improvements in education, for example, may only reveal their ultimate impact in the success of children over a period of several years as they move through and out of the school system. This causes a donor to seek proxies, nearer results. It can result in an even tighter rein on inputs and outputs and a much more controlling atmosphere – the opposite of what was intended. Instead of making more sense, the drive for results has all the making of another aid fad, and perhaps another aid boondoggle.

In conclusion, then, what began in the 1960s as a simple matching grant arrangement has moved, in many countries, through a needs-based grant-making approach to a contracting approach to a much more rigid output-contracting arrangement. In its worst manifestations, the new approach is controlled by government officials who, fearful of their political masters, are determined to transform NGOs from what once made them attractive into contractors, service providers, and government executing agents.

Conclusions

For many NGOs these recent developments are not a problem. There is still money to be tapped. The international CARE network was worth over US$600 million in 1997, more than 75 per cent of it government grants, contracts, or food aid. Such organizations have been called 'public service contractors,'[23] and the demand for their services shows no sign of faltering. Some of the larger multinational Northern NGOs are able to balance the desires and predilections of one donor against those of another, exercising a great deal of independence. Some have become extremely big business, and a few (World Vision, Foster Parents Plan, Oxfam) are not heavily reliant on government funding. In the South the problem of donor dependency is more acute. Despite the donor mantra about the need for NGO sustainability (usually donor-speak for 'self-financing'), there is little assistance available for endowments, productive enterprise, or investments in building a local philanthropic base. Some NGOs have discovered that microcredit operations, if well managed, can become self-financing and can even cover other administrative and programming costs. That helps to explain the mid-1990s stampede towards microcredit as the answer to the problems of the poor. It also reflects donor priorities and pathologies. Ninety-eight per cent repayment rates are about as far down the results chain as many can see, and the cry of 'eureka' rings out long before there is good information about whether a loan is profitable, whether the investment is sustainable, whether the profits are kept by the woman who borrows the money, or whether the loan simply adds to an already burdensome load of responsibilities.

This is not to suggest that all government-NGO relations, learning, and pressure are one-way. Much of what the international development community knows about the informal sector, microenterprise, public health, nonformal child and adult education, gender, and the environment was and still is being pioneered by NGOs. In growing numbers of emergency situations and war zones, NGOs have again demonstrated the attributes that made them attractive in the 1960s: they can move quickly, they can work directly with large numbers of people in great distress, and their workers are both audacious and courageous. Over the years, governments and multilateral agencies have absorbed many of the lessons offered by NGOs, ceding ground to the nonprofit sector on important issues and changing the way in which they think and operate. Perhaps the most striking example can be found in Washington: the World Bank now has an entire unit devoted to the issue of 'participation' in development.

Most predictions about the future are firmly rooted in the present. Even professional futurologists have difficulty getting beyond the here and now – hence the CIA's inability to predict the collapse of the Soviet Union or, once it had happened, the ring of fire (rather than a ring of democracy) that broke out in the Balkans and the Caucasus. If the CIA could not predict the collapse of communism, it is unlikely that this chapter will end by providing a completely accurate picture of the NGO future. Because official development assistance is in decline, many writers believe that a Southern NGO has basically three options. The first is to become a compliant public service contractor, carrying out services on behalf of donors and governments much as the Red Cross does today in industrialized countries. The second is to disappear, because foreign money will dry up, and most NGOs cannot or will not find the means to sustain themselves financially.

A third idea seems to emanate from fast-growing concerns about globalization. If companies can globalize, why cannot NGOs do the same? The Internet provides a metaphor, not to mention a wonderful and inexpensive vehicle for new kinds of networking. Richard Falk talks of 'global citizenship' of the sort that began with the transnational activist movements of the 1980s: the environment, women, and human rights. This, he suggests, consists 'more and more of acting to promote a certain kind of political consciousness transnationally, that could radiate influence in a variety of directions, including bouncing back to the point of origin. Amnesty International and Greenpeace are emblematic of this transnational militancy.'[24] Alan Fowler expresses a similar view: 'The most promising long-term future for NGDOs[25] dedicated to change through the power of third-sector leverage is to become nodes, hubs, enablers and supporters of civic networks. Straddling countries, regions, continents and the globe, and electronically linked, people-to-people networks are set to take the place of NGDOs in shaping world development.'[26]

A first tentative example of this development was the scuttling (or delaying) in 1998 of the Multilateral Agreement on Investment (MAI). A well-organized coalition of non-governmental organizations, some well known and others formed only to operate through the Internet, fought globalization on its own turf. The groups included hundreds of 'hubs and nodes' such as the Sierra Club, Greenpeace, Global Trade Watch, the Malaysia-based Third World Network, the Australian MAI

Community Awareness Site and Preamble Collaborative. A diplomat involved in the OECD negotiations said 'This is the first successful Internet campaign by nongovernmental organizations. It's been very effective.'[27]

A closer examination, however, does not bode well for Northern development NGOs if this is the way of their future. A 'Joint NGO Statement on the MAI' was electronically endorsed by 560 organizations in sixty-seven countries. In fact, over half the endorsements were American, Mexican, and Canadian, many from labour organizations still fighting the North American Free Trade Agreement (NAFTA). One-third of the endorsements were from environmental organizations and two – that is, one-third of 1 per cent of the total – were from operational Northern development agencies: the Catholic Fund for Overseas Development (CAFOD) in Britain and the Canadian Catholic Organization for Development and Peace (CCODP) in Canada.

Southern NGOs still live with day-to-day needs and with real people far removed from the Internet. As somebody who started one NGO and managed another and who works on a regular basis with NGOs in the North and in the South, I always ask a basic question when I hear a bright new idea: 'Who will pay?' Southern NGOs can certainly start raising funds at home. They can perhaps earn some income. But for the next decade at least, most are likely to depend heavily on Northern donors (as long as there are any left) if they want to reach any meaningful levels of achievement. The problem with this is that Northern bilateral and multilateral donors want service providers, not organizations straddling the globe, radiating influence, and shaping world development. And as so many chapters in this volume show, Keith Griffin's in particular, Northern donors have waning resources and few new ideas. Northern NGOs do not look like much of a solution either. The largest are heavily indebted to child sponsorship and emergency fund-raising, which together account for as much as 75 per cent of their global cash income. They too are likely to have problems with the call for electronically linked people-to-people networks that will inevitably be based on $3,000 computers and people who need salaries in order to survive.

What is actually starting to straddle the globe is seven or eight multinational NGOs, headquartered in New York, Atlanta, London, and Monrovia, California. Only one of them – World Vision – has begun to integrate its Northern management and governance structure with its Southern operations, but this form of transnational NGO may become a more prominent kind of actor in the future. Whether it will be a public service contractor or one radiating influence through activist nodes and hubs is another question entirely. But that may be the real question for the future: can those Northern NGOs with meaningful amounts of cash transform themselves into something else?

As for what that something else might be, there is no shortage of suggestions. But perhaps the final challenge is for Southern NGOs. Even if they could become self-financing, it might not be in the best interest of development for them to say farewell to their erstwhile Northern benefactors. For if they are truly concerned about development, they will understand that development writ large will not occur on the basis of aid, projects, or the work of NGOs. These can help, but they are not enough. Much of the answer to global development will lie in the willingness of the North to engage in serious discussions on trade, commodity prices, natural resource depletion, pollution, and consumption patterns. Northern governments will only do this if there is popular support for such a dialogue, and this popular support does not currently exist. It might be generated by the media, but so far, so bad. If schools in Japan and Europe and North America were preparing young people for the real challenges of the future the kind of discussion required might become possible. But mostly they are not. It could be generated by Northern NGOs, but to do it, they will need serious prodding and support from the South.

The most possible kind of transformation under the current circumstances is to change the North-South NGO relationship to one that is not based solely on money. Northern and Southern NGOs do not have to say farewell to projects or money, but they will have to make their relationships transcend money. This is doable. Such a transformation is already being achieved by new organizations based in the South, such as Social Watch in Uruguay, Focus on the Global South in Thailand, and the Third World Network based in Malaysia. Taking it to the next stage, drawing the mainstream NGO movement into this new approach, will be one of the prime challenges of the new century.

Notes

1 L. Salamon and H.K. Anheier, *In Search of the Nonprofit Sector: The Question of Definitions* (Baltimore: Johns Hopkins University Institute for Policy Studies, 1992), 11.

2 Alexis de Tocqueville, *Democracy in America* (1835; Garden City, N.Y.: Anchor Books, 1961).

3 John Steinbeck, *The Log From the Sea of Cortez* (New York: Viking, 1951).

4 Cited in Tim Brodhead and Brent Herbert-Copely, *Bridges of Hope: Canadian Voluntary Agencies and the Third World* (Ottawa: North-South Institute, 1988), 31.

5 World Bank, *Latin America and the Caribbean: A Decade After the Debt Crisis* (Washington, D.C.: World Bank, 1993), 127 and 143. The Brazilian NGO is the Pastoral da Criança, managed by the Catholic Church.

6 A. Matthias and A. Green, 'Government and NGO Roles and Relationships in Policy Making: The Health Sector in Zimbabwe,' University of Manchester Workshop, June 1994.

7 Ian Smillie, *Words and Deeds: BRAC at 25* (Dhaka: BRAC, 1997).

8 Charles Bahmueller, 'Civil Society is the Buzzword of the Hour,' USIA Online Journal at http://civnet.org/index.html.

9 Ian Smillie and Henny Helmich, eds., *Stakeholders: Government – NGO Partnerships for International Development* (Paris: OECD (forthcoming)).

10 See Stephan Dale, *McLuhan's Children: The Greenpeace Message and the Media* (Toronto: Between the Lines, 1996), 46–7.

11 The 1982 figure is taken from the *New Internationalist*, May 1982; the 1996 figures are taken from the 1996 Annual Reports of the three organizations.

12 Alan Fowler, 'Distant Obligations: Speculations on NGO Funding and the Global Market,' Review of *African Political Economy*, No. 55: 9–29, 1992.

13 *New Internationalist*, May 1982.

14 In March 1998 the Chicago *Tribune* ran more than thirty detailed articles on child sponsorship. Although the stories were highly critical and were picked up by other print and broadcast media in the United States and around the world, the net impact on both donors and child sponsorship agencies appears to have been negligible.

15 Akhtar Hameed Khan, *Orangi Pilot Project; Reminiscences and Reflections* (Karachi: Oxford University Press, 1996), 36.

16 Smillie and Helmich, *Stakeholders*, 33 and 318.

17 'The Impact of NGO Development Projects,' ODI Briefing Paper, May 1996.

18 Stein-Erik Kruse, Timo Kyllonen, Satu Ojampera, Roger C. Riddell, and Jean-Louis Vielajus, *Searching for Impact and Methods* (NGO Evaluation Synthesis Study prepared for the OECD/DAC Expert Group on Evaluation), vol. 1 (Helsinki: Ministry of Foreign Affairs of Finland, 1997), vii.

19 OECD, *Development Cooperation, Efforts and Policies of the Members of the Development Assistance Committee* (Paris: OECD, 1995), 25.

20 UNDP, *Beyond Aid: Questions and Answers for a Post-Cold-War World* (New York: UNDP Division of Public Affairs, 1995), 7.

21 David Osborne and Ted Gaebler, *Reinventing Government: How the Entrepeneurial Spirit Is Transforming the Public Sector* (New York: Plume Press, 1993), 138–65.
22 'Strategies for Sustainable Development,' USAID paper, March 1994, p. 1.
23 See, for example, David Korten, *Getting to the 21st Century* (West Hartford: Kumarian, 1990).
24 Richard Falk, 'The Making of Global Citizenship,' in J. Brecher, J. Brown, and J. Cutler, eds. (Montreal: Black Rose Books, 1993), 47.
25 Non-governmental development organization.
26 Alan Fowler, *Striking a Balance* (London: Earthscan, 1997), 233.
27 'How the Net Killed the MAI,' *Globe and Mail*, 29 April 1998.

PART FOUR

Foreign Assistance and Globalization

Globalization brings immediately to mind the juggernauts of economic power, General Motors, Mitsubishi, and Sony, each with budgets many times that of Thailand. These are the merchants who have become lords in the unregulated and unmonitored world of the international market place, and everyone from Lagos to Goa is a subject, in one form or another, of these merchant kings. Everyone is touched by these product empires, whether they be fishermen or market women, rickshaw drivers or Tibetan monks, and their lives are the better or worse for them. What is not clear, however, is what these subject/lord relations mean, how they condition political awareness, how they make and break careers, how they build or tear down opportunities.

The question posed in the following two chapters is not the customary one about globalization, about the holdings and investments of the merchant kings themselves, but rather about the lives of their subjects, of you and me.

Roy Culpeper offers the novel idea that, contrary to their reputations, these merchant kings will eventually rise above their pursuit of accumulations and assume responsibility for social justice on a global scale. As the new barons of the bazaar they are poised to be the arbiters of justice as well. Codes of conduct, international environmental standards, and an emerging corporate ethic may guide transnational corporations in taking up the mantle abandoned by national donor institutions. And they will do so, he argues, since global corporations must inevitably recognize the benefit they reap, or at least the costs they avoid, by maintaining the well-being of the societies in which they operate. By necessity, they are benevolent kings, for the flow of accumulations depends on keeping the peace.

Jonathan Barker examines in turn the lives of some far-flung subjects, in a cluster of neighbouring villages in India, a province in Nigeria, and a market in Uganda. Donors, merchants, fishers, and shopkeepers come together in these places where international capital is sometimes intrusive and other times less so. Here the global and the local intersect and these markets and villages are better places than boardrooms for assessing how global capital affects common lives. Small businesses may grow, labour may be exploited, children may have more or less chance at education, and the threats to local autonomy may extinguish local political action or provide the frustration to make it flare into protest. Verdicts about the consequences of globalization vary from place to place; in India small fishers are losing their livelihood, while in Uganda shopkeepers have organized to manage their market place better. We learn as much from these social junctures where peasants, traders, and farmers react to the push and pull of capital in various parts of the globe as from studying the centres of economic power themselves.

7

Private Markets and Social Equity in a Post-Aid World

ROY CULPEPER

Introduction: The Post-Aid World

In February 1997, a much-noticed article appeared in the *Atlantic Monthly* by billionaire financier George Soros, in which he declared that with the demise of communism, free markets are now the biggest threat to world stability.[1] Excessive individualism, too much competition, and too little cooperation, Soros contended, can cause intolerable inequities. In a trenchant critique of modern 'laissez-faire capitalism,' including what he called the 'robber capitalism' of post-Soviet Russia, he went on to argue that markets are weakening traditional values of community and caring, thus undermining social and political stability as well. He also asserted the need for governments to intervene in and regulate markets in order to redistribute incomes and make society more fair.

Coming from one of the leading architects of globalization, Soros's views are also highly ironic. Partly because of the incessant pressures by banks, investors, and financial speculators like Soros himself, globalization has become the seemingly unstoppable force governing international economic and political relations. Countries in the former Soviet bloc are now open to foreign business; so are most of the few remaining countries, like China, still formally under communist rule. Some rapidly growing developing countries (predominantly in East and Southeast Asia and Latin America) are joining the ranks of the industrial countries, although financial crises in Mexico (1994–5) and Asia (1997–8) indicate that there are few certainties, whether about the process of industrialization or the ultimate destination for any particular country. Despite these setbacks – and in contrast to the rather somber views of Soros – globalization has generally been greeted by the world's dominant powers (the G-7 countries) and institutions (the Organization for Economic Cooperation and Development (OECD), the International Monetary Fund (IMF), and the World Bank) as a trend altogether to be encouraged and in the interest of the world community, particularly the developing countries.

Certainly, the statistics tell a story of global markets eagerly embracing much of the Third World. Until 1990, the total net flow of private investment to developing countries was actually less than the volume of 'official flows' (through bilateral aid and export credit agencies, multilateral development banks, and the UN). By 1997, private flows had grown to six times the volume of official flows, which have fallen somewhat through the 1990s.[2]

It is too soon to tell whether or not the crisis in Asia will lead to a new and much less optimistic phase of globalization. To the extent that the volume of private flows increasingly dwarfs official flows, they suggest that we are already in a 'post-aid world.' However, the trends raise as many questions as they settle. Is official development assistance (ODA) (along with other official flows through the UN and multilateral development banks) truly becoming redundant? Are we in fact on the threshold of an era in which relations between richer and poorer nations will be governed largely by market forces rather than national or international arrangements and institutions (in trade relations as well as through aid programs)? More generally, if 'development' means improved circumstances and prospects for the world's poorest countries and people, do global markets promise to deliver more than foreign aid and all other official flows have done in the past or can deliver in the future? If so, how can we reconcile the views of sceptics such as Soros and a rising chorus of critics who contend that globalization brings with it rising inequities, increasing social instability, and political uncertainty?

Historians have pointed out that economic globalization is nothing new. Indeed, depending on the measures used, the world economy was more 'globalized' a century ago than today. Capital flows and foreign trade accounted for a much larger percentage of economic output at the end of the nineteenth than at the end of the twentieth century.

What perhaps distinguishes the globalization of our own era is the speed and potency with which global transactions take place. This is partly due to the efficacy of modern telecommunications. But it also owes much to the way in which business is organized: the pervasiveness of globalization stems from the agility and power of the modern global corporation. In this context, it is interesting to note the phenomenal growth in the size of the world's largest transnational corporations (TNCs).

By the mid-1990s the largest global TNCs exceeded in size (if measured by their gross revenues) all but a handful of developing countries (measured by their gross national product (GNP) at market prices). The two largest Fortune 500 companies (General Motors and Ford) together had revenues equal to the aggregate GNP of the forty-seven poorest developing countries (saving India and China), with a combined population of over a billion.[3] By such measures, Royal Dutch Shell is larger and Exxon is slightly smaller than Saudi Arabia, the world's largest oil-exporting country; the revenues of Wal-Mart Stores are more than half as much as the entire GNP of Indonesia, a country of over 190 million people.

It would perhaps be too simplistic to identify the relative size of a TNC with its 'influence' or 'power.' But when particular TNCs are involved in dealing with the governments of particular countries, it is worth noting the resources each party has at its disposal. Much of the language of international economic diplomacy is couched in terms of a 'level playing field' for international business when dealing with various national governments, but it seems clear that many of the business players represent economic entities considerably larger than those of the officials trying to oversee and adjudicate the games being played.

It would be a mistake, however, to identify economic globalization as a phenomenon involving only large TNCs. Because of modern information and telecommunications technology, small and medium-sized enterprises are able to undertake business in remote markets in a manner unthinkable even half a century ago. Individual private investors are getting into the act as well. One of the most remarkable and unprecedented developments in the 1990s has been the growth of cross-border portfolio equity investment. The purchase of share capital, once almost wholly an activity confined within national boundaries, now occurs between countries in a number of ways. And an increasing proportion of the transactions takes place between industrial and developing countries. Many developing countries have for the first time opened their stock markets for investment by non-residents. Individual investors in industrial countries now participate in such cross-boundary transactions through the purchase and sale of 'emerging market' shares through mutual and pension funds, and through brokered deals involving particular Southern firms.

This chapter is concerned with, first, the implications of these trends for corporate behaviour in the global economy. Can private firms and investors be 'part of the solution' in enhancing the conditions and prospects of the poorest countries and their people? The conventional response to this question tends to regard development as a process driven largely by the investment of physical capital via its impact on economic growth. On this view, if private investors are providing six times the resources of official agencies, they are making six times the contribution.

Stated this way, the conventional view of development is rapidly becoming dated. By the late 1990s, development has come to connote a multidimensional process involving not only aggregate economic growth, but also the reduction of poverty, preservation of the environment, and improvement of human resources through investments in health and education, with particular regard to the circumstances of women and children.

This chapter also addresses the role of public agencies and policies in a world increasingly dominated by private financial flows and corporations. The 1990s have not been kind to official development assistance (ODA). Aid budgets have fallen victim both to fiscal deficit-reduction in most donor countries, and to a growing disillusionment with foreign aid, perhaps more among officials and politicians than among the public at large. Other contributors to this volume, Keith Griffin in Chapter 5, for example, chart this decline. Jim Freedman's introduction, while not so pessimistic, clearly shows that from 1990 to 1996 there was a sharp drop in official flows (comprising both ODA and other official flows, such as bilateral and multilateral loans).[4] After a sharp fall in 1993 and a partial recovery in 1994, ODA dropped by nearly 10 per cent in real terms (adjusted for inflation and exchange rates) in 1995. As a share of the GNP among the principal aid donors, ODA fell to 0.27 per cent, its lowest level in forty-five years. The ODA/GNP ratio fell in fifteen out of twenty-one OECD Development Assistance Committee (DAC) member countries, including all the G-7 countries. Huge cuts in the ODA program of the United States had reduced that country, until recently the world's largest donor by a wide margin, to the rank of fourth-largest donor by 1995, with a program less than half the size of Japan's, and less than that of France and Germany combined.[5] Canada, until the 1990s known as one of the more committed aid donor countries, cut its aid budget by 40 per cent between 1989 and 1997.

This chapter is organized as follows. The next section takes a closer look at the phenomenal rise of private investment in developing countries in the 1990s. Following that is a discussion of whether and how markets and corporations contribute to social equity, and how the objectives of social equity are particularly challenging   in the context of developing country markets. A concluding section reviews the strengths and shortcomings of private markets and corporations with regard to social equity, as well as the future roles and responsibilities of public agencies and policies in a post-aid world.

Private Foreign Investment and Developing Country Markets

There are two reasons to doubt that the spread of global markets to the developing world in the post-Cold War era has removed the *raison d'être* for foreign aid, or that private flows by themselves can serve as the 'engine of development.' As mentioned, the first relates to shifts in the conceptualization of development, from one anchored in economic growth driven by investment and capital to one concerned with a broad spectrum of economic, social, and political objectives. The second relates to the inherent shortcomings of markets and the conceptual underpinnings of market-based economies. This is not to deny that international markets can make an important contribution to development. It is simply to point out the limitations of that contribution.

To begin with, it is by no means certain that the trends of the 1990s, with their phenomenal growth of private foreign investment in developing countries, will be sustained, stable, or durable. Private flows over the past two decades have been extremely volatile: witness not only the recent financial crises in Latin America and Asia but also the earlier explosion in bank lending during the 1970s followed by the debt crisis of the 1980s.

Moreover, large influxes of foreign capital, even if they are not volatile or subject to sudden reversals, can have adverse macroeconomic impacts, including exchange rate appreciation, a commensurate erosion of export competitiveness, and balance of payments deficits. Nor are the policy choices to contain these impacts easy ones.[6] In other words, even though foreign savings can provide resources for investment and economic growth in developing countries, large inflows of capital are not an unmixed blessing and may even undermine growth if domestic authorities pursue macroeconomic stabilization (anti-inflation) policies.

TABLE 7.1
Recipients of private foreign investment, 1996

Country/region	Billions of U.S.$
All Developing countries	243.8
Sub-Saharan Africa	11.8
East Asia and the Pacific	108.7
Latin America and the Caribbean	74.3
Top country destinations	
China	52.0
Mexico	28.1
Brazil	14.7
Malaysia	16.0
Indonesia	17.9
Thailand	13.3
Argentina	11.3
India	8.0
Russia	3.6
Turkey	4.7
Chile	4.6
Hungary	2.5

Source: World Bank, Global Development Finance 1997, 7.

Even if private flows are sustained in the longer term, there are some obvious shortcomings in the nature and direction of these flows if they are expected to contribute to development. First, it seems clear that the lion's share of flows is attracted to markets in which purchasing power is high and growing fast. Such countries are not necessarily 'high income' countries, but may include, as in the case of China and India, 'low income' countries (that is, with low average per capita GNP) containing a sizable 'middle class' of consumers.[7] World Bank data indicate that in 1996, the top twelve recipient countries received 72.5 per cent of private flows (Table 7.1). Sub-Saharan Africa received less than 5 per cent of total private flows, although during the 1990s some African countries have been experiencing the greatest increase in private foreign investment. Low-income countries, excluding China and India, received net private flows amounting only to 1.5 percent of their GNP, while middle-income countries' flows amounted to 3.2 per cent of their GNP.

Markets, Efficiency, and Equity

The fact that private foreign investment appears to prefer countries with higher purchasing power suggests fundamental problems underlying the notion that market forces can act as engines of development – even if 'development' is understood in the more traditional sense of economic growth and investment. These relate to the motivations of private market agents, which stem from maximizing profits or other self-interested objectives (accumulating assets, increasing market share, etc.).

Private investors may indeed act to allocate their resources in the most efficient manner possible. Their actions may serve to boost investment and economic growth in certain countries and regions. However, such outcomes say little about equity – the fairness of those outcomes – for example, the distribution of wealth and income. Whatever economic growth occurs may do little (directly or indirectly) to reduce the incidence of poverty or to raise the level of investment in human resources (e.g., through education or better health services). As indicated above, there is growing consensus that these dimensions of development are as essential as economic growth to the well-being of people.

Without passing judgment on the nature of the motivation of private investors, it is typically assumed that their fundamental rationale is to earn profits and not necessarily to achieve other social objectives. The question is whether, or the extent to which, private investment can or should do both. Indeed, at the centre of current debates about business ethics is the question of how responsible corporations should be for such social outcomes. Defenders of the more conventional view argue that businesses are abdicating their principal obligation (to maximize profits) by indulging in expenses to demonstrate their 'social responsibility.'[8] At most, this viewpoint might support actions, such as voluntary codes of restraint, that enhance corporate image or serve to preempt formal regulation and hence contribute towards long-run profit maximization.

Critics of the conventional view, on the other hand, argue that businesses do not exist in a vacuum but operate in a framework of laws, rules, and conventions.[9] Indeed, the notion of *laissez faire* is a serious misdescription of what free markets actually require and entail. Free markets and the system of private property depend for their existence on law. Markets, in other words, are a legal construct that facilitate certain transactions (such as contracts) and prohibit others (such as trespass). Moreover, the legal framework goes far beyond defining property rights and contract obligations to defining social norms that may also limit freedoms (for example, laws forbidding racial discrimination).

The laws, rules, and regulations within which businesses operate generally reflect the standards, objectives, or conventions of each particular country or jurisdiction. For example, there may be regulations governing workplace safety and health standards, environmental impact, or laws permitting collective bargaining or minimum wages. The national (or provincial) framework establishes the obligatory responsibilities of all corporations operating under the national (or provincial) jurisdiction. This framework is frequently contested terrain on which political struggles are waged between businesses seeking to limit the costs they must bear associated with such obligations and workers or other stakeholders seeking to establish, protect, or widen their rights. Once the framework is established, however, meeting legal obligations becomes part of the cost of doing business.

Two points are at issue. First, what should be included in such obligatory social responsibilities (particularly since there may be disagreement as to community standards on which to base these)? Second, do businesses also have supererogatory responsibilities beyond the legal requirements? For example, some companies may decide to exceed the legal minimum wage for their lowest-paid employees, adopt affirmative action policies, or go beyond environmental quality standards. In so doing they may incur additional costs or reduce their profits.

Perhaps this puts the matter too starkly as a 'win-lose' proposition – society stands to gain what corporations must lose in discharging their social responsibility. Scholars like Amartya Sen point out that commercial or economic success is not simply a matter of the self-interested pursuit of profits, and that moral codes of behaviour can in fact enhance corporate productivity and competitiveness.[10] If so, the choice between the interests of society and those of corporations is a false dichotomy, making plausible win-win combinations between corporate responsibilities and social interests.

Sen's critique of the conventional (win-lose) view runs much deeper. A premise of that position holds that maximizing self-interest constitutes the only form of 'rational market behaviour' and other forms of behaviour (involving duty, loyalty, goodwill, or ethically motivated conduct) will undermine the efficiency of markets. An even stronger assertion maintains that self-interested behaviour approximates actual behaviour in the real world. Both of these assumptions are highly questionable: non-self-interested behaviour is not irrational nor does it necessarily undermine efficiency. For example, in Japan, despite its market-based economy, many commercial relationships are based on duty or loyalty (including labour market conventions such as lifetime employment), and while they have no doubt exacted an economic cost, these relationships have arguably enhanced productivity and played an important role in Japan's industrial competitiveness – notwithstanding that the current crisis in Japan and the Asian 'tigers' has called into question the sustainability of such traditions in a global economy. The implication is that it is quite plausible to conceive of corporations both competing in the marketplace and taking on social responsibilities (obligatory and supererogatory) that actually enhance their commercial success.

Global Markets, Codes of Conduct, and Equitable Development

The issues of markets and social equity are contentious enough within a single political jurisdiction, such as the nation state. They become far more complex when business transactions take place across jurisdictions between which the laws and regulations are substantially different. Within the nation state, to the extent that the standards of corporate behaviour are prescribed by law or custom and commonly observed (and this may be far from being the case), there is no leeway to gain a competitive advantage in the domestic market place by diverging from the norms. But the globalization of trade and investment has profoundly changed the context of social norms in the market place.

Globalization has posed a basic conundrum for all international transactions. Whose standards of behaviour should apply? Those of the home or host country? The dilemma is that if foreign investors or traders abide by host country standards that are lower (e.g., labour standards), they are open to the charge of exploitation. If they abide by higher home country standards, they may render their foreign ventures uncompetitive and doomed to failure. Thus accusations of 'a race to the bottom' are levelled by labour critics against corporations' investments in developing countries. Likewise labour critics wanting to impose trade restrictions on goods produced with child labour or under conditions below acceptable Northern safety or environmental standards are often accused by business and advocates of economic liberalization of 'protectionism.'

The problem has been made considerably more complex by an attitudinal transformation on the part of the developing countries. Two decades ago, private foreign investment was generally greeted with scepticism if not hostility, and it typically confronted considerable red tape and large or uncertain tax liabilities. Today, such investment is eagerly sought for its creation of employment and incomes and access to specialized technology and industrial country markets. Accordingly, tax or other incentives are becoming more prevalent than the threat of expropriation, whether 'creeping' or otherwise. And the enthusiasm in developing countries for the more basic attributes of foreign invest-ment has often swept aside concerns about workplace standards or community and environmental impacts. In other words, corporate social or environmental responsibility may typically be more of an issue for guest investors and their home countries than for the host country.

There are no simple ways out of these quandaries. But several strands in the argument can now be brought together. First, there are signs of growing sensitivity by international business people that glo-balization may be contributing to widening social disparities and to social and political instability. Some business leaders are accordingly calling for a more proactive role and enhanced corporate social respon-sibility in order to foster goodwill among stakeholders. Second, although it is dangerous to extrapolate past trends, private foreign investment seems destined to supplant official development assistance as the primary interface between industrial and developing countries in the twenty-first century. Third, there has been a profound reconcep-tualization of what is, or should be, entailed by the development pro-cess and thus what ODA should strive to achieve. Twenty-five years ago emphasis was placed on achieving high rates of economic growth; today, this goal must be shared with increased equity and tangible social and political progress.

It seems obvious that private foreign investment will make at best only a partial contribution to this broad spectrum of development objectives. In certain areas targeted by aid programs (aimed at basic human needs, women, children, health, education, human rights, and environment) the contribution of private markets is likely to be at best indirect, and in fact private agents could act in ways harmful to these objectives (e.g., through degrading the environment or by exploitative child labour).

In any event, the established pattern of private flows indicates signif-icant limitations if they are to be relied on as an engine of development. The herd mentality of financial markets makes them susceptible to vol-atile shifts. They have a proclivity towards the better-off countries and their wealthier citizens. They can have destabilizing macroeconomic impacts that will jeopardize growth. None of these characteristics serves as a strong recommendation for private markets as agents in the struggle for equitable and sustainable human development. The case for continued flows of ODA, at least for the next two or three decades, seems solid insofar it can be demonstrated that ODA can deliver the full spectrum of development benefits that it now attempts to achieve.

That being said, it may also be true that private market actors can accomplish more in the way of social equity in their operations in developing countries. For example, multinationals could – and an increasing number actually do – invest in the local workforce and community by training and educating employees, setting high safety standards, and providing health services. In so doing, foreign businesses make important contributions to objectives such as meeting basic human needs; enhancing gender equity; reinforcing respect for human rights, good governance, and democracy; and fostering environmental stewardship.

An increasingly common corporate tool designed to deal with these challenges is the Code of Conduct. Such codes serve as proof that the corporation recognizes the concerns of its stakeholders (i.e., the shareholders and others) regarding its standards of corporate behaviour. Typically the codes are conceived in an essentially national or domestic context and articulate supererogatory standards of behaviour – standards by which the corporations will abide, whether or not they are explicitly prescribed by law. However, such codes represent only intent (cynics might say they are primarily intended to boost corporate image) rather than plans of action to which firms are held accountable.

A recent survey commissioned by the International Centre for Human Rights and Democratic Development (ICHRDD) of fifty-five Canadian firms indicated that only six engaged independent audits to oversee and enforce their codes.[11] In the absence of independent audits, there is no guarantee of the extent to which the actual standards of corporate behaviour adhere to its code of conduct. In other words, while codes of conduct may to some extent demonstrate corporate social responsibility, what seems more important is corporate social accountability. Actions count far more than words. But if, on the other hand, a code of conduct does not aspire even to a minimal set of standards, accountability to those standards may not mean much. For example, only six firms of ICHRDD's sample of fifty-five included all four 'core' OECD labour rights.[12] The other forty-nine firms could adhere to their codes without meeting the core labour rights.

At the end of the day, the pervasive forces of competitive markets can and usually do quickly undermine the resolve even of the most socially responsible corporations to be held accountable. Accordingly, there is scope for devising codes of conduct or conventions that would help to level the playing field by raising or simply enforcing minimal labour, environmental, and other standards. Depending on how they are monitored and enforced, such mechanisms would reduce the possibility of socially responsible firms being undercut by less conscientious competitors. Collective action to deal with competitive pressures may take several forms and occur at several levels. For example, codes of conduct such as the one recently signed by fourteen Canadian companies[13] could become standardized for all Canadian firms with significant operations abroad. But if Canadian firms signed on to such a code (and the particular code in question has been criticized for lacking any mechanisms to monitor or enforce compliance),[14] they might be at a strong disadvantage in developing country markets if their major competitors (from the United States, Europe, and Japan) operate without similar codes or with lower standards.

Broader action on an international level thus seems warranted. Such action may in turn take place at two levels: in individual host countries, where all foreign firms cooperate on standards appropriate to each particular host country, or at the global level. A recent example of an initiative at the international level is the OECD Convention on Combating Bribery of Foreign Public Officials in International Business Transactions, signed by twenty-nine industrial countries in December 1997. While several shortcomings to this convention have been noted (in particular, it is up to signatory countries to apprehend and prosecute offenders), it still constitutes an important initiative that would have been unimaginable a few years ago.[15]

Conclusion

It is clear that in the 'post-aid world' of the twenty-first century, progress on social equity in developing countries will involve closer collaboration between donor agencies, international organizations, foreign business operations, and national or local authorities in developing countries. There is no question that the dramatic rise of private investment and trade internationally, even if it is subject to cycles and setbacks, is profoundly and unalterably transforming relationships between rich and poor countries and their people. This does not mean that private market agents are good substitutes for public agencies, whether national or international. To some extent, private investors can provide public goods, such as clean water or adequate housing in remote mining communities, but ultimately the responsibility for such services – when the mine runs out and the company moves its operations elsewhere – must fall to local governments.

More generally, the quest to enhance progress in all the dimensions of development – economic, social, and political – will require ongoing and active ODA programs, reinforced by other aspects of public policy. For example, diplomacy must play an important role in the struggle to achieve and sustain democracy and human rights. But international market actors must also use their growing influence through the channels of trade and investment to enhance social equity considerably more than they have in the past.

Indeed, as a number of business critics have recently commented, enlightened business enterprises will regard a positive overall impact of their operations on society as integral to their responsibility.[16] In the twenty-first century, the success of corporations is likely to be intertwined with the overall benefits they bring to the communities and countries in which they operate. As Courtney Pratt, a former senior executive of Noranda Inc., put it: 'A business's success is ultimately dependent on the success, strength and optimism of the society in which it operates. I consider it to be a responsibility of business to be one of the key contributors toward the evolution of our society in a direction that will benefit every stakeholder.'[17] The issue can no longer be framed in terms of the trade-off between profits and social responsibility, or between corporate shareholders and the rest of society. Rather, the issue is one of how businesses can contribute towards the common interests of their shareholders and of society at large.

However, ensuring corporate social responsibility in a post-aid world must go beyond statements of intent. While corporate codes of conduct are important, the details of such codes are crucial. Moreover, ensuring performance in line with the code (ensuring 'accountability, not just responsibility') is essential. As this chapter suggests, the forces and incentives of competitive markets present major stumbling blocks to transforming corporate intentions into consistently good corporate practice. While more reflection and research is required, two elements seem to be vital to point incentives and competitive forces in the 'right' direction. Only independent monitoring of corporate conduct will ensure accountability. Ensuring accountability is essential if corporate adherence to codes of conduct is to be credible. Unfortunately, many firms are not yet prepared to abide by external monitoring of their conduct, preferring 'self-regulation.' In time, however, it seems inevitable that firms will be subject to external audits of their environmental and social behaviour, much as they are already subject to audits of their financial probity.

Finally, there are also some questions about the future of official development assistance in the post-aid world. These flow from the fact that the object of ODA has been the recipient country rather than its people. Eligibility for ODA or for concessional assistance from the World Bank and other multilateral development banks is usually geared to the recipient country's per capita GNP. And there is a prevalent assumption both among aid policy makers and aid critics that countries should 'graduate' from ODA once they access private foreign capital markets. But this chapter has argued that there is no guarantee that a country's graduation to private capital markets will deliver the panoply of social and economic benefits that ODA attempts to deliver, albeit very imperfectly. Even if foreign private investors become paragons of virtue in discharging their social responsibilities abroad, the benefits may simply not be shared by a large portion of the citizenry, who will continue to be left behind.

Accordingly, especially where there are wide disparities between the winners and losers of globalization, many aid programs and agencies face a dilemma. In concentrating constrained ODA resources on the poorest countries, that is, those in which per capita GNP falls below some threshold, it overlooks a possibly growing number of poor people who fall below the poverty line but happen to live in countries where the average level of income is high. Ultimately, however, foreign aid cannot possibly hope to be the great equalizer. Perhaps the most that ODA, along with public and foreign policies generally, can reasonably aspire to do in a post-aid world is to act as a catalyst for economic and social change and as a countervailing power against elites and vested interests everywhere.[18]

Notes

1 'The Capitalist Threat,' *Atlantic Monthly* (February 1997), 45–70.
2 World Bank, *Global Development Finance 1998*, 3.

3 Computed from data in *Fortune*, 4 August 1997; World Bank, *World Development Report 1997*.

4 The drop in 1996 was dominated by a prepayment by Mexico of its 1995 emergency bilateral loan from the United States – a loan that also inflated ODA in 1995 when it was made.

5 World Bank, *Global Development Finance 1997*, 35–6.

6 For a discussion of the complex policy dilemmas involved in the Latin American case, see Ricardo French-Davies and Stephany Griffith-Jones, eds., *Coping with Capital Surges: The Return of Finance to Latin America* (Boulder, Col.: Lynne Rienner, 1995).

7 The Indian 'middle class' (defined as those with incomes equivalent to Western European averages) is thought to be anywhere between 100–200 million strong, in other words, larger than any European country. On the other hand, the remaining 700–800 million in India include a large portion of the world's poorest people.

8 See, e.g., Norman Barry, 'What moral constraints on business?' in S. Brittan and Alan Hamlin, eds., *Market Capitalism and Moral Values* (Aldershot: Edward Elgar, 1993).

9 For example, Cass R. Sunstein, *Free Markets and Social Justice* (New York and Oxford: Oxford University Press, 1997).

10 *On Ethics and Economics* (Oxford: Basil Blackwell, 1987) and 'Moral Codes and Economic Success,' in Brittan and Hamlin, *Market Capitalism and Moral Values*. See also Sunstein, *Free Markets and Moral Justice*.

11 Craig Forcese, *Commerce with Conscience? Human Rights and Corporate Codes of Conduct* (Ottawa: International Centre for Human Rights and Democratic Development, 1997).

12 Freedom of association and the rights to organize and bargain collectively, proscription of child labour, of discrimination in the workplace, and of forced labour.

13 The initiative was spearheaded by Canadian Occidental Petroleum and supported by Alcan, Beak International, Cambior Inc., Chauvco Resources Ltd., John Neville Inc., Komex International, Liquid Gold Resources, Profco Resources, Pulsonic Corp., Reid Crowther International, Sanduga and Associates, Shell Canada, and Wardrop Engineering.

14 See the North-South Institute, *Canadian Development Report 1998: Canadian Corporations and Social Responsibility* (Ottawa, 1998), 16, 29.

15 Ibid., 15.

16 See, for example, Samuel Brittan, *Capitalism with a Human Face* (London: Fontana Press, 1995) and John Dalla Costa, *The Ethical Imperative: Why Moral Leadership Is Good Business* (Toronto: Harper Business, 1998).

17 'Business does well by doing good,' *Globe and Mail Report on Business*,

2 October 1997. Emphasis added. Mr Pratt went on to elaborate three critical areas of 'multistakeholder responsibility' of business beyond its immediate shareholders: towards its employees, the environment, and the community.

18 See Richard Jolly, 'The Myth of Declining Aid,' in R. Culpeper, et al., *Global Development Fifty Years after Bretton Woods* (London: Macmillan, 1997).

8

The Small, the Big, and the Ugly

JONATHAN S. BARKER

Introduction

There are very different perceptions about the relationship between local action and global economic forces.[1] At one extreme globalization is seen as a positive development which, by stripping away the dead hand of bureaucracy and the twisted hand of political corruption, allows local economic entrepreneurs and social activists to get on with building local economies on their own or in collaboration with external investors. This view of globalization also stresses the progressive benefits that local action, both economic and social, can achieve. Globalization, so runs the claim, expands the opportunity, the incentives, and the resources for local entrepreneurial and civic action.

At another extreme global forces and the businesses and institutions that drive them are criticized for weakening the autonomy of small-scale producers by drawing them into exploitative labour contracts, undermining relations of social support, and destroying organizations of civic action. Governments are forced to curtail their social welfare activities, leaving people vulnerable to ill health and misfortune and depriving them of basic support for self-help. If there is any scope for small business, it increases local inequality and fails to improve local living conditions in general. Globalization, from this standpoint, makes collective local action difficult and confines it to defensive reactions against the assaults on livelihoods and local social support organizations.

Although all analysts do not see global forces in quite the same way, most have in mind an expanding international trade for goods and services, an intensifying pressure to reduce or eliminate government controls over market transactions, a rising volume of transnational communication, an increasing movement of people across national borders, and growing numbers of people worldwide who participate in a common global culture of symbols and values. Views of local action also differ, but most refer to people doing things to defend or to promote livelihoods and ways of life in particular urban and rural places, whether it be through business activity, voluntary associations, social movements, or civil society in general.

Local actions are, by definition, local, and the forces of globalization do not operate uniformly in every part of the globe. The very different consequences of introducing sophisticated information technologies, such as those Einsiedel and Innes describe in Chapter 14, provide ample testimony. What pertains in Costa Rica may not pertain in Tanzania or Bangladesh. Variations within countries may also be enormous. The ugliness of globalization has high visibility in the union-hostile footwear, clothing, and computer chip factories of Central America and Southeast Asia, where investment exploits young women. Ugly, too, are living conditions in the burgeoning shanty towns of Africa, where both global investment and paying jobs are scarce. Conversely, the beauty of globalization was seen (until the crisis of 1998) in the rising incomes and decreasing incidence of poverty in the senior and junior tiger economies of Asia; it is also detected in the growing export sector in Chile and, more faintly, in the small per capita expansion of agricultural production in Africa.

This chapter addresses the question of how global forces and local action interact with one another in practice and in detail by reflecting on the fates of three social milieux: a market in Uganda, a cluster of neighbouring villages in India, and a province in Nigeria between the years 1992 and 1995. In each instance, an account of the tensions that arise as local organizations react to global influences is guided by observing these specific social milieux through five windows, or frames, within which distinct types of social action occur:

1 changes in the national or regional political climate and rules;
2 changes in the spatial patterns of social life
3 changes in the pattern of ownership and labour relations;
4 changes in the pattern of gender relations; and
5 changes in the pattern of cultural relations.

We begin with a brief description of these five dimensions at the sites of the case studies.

National Political Climate and Rules

Uganda under the National Resistance Movement had no open party politics, but there was extensive party activity below the surface. Political expression, including criticism of the central government, was quite open. Strong memories of the horrors of political oppression and violence made many Ugandans determined to avoid old-style political conflict. In India, party competition was well established and there was experience with changing party dominance in Tamil Nadu State. Local administration was strongly hierarchical. Techniques of popular action bordering on violence – road blockages, sit-ins, strikes, hunger strikes – were utilized to goad otherwise unresponsive officials into doing their work. Nigeria under General Babangida had an autocratic administration with local elections, and consequently political discussion, except about national political leadership, was open, if careful. None of the case study sites had a highly repressive regime that used terror or directly attacked public political organization.

Spatial Patterns of Social Life

All three sites can be called pedestrian zones, although each was served by public and private motor transit. Kanyakumari in India had particularly dense and frequent social encounters. The beach where men gathered each morning to mend nets was a place for work and for socializing. Inside the church and its related buildings and outside in the public plaza were many potential meeting places. The streets between rows of small houses were also places of casual encounter and were sometimes used for formal neighbourhood gatherings.

In Owino market in Kampala, Uganda, the office of the Market Vendors' Association was built to be a meeting place as well as an office. Neighbouring vendors often gathered for short meetings in an uncluttered stall. For larger meetings there was an auditorium near to the market. The close proximity of vendors' stalls made communication among vendors relatively easy; meetings could be called on short notice. In Yobe State in Nigeria the two small towns, Machina and Dagona, had several public places where people often met. In Machina meetings were held in the space in front of the Emir's palace, in the school, and in the market place. The grounds of the government office building and of the two government-sponsored political parties were used for some official functions. Dagona had similar meeting places while the bank of the river provided an additional place for informal social gatherings. All of these localities used messengers or town criers to announce meetings and citizens could walk to all of the main meeting places. Compared to these three localities scattered farmsteads, sprawling suburbs, or dangerous shanty towns would be less conducive to social interaction.

Pattern of Ownership and Labour Relations

Ownership was spread among a large number of small production units in all three sites. Although wage labour had a significant presence in all three of the case study sites, it existed alongside work partnerships, working on shares, and family-recruited labour. A tradition of labour union organization was present in the Indian villages and among government employees in Nigeria. The sites chosen do not include examples of industrial or plantation employment that subjects a large number of employees to the economic and managerial power of a small number of employers. Such conditions would obviously have a deep affect on local political action. In all three locations the great majority of people were struggling to meet basic needs.

Pattern of Gender Relations

Patriarchy was culturally most prominent in Yobe State, Nigeria, where most adult women stay inside their homes, except for specified activities, and where they do not attend public meetings. In Owino market in Uganda and in the villages around Kanyakumari in southern India, the formal rules placed no restrictions on women's political participation but informal rules and practices presented women with definite obstacles to full participation.

Patterns of Culture

Significant cultural pluralism existed in each location studied, but a majority in each locality belonged to a single cultural category. Cultural pluralism was greatest in Owino market, although more than half the vendors were Baganda and Christians. In Yobe State, the town of Dagona had a Bade majority while in Machina most of the population was Manga, but both towns included several other ethnic groups.

In Kanyakumari the fishing villages were inhabited almost entirely by members of two fishing castes, Mukkuvar and Paravar. In all of the research areas social stratification was evident, with a dominant family most apparent in Machina, where the Emir held sway. Meetings within the localities that involved collaboration with outsiders and translocal organizations presented local organizations in all three countries with immediate issues of what language to use and how to manage translation.

Method and Perspective

This chapter investigates a fundamental issue: what kinds of civic action exist and how do they relate to global forces? We claim no Olympian standpoint, but only record the features of local collective action and its relation to global forces.

We have chosen to examine instances of public collective action and sought occasions where groups of people discuss openly matters considered to be of great common concern. These venues of public discussion, decision, and action have been given the name "political settings." They include meetings, demonstrations, and offices where officials meet the public, but meetings are of special importance for the quantity and quality of political discourse and collective action.

We looked for meetings in which matters of public concern were addressed, then analysed the rules and customs used to control participation in the meeting, the way the agenda was set, the nature of the issues raised, and the way in which they were discussed. We also examined the role different categories of people played in the political setting: men and women, officials and ordinary citizens, rich and poor, and different cultural groups.

The subject matter of these meetings was overwhelmingly oriented to issues of livelihood, social welfare, social peace and conflict, and control of local power structures. In these localities, politics had a gritty and down-to-earth content. The emotional temperature varied from cool and conversational to hot and conflictual. A certain apprehension of the danger of opening the floor to unpredictable tensions was often evident, although the skill and self-control of chairpersons and participants almost always kept the political settings orderly. It was very common in all of the localities for chairpersons to open meetings with a prayer that invoked the values of tolerance, respect, and harmony.

The Small

The relationship between local action and global forces, discernible in these three localities, ranged widely from the absence of any relationship to profound mutual influence. This section sketches the background to each place, demonstrating, in a preliminary fashion, the range of variation.

OWINO MARKET IN KAMPALA, UGANDA

Owino is the largest organized market in Uganda, and possibly in East Africa. In a city of about 800,000 people it had in 1992 5,000 vendors and 30,000 employees. Owino was built in the 1970s for a few hundred vendors and has since expanded with little control and few amenities. A spurt in growth occurred with the fall of the Amin regime in 1979, when goods looted from nearby shops were brought to the market for sale, adding hardware, sugar, and salt to the lines of available merchandise. It is the largest wholesale and retail market in the country. In 1992 vendors sold everything from used clothing to electrical fixtures to meat to bananas, but cereals and used clothing were the most widely sold items, accounting for almost half of the stalls in one sample. Owino Market is a crowded and hurried place with strong smells and narrow paths in which buyers and transporters compete for space. Most of its walkways are uncovered to the rain and open drains carry sewage as well as rainwater. Many Kampalans are reluctant to shop there, disliking the discomfort and fearing thieves.

The ownership of market stalls is not easy to decipher. Operators are often not the owners, but owners rarely own more than a few stalls. Most stalls are relatively small businesses, although among vendors there is a considerable range of wealth. Most of the vendors, like the other workers in the market, can be classified as belonging to the large category of 'urban poor.' Half the vendors are men and half are women; many ethnic groups are represented, with Baganda predominant; and the Catholic, Protestant, and Muslim faiths are all well represented. Competition is fierce and direct with many vendors selling the same goods. The vendors bargain with both suppliers and customers; contract with employees, transporters, and security firms; pay fees to the market authorities and the Market Vendors' Association (MVA); and make contributions to market-based football clubs and social groups.

During the period under study the Owino Market, like the economy of Uganda, was subjected to considerable pressure from global forces.

A structural adjustment program limited government spending and kept the salaries of municipal and central government employees much below the level of a living wage. The same structural adjustment program provided a large inflow of loans and assistance that fuelled trade and construction in Kampala, contributing to the expansion of Owino. And there was a commitment on the part of the World Bank to invest in rehabilitation of the markets in Kampala, once a series of issues – including ownership of the land on which the markets were built – was resolved. In addition, formal markets like Owino were facing competition from large and rapidly expanding evening markets along the well-travelled roadways and in the streets adjacent to Owino itself. These were, strictly speaking, illegal markets, but they were more than accepted by the officials who collected fees and undocumented payments from the vendors. Many Owino Market vendors also operated stands in the evening market after the main market closed.

Here in the home terrain of small competitive commerce we found a great proliferation of local action in the form of an astonishing number of meetings and came to appreciate the detailed organization of the market as a whole. The Market Vendors' Association was the most comprehensive organization dealing with livelihood issues. It had a pyramid of committees from fifty-seven departments (based largely on contiguity and type of merchandise), to four zones (based on the history of Owino's expansion), to the market as a whole. The committees met to discuss waste disposal, market plans, market fees, government administrative practices, security, transport, and many other issues. Small committees heard a wide range of disputes, resolving some of them and transferring others to higher-level committees. The more central bodies held meetings about market redevelopment plans but also about immediate issues like security and conflict and what to do about the evening market.

It was striking that men dominated the meetings, except in the departments in which almost all the vendors were women. Equally striking was the wide acceptance of open discussion, usually begun and closed with a prayer about the importance of peaceful dialogue.

There were many other groups in the market, including more than thirty football clubs plus a football club for the whole market and cultural groups, which were often run by women for women. Even the head police officer in the market held educational meetings for departmental leaders to learn about the rules of law enforcement in the market.

A great deal of the work of the MVA meetings could be classified as social repair work. Small-scale trade is strenuous and conflictual activity that does social damage; both the tensions and the damage were magnified by economic and administrative pressures derived from global forces like structural adjustment and inflowing economic assistance. Vendors generally seemed to accept their strong common interest in resolving conflicts, punishing theft, and retaining some recreational and symbolic activity for the market people. Many of them, especially the MVA leaders and some of the bigger merchants, saw the need for policy and pressure with respect both to the redevelopment project the government was likely to hand to them and the dangerous competition from the evening market. Thus there was a politics of larger issues, both defensive and proactive, in the political settings of Owino market. The MVA leadership feared a redevelopment process that would ignore the voices of the vendors. As the market redevelopment project moved along in fits and starts, the MVA played a small role in negotiations in which the Kampala City Council, a Ugandan engineering firm, and a Chinese contractor were the principal actors, but when it came to the actual implementation of changes and the management of relocating stalls and offices it had a strong voice and exercised effective veto power.

KANYAKUMARI DISTRICT AND VILLAGE IN TAMIL NADU STATE, INDIA

The coast of Kanyakumari district in Tamil Nadu State at the southern tip of India is the home of an ancient fishing industry. Two hundred thousand people live in forty-two villages along the coast. The men who fish live in villages just above the beaches where they keep their narrow raftlike catamaran vessels or larger open boats called vallam, some of recent design. Merchant-owned trawlers are docked near the villages that have appropriate facilities. The foreign-owned factory ships that work the deeper waters further out are usually invisible beyond the horizon. The catamaran and vallam may be equipped with outboard motors, increasing their range of operation, but many use sails and oars. The larger motorized open boats approach the small trawlers in range. In the last forty years the fishery has changed profoundly in response to globalization. The markets are now national and international as well as local. The species that can be sold and those that can still be caught have changed radically as the intensity, range, and equipment of fishing have changed. Artisanal fishers have adopted nylon nets, outboard motors, and bigger boats. Trawlers with inboard motors and even larger nets can fish many of the same waters as the smaller vessels. Agreements to divide the fishing zone into a near-shore zone for small craft and a zone further out for trawlers have failed to endure; verbal and violent conflicts repeatedly threaten and occasionally break out. In recent years the government of India has licensed deep-sea fishing by large factory ships, a practice which both trawler fishers and small-boat fishers perceive as a mortal threat.

As more fish were sold in more distant markets the fishers organized to defend their interests against the fish merchants. Much of the fish marketing in 1994 was in the hands of cooperatives of fishing people rather than private fish merchants. The trawlers, usually owned by local merchants, have entered into competition with the open boats in the last two decades, competition in which merchant capital employing labour is pitted against production units retaining family labour at their core. Some fishers now work on the trawlers instead of operating their own boat or working on shares with their fellows. Social differentiation is increased by the wage labour some local men undertake in the Gulf States. Women formerly made nets from local cotton, but now the nets are nylon and machine made. The outboard motors used by a minority of fishers are costly and imported. Artisanal fishing now requires a considerable cash outlay. In their search for paid work, women market fish for local markets, and to make their earnings go further they form savings and credit societies.

Profound changes have occurred at the cultural level as well. Schooling has expanded, dividing boys who stay in school from their peers who apprentice with their elders to learn the demanding trade of fishing. Seldom do scholars or fishers change to the other path. Television is widely present in all the villages, and the deep interest in film and film stars for which Tamil Nadu is famous penetrates the villages. Some observe that television has gravely eroded participation in meetings, especially at the times when the very popular soap operas are broadcast. Party politics is also well entrenched in the villages.

The people of the fishing villages are overwhelmingly Roman Catholic and have been so for more than four centuries. The architecture of most villages is dominated by a large and centrally located church, often with the priest's dwelling, a ceremonial stage, and an open meeting place nearby. In recent years young priests influenced by liberation theology have brought ideas and practices of base communities and social action to the work of the church.

The economic, cultural, and social changes underway in the fishing villages constitute direct and indirect sources of great tension. Handling the day-to-day conflicts takes a great deal of political work, and some of the everyday conflicts have direct connection to national and international forces. Because of their growing expenditures for equipment, fishers are under great financial pressure to bring in a cash income. On the whole, fishers do more work with more equipment covering more water in order to keep their incomes more or less stable. Trawler owners face similar pressures.

Much effort is being made to adapt to changes locally. The church and certain parish priests were the immediate instigators of many political settings, most recently of neighbourhood base groups to discuss all kinds of social issues, from alcohol consumption by men (an ancient source of contention by all accounts) and education for girls to noise and litter in the streets. Organizations like the National Fishworkers' Forum, the union of small-vessel fishers, and the fish marketing cooperatives had their origins a generation ago in the activities of both church and social-political activists and the fishers themselves.

The sheer number of political settings was impressive. Saturday was a day of meetings. And when collective action was called to get more government services or to end the deep-sea fishing licences a whole array of techniques of collective action was there to draw upon: delegations to the government administrator's office, road blockages, blockades against police entry into villages, demonstrations near government offices, and fasts.

Women played a strong role in their own economic and social organizations: associations of widows and associations of women who market fish, for example. They also took centre stage in the sit-ins that closed the nearest major highway and the delegations that demonstrated before government offices. Women were believed to be less prone to physical combat than men and less likely to attract assault and arrest by the police. In most meetings, however, women were less well represented than men and those present tended to speak little or not at all. The meetings of neighbourhood base groups to discuss local welfare issues were an exception: in this forum women spoke actively. Many men regarded these meetings as being for women, children, and priests and consequently stayed away.

Conflict within the locality also produced much local action, action that often flowed beyond the confines of meetings and demonstrations. Artisanal fishers went on expeditions to burn trawlers and trawler crews cut loose expensive fishing nets placed by small-boat

fishers. The intralocal conflict had a long history and, except temporarily, pacification seemed beyond the power of church or state. It
interfered with the efforts led by national and international organizations to demonstrate against the Indian government's licensing of deep
sea fishing vessels from Taiwan, South Korea, Russia, and many other
places. But priests and other local leaders were successful in 1996 in
persuading trawler and artisanal factions to support the one-day strike
and to join in the action that eventually succeeded in getting the government to declare a change in policy that would favour local fishers.

TWO TOWNS IN YOBE STATE, NORTHERN NIGERIA
Machina and Dagona are towns of 8,000 and 5,500 people respectively
in a region of limited seasonal rainfall known for its production of food
grains (principally millet and sorghum) and livestock (mainly cattle,
sheep, and goats). There is hardly any export production, but grains
and livestock are sold in Nigerian cities and there is some trade with
neighbouring Niger. Dagona is located on a tributary of the Yobe River
and the nearby farmland benefits from irrigation and flood-recession
cultivation. Farther from the river farmers engage in rain-fed, upland
farming and in stock raising. The better water supply makes Dagona's
agriculture more productive than that of Machina and, when farm
work is not pressing, Dagona's farmers can go fishing for an additional
source of food and income. However, Dagona is the destination for a
large inflow of immigrants from other parts of northern Nigeria and
their relation to the inhabitants who consider themselves to be indigenous can be tense.

Dagona also differs from Machina in having a more pluralistic structure of social power. There is no single leader or family that compares
with the Emir and his family in Machina, perhaps because Dagona is a
newer town. Machina is ancient, with remnants of walls built in the
twelfth century to defend the ruler's palace. The Emir, with more than
fifty years in power, still skilfully dominates most local institutions of
influence through his personal networks and often through his numerous offspring. However, the town is gaining in diversity, partly
because of the Emir's success in getting it designated a centre of local
government, with all the offices and officials pertaining thereto.

Our research centred on a comparison of three development institutions active in Yobe State, two of them government-managed (the Better Life Program for Rural Women (BLP) and the Directorate of Food,
Road and Rural Infrastructure (DFRRI) and one financed by the Euro-

pean community and administered under its auspices (the Northeast Arid Zone Development Program (NEAZDP). NEAZDP provided the most obvious evidence of globalization in the area, although one could argue that most government activity was linked to globalization, since almost all of its financing came ultimately from revenue taken by the government from petroleum sales abroad. Even in its economic difficulties, the national, state, and local governments of Nigeria maintained a visible and active presence in both Machina and Dagona.

Most striking among our findings was the extent to which NEAZDP succeeded in establishing political support groups as integral components of its rural development schemes. Establishing grain mills and credit schemes, training bulls as draft animals, improving water supply, instigating small irrigation schemes, creating more efficient clay cooking stoves, setting up tailoring groups, and many other activities utilized a methodology that implemented meetings and education groups requiring participation by beneficiaries. In contrast, government-sponsored projects were less numerous and tended to be run from the top down, despite rhetorical invocation of participatory principles.

A related finding was that the less centralized power structure of Dagona made it easier there, than in Machina, for NEAZDP and other associations to hold meetings and initiate activities.

The Big

The changes that resulted in local dramas in Kampala's Owino market, among fishers of Kanykamuri, and among resident farmers of Nigeria's Yobe district were shaped by global or transnational forces. In this way, 'the big' incited 'the small' to respond, even though the nature and success of the response was difficult to predict and depended on the capacity of local political sensibilities to comprehend and respond to global challenges. Local response depended on how local groups coped with the threat of technological innovation which, in some instances, threatened local economic activity. It depended on how they responded to the exhaustion of local resources, such as water and trees, occasioned by local growth and expansion of economic activity. It depended on how local political actors, pressure groups, and neighbourhood organizations responded to global political actors such as government and business, armies and non-governmental organizations. And it depended on the extent of influence that global culture, via media transmissions, had on local political sensibilities.

Owino was faced with the rapid degradation of material conditions in the market, as its activity and population expanded without improvement of infrastructure and as the evening market swelled around it. At the same time there was the impending possibility of large external organizational intervention in the form of a World Bank–funded 'upgrading' managed by the government. Impressive in Owino was a kind of balance struck between local organization in the form of the Market Vendors' Association and the World Bank–government nexus. In the background was a generally expanding urban economy fuelled by inflows of aid and improved production and trade made possible by civil peace.

The villages of Kanyakumari district had for decades been affected by ecological changes, by changes in fishing technology, and by the way the market exploits the fishers. Some of these changes divided local society between villages competing for the same fishing grounds and between merchants and their employees using trawler technology and small-boat fishers with less capital. The advent of deep sea fishing by foreign ships licensed by the Indian government created a line of conflict that united villages and trawler owners and workers, as well as small-craft fishers, against the high-technology outsiders. Fishers, too, had adapted to change in the value of different species and the relative decline of the local market in favour of external markets, changes that undermined local nutrition by removing a large source of protein from the local food economy. At the same time organization by labour unions, political parties, and the Catholic Church, together with ideologies of socialism, liberation theology, and self-help, directly targeted the construction and use of political settings in the fishing villages.

In Yobe State global forces were less directly evident than in the other two cases. There was long-term environmental degradation, part of a global trend, but the trend is hard to link to any particular global force. Oil money funded the state and its continuing autocratic politics. Most directly global was NEAZDP, with its central administration and its differential effect on Dagona and Machina, undermining local political officers in favour of development personnel. It stimulated the founding of public forums for discussion of broad issues of the direction and quality of change in the area, something that had never before occurred. When the local elections in Machina by a narrow margin removed the son of the Emir from the position of local government head it was hard not to think that NEAZDP's presence had encouraged a freer vote. However, to underscore the subtle complexity of the forces at work, the Emir himself worked closely with NEAZDP and another one of his sons served as its chief field officer in the Machina area.

One pattern that was common to all three cases was the striking weakness of governments as compared to other agencies as creators or sponsors of participatory political settings. In Owino the Kampala City Council's market authorities opened offices and tried to sponsor meetings, but these were invariably held inside administrative offices with a clear hierarchy exercised by the officials behind their desks. Few participants were attracted. In contrast, the MVA's meetings were models of participation. In Kanyakumari the government made feeble efforts at forming participatory settings, but the church, the fishers' cooperatives, and the fishers' union all made extensive use of meetings in which grass-roots participation was significant. In Yobe State the government-sponsored projects held few public meetings and those held were information sessions in which officials explained things to the assembled people. In contrast, NEAZDP initiated a large number of gatherings in which people could and did express their ideas and concerns about the project in question or about general development issues, which usually meant how to increase the provision of water.

Government, on the other hand, played an important indirect part in occasions of significant participatory accomplishment in all three cases. In Owino the government was a key player in the process that finally accorded a large role to the MVA in upgrading the market under a World Bank project. In Kanyakumari, the government of India responded to the widespread demonstrations and the one-day fishers' strike by putting a moratorium on deep sea fishing licences for foreign vessels and promising to withdraw the licences it had already issued. In Yobe State the government contracted with NEAZDP to provide development services, and it organized the local elections that changed the local governmental leadership in Machina.

The Ugly

How do we evaluate 'small' and 'big' and their relationship to one another? Small is not necessarily beautiful. Political settings in all three cases, despite the formal affirmation of gender equality in Owino and in Kanyakumari, reflected in their actual operation a powerful bias against participation and leadership by women. Moreover, local public institutions were unable to resolve the long-running destructive conflict between trawler people and small-boat people in Kanyakumari.

Conflicts between herders and farmers and between older residents and newer immigrants in the localities of Yobe State were similarly intractable and destructive. The cases brought for adjudication that we learned about in Owino revealed at least occasional raw deployment of economic power in relations between male employers and female employees and between wholesalers and retailers.

If small is not always beautiful, big is not uniformly ugly. Economic expansion in Kampala created many new jobs in Owino market and some of the income therefrom was contributed to the MVA and its impressive works. And the World Bank did stimulate great interest and some action with respect to improving basic living and working conditions for the 30,000 people who worked in the market. In Kanyakumari new international fish markets allowed more fishers to gain a livelihood from fishing and gave economic utility to a wider array of fish species. In Yobe State international markets played little direct role, although oil indirectly financed much government activity in the area.

The church was the conduit for liberation theology and before that for socially relevant action in the villages of Kanyakumari District. And the fishers of India, together with those of other lands plus numerous academics and activists, had been able to shape a small but significant counterweight to large-scale global fishing interests. In Yobe State, the main instigator of meaningful participatory development was using European Community money and an international participatory economic ideology to build a small infrastructure of locally controlled economic and social service activities. The global forces for informed and democratic local organization seem far from ugly indeed, even though, someday, they might be turned into forms of domination and manipulation and require further reassessment.

Local political and economic autonomy is vulnerable, to be sure. It is equally certain that its preservation depends on the strength of local political groups, in which local people, informed by connections to transnational sources of information and ideas, address those issues. National and regional governments, furthermore, have key parts to play in strengthening local response to potentially devastating global forces.

There can be no uniform recipe for reinforcing the beautiful against the ugly, and local realities include the particular constellation of global forces and state institutions that bear upon the locality. If local political settings and local social action are to be effective, they must draw upon the social and institutional strengths of the locality. In Kanyakumari parish priests with strong church bases and personal ties to the area could take practical action on the inspiration of liberation theology. But like the secular activists they could also draw on the tradition of labour organization among plantation and farm workers and government employees in the region, a tradition honoured in the Marxist political parties. No less important were the traditions of direct action and self-help of the men and women of the fishing villages. In Owino skills of organization, leadership, and record keeping were joined with determination to avoid the disastrous forms of politicized conflict of the past. In Yobe State, administrative skills and a strong desire for effective action by a well-paid administrative cadre combined with popular receptiveness to participatory techniques.

Global forces have a double-sided relationship with local action. Directly and indirectly they often push local action into a defensive posture while provoking social divisions and local conflicts. However, global forces also strengthen the capacity for local action by weakening old political monopolies and introducing useful information, resources, and models of action. There is room here for transitional activist groups to put their energy, information and money at the service of networks that support local action for equality, participation, and livelihoods. There is room, too, to import ways of making such networks accountable to the people they aim to serve.

Notes

Research for this chapter was funded by the Social Science Research Council of Canada. I wish to thank the collaborators in the research: Christie Gombay in Uganda, Kole Shettima in Nigeria, and Aparna Sundar in India. In each case, my focus was on political settings; the collaborators worked both on that subject and on broader topics of their own. Thanks to Bob Shenton for his helpful comments on an earlier and uglier version of the paper.

1 Compare, for example, Mander and Goldsmith (1996) with the World Development Report (1997).

PART FIVE

The Pay-offs of Social Capital

Development assistance has obliged the social sciences to take the canonical ideas in economics and politics, geography and sociology off the shelf and put them into practice. In this way development assistance has given its disciplines an experimental ground to check its principles against a diversity of social realities. The experience has been a sobering one, as in many instances they have not worked terribly well.

One lesson in particular stands out, and this has to do with the relative importance of economic and social capital in making economies grow. The question is whether the hard currency of physical infrastructure is more or less important than the softer stuff of authority and equity in how societies are governed. The most conspicuous failures in development's record can be found where these two types of capital are treated as separate, as mutually incompatible, or as if one mattered and the other did not. Ignoring or excluding either economic or social capital seems to have contributed as much as anything to sabotaging decent solutions. Conversely, treating the two as complementary seems to hold considerable promise.

As much as anyone in the development disciplines, Norman Uphoff has made the case for a mode of thinking that marries once exclusive categories. He asks how large consequences can come from small inputs, or how hard pay-offs can be won from soft resources. Uphoff's essay introduces the principal idea underlying this section of the book: that economic capital can emerge from sensible social reforms. The rising currency of this idea is an auspicious sign of the times. A dismantling of the walls that have conventionally separated 'hard' economics from the other, 'softer' disciplines has made possible a merging of the economists' answers to growth and the sociologists' answers to poverty: the social efficacy of the market place may now consort with rural empowerment schemes.

A decade ago, the economists' view of poverty relied heavily on the notion that poor farmers were too poor and knew too little about economic growth to participate in the development process and that they had to be led out of poverty by the more powerful investors or the more prudent savers. It was unthinkable that a poor woman could pretend to tell experts what was best for her children, her neighbour, or her village about how levels of health or income stagnate, much less improve. Poor people did not qualify as actors in the process of growth because they were poor; only those with resources qualified as actors in the market place and among these, only those who could spend and produce in more or less the right way.

The alternative perspective (typically that of progressive sociologists, anthropologists, geographers, and political scientists), in objecting loudly that the economists ignored poor people entirely, saw only the urgent necessity to supply them with essentials, to relieve their suffering and their hunger. But advocates of this alternative perspective were just as dogmatic in their approach to supplying basic needs as the economists were in nurturing investments. Neither had lasting insights, for the poor benefitted little more from participating in a market place to which they had little access than they did from the influx of commodities about which they had little say. Now that the different intellectual dispositions have softened, a common ground is emerging where the rights of the poor to choose and to act as individuals are enshrined in support to local institutions, in autonomous microcredit schemes, in the creation of marketlike institutions through which both the disenfranchised and the affluent can situate themselves along a demand curve. Equity and growth are becoming comfortable bedfellows in a domain of inquiry some call economic sociology or political economy (Alesina and Perotti, 1994).

This common ground embraces the democratic potential of programs sensibly driven by market competition. Free trade is tempered with the realization that trade is never really free. At the same time, even some of the more blatant instances of dependency and clientage, both at the international and village level, can be undermined by more efficient, more democratic participation in the economy.

In Chapter 9, using the example of development experience in Sri Lanka, Norman Uphoff shows how changing the way in which people collectively think about their role in maintaining an irrigation system can revive the system itself. Social equity builds economic capital. In Chapter 10 Jim Freedman then demonstrates the economic costs of social inequities, drawing on a long-term study of an irrigation system in Northern Pakistan.

9

Hard Pay-offs from Soft Resources: Transforming Irrigation System Performance in Sri Lanka

NORMAN UPHOFF

There is much about the enterprise of 'development' that is paradoxical, as Albert Hirschman has been fond of pointing out (e.g., 1963, 1967, 1984). Why should richer countries help poorer ones to advance economically and socially? This makes them stronger competitors in the world market, less easily exploitable. Yet by the magic of positive-sum processes, both can be better off as a result of the progress of the poor. When poorer countries, households, or individuals remain at lower levels of productivity, not only are they worse off but others are denied the benefits of whatever goods and services, ideas, technologies, markets, cultural creations, and even sociability that the poor could otherwise have contributed to the greater good of all.

Another paradox concerns the genesis of development. Decades of unsatisfactory experience with 'top-down' efforts to promote the development of the poor have led to the realization that broad and sustainable success depends upon the active participation of the poor in their own advancement. Yet we find that effective 'bottom-up' development often requires initiative and support from above, that is, from the 'top down.' The paradoxical strategy of assisted self-reliance is one of the most promising ways to create local capacities for broad-based development (Esman and Uphoff, 1984: 258–61; Uphoff, 1988; also cases in Krishna et al., 1997). To be sure, paradoxes do not produce only positive results. The provision of opportunities for local participation does not necessarily produce greater democracy but it can create legitimate channels for oligarchic dominance, as Robert Michels cautioned many years ago when he proposed 'the iron law of oligarchy' (Michels, 1915; but see also Fisher, 1994).

Appreciating this kind of complexity and contingency should disabuse us of our love affair with linear models, which has come from the so-called Age of Enlightenment. Many material and cultural accomplishments have resulted from such simplifying assumptions, but these should be regarded as opportune and useful rather than true. Reality itself is much different and more complex, as we have learned from the body of discoveries and analyses grouped under the rubric of chaos theory (Gleick, 1987), which feeds into a larger, expanding body of knowledge known as complexity theory. Even our conception of mathematics is being altered by the unfolding advances of computers and the exploration of ever-more complex problems.[1]

One of the central and thoroughly paradoxical tenets of chaos theory is that small causes can have large effects. Conversely, one can say that large causes can also have no effect, as when a planted crop fails totally or big research projects produce no results. Neither outcome is proper or predictable in a universe that operates according to classical linear notions of causation, where effects should always be proportional to causes. Yet we know from experience in development that both dynamics are at work in the real world. Very small impetuses, as a result of careful calculation, persistence, or just luck, can contribute to large changes, while immense efforts can come to naught. This realization should shake the confidence of all who hold to mechanistic images of reality, though it will probably take a decade or more before the insights coming from the natural sciences in this century alter the worldview of social scientists who have had their thinking shaped by physical science principles from a much earlier era.

A particular paradox I would like to explore here is the dialectic not between small and large but between 'hard' and 'soft,' between things that are material and things that are not.

In development, we need to understand and explain how, as Popper has put the question, non-physical things such as purposes, deliberations, plans, decisions, theories, intentions, and values can play a part in bringing about physical changes in the physical world (1972: 228–9).

For many years, the major concern in the study and practice of development was economic development. This was commonly defined and evaluated in terms of gross national or domestic product (GNP or GDP). These measures estimated the volume of goods and services produced as valued by some agreed set of prices. The corollary of this was national income, best represented in per capita terms, which represented the amount of goods and services that people could consume. There is no need to go into the criticisms of this concept of development, as its many shortcomings are now well known. However, it is worth noting that the first major alternative to assessing development in terms of per capita product or income – the physical quality of life index (PQLI) – was equally material in its construction (Morris, 1979).

Economic development, however much it was considered as a proxy for broader ranging concepts of development, was treated primarily as a material process, propelled for the most part by material causes. Land, labour, and capital as the factors of production were the variables that received the lion's share of attention, as they were deemed the most important and reliable means for expanding the output of goods and services. Some nonmaterial factors like entrepreneurship and X-efficiency were proposed by some eminent economists (Schumpeter, 1934; Leibenstein, 1976).[2] And in spite of many critiques of this orientation, the mindset that reduced development essentially to physical dynamics and relationships has remained prevalent. Objections have been growing stronger, however. The quality and not just the quantity of human resources is now an issue, and the study of social capital presents a potentially powerful challenge to the conventional economic paradigm by going beyond the inputs of land, labour, and capital (Coleman, 1988; Serageldin, 1996: 1–7).

In this chapter, I would like to explore how ideational factors can contribute to concrete and commendable outcomes in development, drawing on intense and successful development experience in Sri Lanka. This line of explanation is not one that I started with, having been trained to regard material investments and incentives and measurable results as the most important considerations. But less tangible factors became more plausible and eventually compelling as researchers from the Agrarian Research and Training Institute (ARTI) in Colombo and from Cornell University together sought to improve irrigation management in the Gal Oya scheme, reputedly the most difficult and rundown system in the country, starting in 1980.

Working with and through a cadre of young organizers who operated as 'catalysts,' we established a network of farmer organizations that greatly increased water use efficiency and agricultural production, simultaneously addressing social and cultural needs. Nobody, ourselves included, had anticipated so much and such rapid improvement. To comprehend this experience and make it useful to others we had to move beyond the easier and more fashionable explanations invoking incentives and material self-interest to ascertain the influence of ideas and norms that produced some powerful material effects. The transformation of soft resources into hard ones presents both challenges and opportunities in development that have been too long overlooked.

Improving Irrigation System Performance in Gal Oya

Water is usually seen as a quintessentially scarce, zero-sum resource, one that cannot be allocated to two different uses (unless these uses can be sequential and the water can be recycled, which is not uncommon). We know that conflicts over water can be severe, even lethal. The Gal Oya irrigation system, built in the early 1950s, was perennially short of water. The catchment area had seldom harvested as much water as expected and the reservoir filled only twice in the first thirty years. Within the Left Bank area, which was the largest part of the system, at least 25,000 hectares seldom got irrigation water down to the lowest third of the command area.[3] The middle third of the Left Bank received only irregular supply during the dry season, when all rice crops depend on the irrigation system because there is no rain, and even many parts of the upper third, nominally having the best water supply, never got enough to grow a reliable crop. Farmers cultivating fields at the tail end of channels, whether in the head, middle, or tail of the system, suffered water shortages ranging from moderate to total.

The 'hardware' for the system – the channels, canals, gates, and measuring devices – had greatly deteriorated during the first three decades of operation. This was partly for lack of maintenance, but also because farmers seeking more water broke open or removed gates that controlled water flow to increase their supply. In the Left Bank, over 80 per cent of gates were broken or missing, and water was reliably measured and controlled at only seven points for the more than 25,000 hectares (Murray-Rust 1983). A condition of virtual anarchy prevailed in 1980 when we started planning to introduce the 'software' of farmer organization into the system to improve its operation and maintenance.

Actually, farmer organizations were not part of the original design of the project through which the U.S. Agency for International Development (USAID) expected to improve water management in Gal Oya. However, we believed that they could make significant improvements, based on experience of the Philippine National Irrigation Administration (Korten and Siy, 1988). As this was a settlement scheme, where 20,000 households had been brought in from different parts of the island during the 1950s, there was little history of cooperation among farmers and indeed much conflict. Our challenge was to bring about such cooperation, and for this we recruited, trained, and deployed organizers to help establish farmer organizations. We started at the field channel level, where ten to twenty farmers were getting a common water supply from the distributary canal. Within several years we had a four-tiered structure in place with over 12,000 farmer-members.

ARTI and Cornell's involvement in Gal Oya terminated at the end of 1985 but the farmer organizations are still operating effectively (Uphoff, 1996: vii–xi; Wijayaratna and Uphoff, 1997). The structures and processes that they pioneered have become the basis for a national program of participatory irrigation management, endorsed by the Sri Lankan cabinet at the end of 1988. There are now about 250,000 farmers participating in organizations based on the Gal Oya model functioning in all the major irrigation systems in the country.[4]

Although water is usually considered to be a scarce resource, farmers have been able, by collective action, to practically double the efficiency of water use, reducing seepage, conveyance, and evaporation losses. In practical terms this has meant that the supply of water is effectively doubled, since twice as much area can be cultivated satisfactorily as before with the same amount of water.

The program of participatory management started during the dry season in 1981, when the main reservoir was only 25 per cent full and the possibility of crop failures loomed. One Cornell adviser suggested that we postpone the start of the program until the next season, so that it could not be blamed for any failures that might occur and that could jeopardize our mission. Indeed, most social scientists would predict that greater scarcity of a valued resource would probably result in more conflict. In fact, the opposite occurred, thanks in large part to the efforts of the young organizers.

Within six weeks, 90 per cent of the field channels in our pilot area, over 2,000 hectares, were doing some combination of:

- cleaning silted-up channels by voluntary group labour, some channels not having been cleared of weeds, stones, and silt for ten years or more;
- rotating water deliveries among all farmers so that each got a fair share of whatever water was available, which was quite amazing in Gal Oya at the time; and
- saving as much water as possible to be donated to farmers downstream who were even more water-stressed; in some cases, Sinhalese

farmers gave up water for Tamil farmers, remarkable behaviour in a country where ethnic tensions were rising.

We calculated that upstream farmers were willing to give up about one-sixth of the amount of water allocated to them, usually to farmers whom they did not even know.

Such cooperative behaviour 'produced' water by cutting transmission losses. Once channels were better maintained, the water could run more swiftly and with less loss through percolation into the soil during conveyance. If water was rotated at field level among water users, with each receiving a larger volume in turn rather than all of them trying to get a continuous but smaller flow, the water could more quickly saturate the soil in a field. Indeed it was more likely to reach the end of the field than when all of the farmers only received a trickle at the top of their fields. With a system of rotation, their fields would be watered within a few hours and farmers could go about other business rather than having to guard their small flow around the clock. Unguarded water was likely to be stolen, so farmers had stayed up at night, possibly to steal water from others as well as to protect their own supply. One benefit that farmers remarked about most enthusiastically when asked about the new system of cooperative water management was that they could sleep at night!

Before the project, overall water deliveries during the dry season were 8 to 9 acre-feet per acre for the Left Bank and 5 to 6 acre-feet in the wet season (FAO, 1975). In 1985 and 1986, after the organizations were in place, the water issued per acre was only half as much, down to about 5 acre-feet in the dry season and about 2 acre-feet in the wet season (well below the national norm of 3 acre-feet). More importantly, in terms of human welfare, after the project ended in 1985 the whole Left Bank could be given irrigation water during the dry season to ensure a proper crop once farmer organizations were in place and working with the Irrigation Department (ID).[5]

The extent of area cultivated is not the only or best measure of successful irrigation. The amount of crop, in this case rice, produced per unit of water provides a summary measure of performance. A study conducted for the International Irrigation Management Institute (IIMI) found about a four-fold increase in production per unit of water issued (Wijayaratna and Uphoff, 1997: 178). One might like to attribute this to the much larger investment that USAID made in improving the hardware of the Gal Oya irrigation system; the investment in software was less than 10 per cent of the total project cost. But water use efficiency gains were made in the first few years of the project, before much of the physical rehabilitation work had been done.

What occurred was a dramatic change in farmer behaviour, and a corresponding change in engineers' performance. The chairman of one organization (for the most conflict-ridden and difficult area on the Left Bank) told me: 'There used to be lots of fights among farmers here over water, even murders. You can check the records of the police if you don't believe me. Now there are no more.' This testified to the difficulties that farmers fighting over scarce water can make for each other. Another farmer chairman told me as the project ended that before it began relations between farmers and officials were not good: 'We were like snake and mongoose.' (He did not say which was which, and I did not ask.) While some engineers were initially unwilling to cooperate with farmer organizations, seeing them as a threat to their status and authority as well as to income 'supplements,' within two years there was substantial acceptance and collaboration.

The benefits to farmers from collective action were various. In an area with a long, harsh dry season, irrigation is essential for getting a second crop each year, and this second crop makes the difference between a fairly secure subsistence and painful deprivations. Yet one of the first things farmers mentioned when asked about the benefits of the new system of cooperation was that they could sleep at night. In Sri Lanka, there is a well-established cultural value of *ekamutekame*, which refers to a spirit of unity or oneness, that is much appreciated. When villages have this quality, there is a sense of harmony and well-being; when it is absent there is strife and insecurity. Since Gal Oya was a settlement scheme, most communities in the area had lacked *ekamutekame*, being made up of households brought in from diverse villages. It was amazing to us how quickly a new atmosphere of cooperation could be created by the young organizers, indicating that an unfulfilled demand was being met, rather than a change made in people's values. Thus a mélange of material and nonmaterial benefits arose from the new system.

Why engineers should accept this system was less easy to see. It seemed that they had much to lose from it, including material advantages. Yet with some positive leadership from within the Irrigation Department, and with endorsement from the top political and administrative figures in the district, most technical staff began cooperating with the farmer organizations. Apparently they needed a rationale as much as incentives. One of the Cornell faculty advisers, an agricultural engineer, told the leadership of the Irrigation Department in 1982 that the ID should not try to 'retail' water to each farmer's field because it lacked the information, personnel, and budgetary resources to do this properly. Rather, it would be wiser for them to 'wholesale' water to farmer organizations at the distributary canal level. These, in turn, undertook to 'retail' the water to farmers' fields through the new field channel groups. At first this idea was resisted, presumably at least in part because it implied some loss of personal revenue to officials from farmers who were willing to pay for supplementary water issues.

Interestingly, within a year or so the new concept of ID responsibility had taken root among engineers or percolated into their thinking. The rationale for maintaining control had given way to a shared-management model of operation. While some reduction in personal incomes for technical personnel might ensue, there were fewer hassles. Farmers not getting water could only blame themselves or each other if the right amount of water had been issued to the distributary canal area. Job satisfaction for engineers and other officials increased as the irrigation system met more of its production goals, the system was maintained better, and interpersonal relations were greatly improved.[6]

Puzzles of Tangibility

People are motivated by a wide range of benefits and satisfactions on the positive side and by a variety of negative costs, penalties, or sanctions. Reductionist reasoning suggests one can decide whether people are more influenced by material or nonmaterial influences. But this reflects the analytical propensities that academic disciplines have promoted. Usually both material and nonmaterial incentives are present. Which is more important? We cannot answer this question unless all the material considerations produce positive inducements while nonmaterial ones create negative incentives, or vice versa.

Trying to explain motivation is one of the most inconclusive things we can do. It is hard enough to know our own motivation with certainty, let alone to determine what motivates other persons. All of us represent some combination of self-oriented and other-oriented thinking, some mix of selfishness and generosity (Uphoff, 1996: 326–56). Rather than categorize our behaviour as being prompted by one motivation or another, we might better be understood as proceeding always with mixed motives, that is, a set of motivations attuned to considerations like self-respect and reputation as well as of self-interest and material aggrandizement.

It is probably true that material incentives (inducements or sanctions) are more tangible and even more predictable than nonmaterial ones. They can be invoked more easily and demonstrably. Payments of wages or bonuses, the imposition of fines or other penalties, the provision or deprivation of material comforts, these have some definite qualities that praise, recognition, and other social rewards cannot match in terms of quantification or documentation. But we know that some of the latter kinds of reward and reinforcement for cooperative behaviour were at work in Gal Oya.

Farmers whose fields were located at the head of a channel had no material interest in a system of maintenance that would clean channels. The more silted up these were, the more water would run into head-end fields. Yet with virtually no exceptions head-enders agreed to participate in channel cleaning whenever it was proposed as a solution to tail-end water shortages. Some assurance was given that everyone would receive a fair share of water, so that there would probably be no loss of crop at the head. Implicitly, farmer organizations adopted a rule something like Pareto optimality. Water would be redistributed to the extent that head-enders would not be worse off but other farmers would be better off. The latter would get the excess water that head-enders had been wasting, taking more than they needed and letting it run into drains and from there into the groundwater or out to the ocean. Some labour, a cost, was required of head-enders along with everyone else, to clean the channel so that water could flow unobstructed (past the fields of head-enders when it was not their turn).

What did head-enders receive for this cooperation? They too benefitted from a system of rotation that let them sleep at night rather than having to stay up to make sure nobody closed off their field inlet to take water downstream. There was a sense of social harmony with neighbours, which had been missing, once a regime of cooperation was established. Neighbours would be more willing to inform a head-ender if cattle got into his field and were eating his rice crop, rather than taking vengeful satisfaction in the fact that their rich neighbour was going to suffer. When a system of cooperation was in place, farmers often grazed their cattle away from the rice-growing area, taking turns tending the herd.

Such considerations provided a rationale, if not motivation, for cooperation. One of the most telling explanations came from an organizer when asked why head-end farmers acquiesced in new practices that shared water more fairly: 'It is hard to be selfish in public' (Uphoff, 1996: 85–7). Self-respect was a factor in people's choice about whether to participate or not in a water management regime. It was easier to be selfish in private, when nobody was paying attention to the consequences of individuals' actions for others. Cooperative behaviour also had some quick and substantial material pay-offs. On balance, it could be said that nobody was made worse off, social and psychological considerations included, whereas many became better off as a result.[7]

One could try to explain the changed behaviour as due to the material benefits alone, and quite possibly there was a balance in favour of cooperation with economically measurable benefits outweighing any and all measurable costs. But head-enders, by entering into a system of management whereby they let water run past their fields to the tail end before they were given their turn (the usual rotation system), were incurring considerable risk that they might not get water during that five-day turn, because the system was at the outset managed unpredictably.[8] Some combination of material and nonmaterial motivations sufficed to win cooperation in a management system that produced substantial tangible results.

We have seen that at least some engineers and other officials involved with system management had financial interests at stake that were compromised by the new approach. Since it was illegal to take bribes or side payments, 'what was stopped or lost was not publicly defensible.[9] But the new system was accepted in large part I think because it made irrigation management easier for officials. There were fewer headaches and hassles and more cooperation with decisions. Water was being used more efficiently and productively. Farmers were even undertaking some preventive maintenance at their own initiative, which reduced cost and trouble for the Irrigation Department. The antagonism towards engineers largely evaporated. A complex set of considerations and incentives emerged, touching on motivations as diffuse as pride and conflict aversion. The material benefits that resulted were primarily for the farmers, not government personnel, but that did not prevent the latter from cooperating.

What motivated the organizers, the key personnel who initiated and spread the program? We enlisted unemployed university graduates who had little if any prior work experience. They were enthusiastic about having a first job and the possibility, admittedly no more than that, of permanent employment. Because they were all appointed as temporary employees, on one-year contracts, whenever the chance for regular jobs elsewhere came along, most accepted these, however much they liked the organizing work, because permanent employment was hard to find. (We had over eight hundred applicants for our first thirty-two openings.)

During the early 1980s, the government periodically took large numbers of graduates into the teaching cadre, so that we lost the majority of our organizers at least once a year. Of our first thirty-two we lost twenty-six; we trained thirty more and then lost twenty-five; and so forth. Of the 169 recruited and trained during the four years of the program, only eight organizers were left in December 1985. How many programs have sustained a turnover of 95 per cent of their field staff and still succeeded? The motivation of these organizers was remarkable. The few who remained behind, often because they were too old to be hired as teachers, managed to convey both the knowledge and motivation needed to be effective organizers, since the formal training could never be as useful as apprenticeships in the field.

That the organizers had individual and collective responsibility for planning and evaluating their work in the first instance was a strong motivating factor. Although they had no time clocks to punch, most worked far more than forty hours a week. Cynics could say that there was not much else to do in Gal Oya villages besides spend time with villagers, which was true. But there was no need for organizers to become so engaged with farmers and their families that they became regarded as 'sons and daughters.'[10] The fact that young people were given opportunity as well as responsibility to make a difference in other people's lives was probably the strongest motivating factor. Their salaries, paid by the Sri Lankan government (not USAID), were fairly good but this reflected that the jobs had no permanence. Conditions of work were very difficult, such that one of the Sri Lankan university professors who advised our program was surprised to see how the organizers were living.[11]

Although we were unable to keep most of the organizers in the program without the promise of permanent jobs, all those who gained experience in the program went on to probably better employment than they would have had otherwise.[12] But perhaps the strongest motivating force in the field was the friendship among organizers, which was palpable when one met them in small or large groups.[13] Ten were eventually given regular appointments, five years after the Ministry of Lands had agreed to create a permanent cadre, with responsibilities to initiate and oversee farmer organization efforts in other systems. For some, this kind of work was seen as a vocation, something they were good at and enjoyed. Most, however, had to regard it as a challenging period in their young lives, averaging about nine months only, before they went on to do something else. Despite the transitory nature of their work, organizers threw themselves into it, usually with energy and imagination.[14]

Social Energy

We all think we know what physical energy is. We see and live with its effects all around us: heat, electrical power, chemical reactions, and other manifestations. Yet for all its evident material nature, it seems to have an ambiguous existence. We always need to denominate one form in terms of another, such as kilocalories or British Thermal Units (BTUs). The parallel concept of power has been elusive in the social sciences, so elusive indeed that its definition according to Max Weber, the most widely cited writer on the subject, represents power not as a thing in itself but as a probability within a relationship (Uphoff, 1990).

Yet despite its ambiguity, energy and power are some of the most 'real' things that we encounter in the world, however they are defined and measured. Based on his observations of development experiences in Latin America, Hirschman (1984: 97) suggested that there is something in human society that could be characterized as 'social energy,' somehow similar to physical energy. Hirschman cited the example of a rural community in Colombia that initiated its own land redistribution, taking excess land from large landowners, when the government's land reform program was moving very slowly. The landowners got the initiative suppressed by the courts and police, so the community migrated en masse to the sea coast, where they learned fishing and started up a fishing cooperative. The same kind of solidarity and commitment to social justice that had animated the land reform efforts reappeared to energize this new venture. Social energy suppressed in one location at one point in time re-emerged later in another place from the same community, suggesting that it was somehow conserved, in a manner akin to the law of the conservation of physical energy.

The marvel of social energy is that it is apparently derived from nothing, at least nothing material. It stems, as best we can tell, from the attraction that people can feel towards one another, a dynamic often referred to as solidarity, which is the macroequivalent of the microphenomenon of friendship. Friendship can be defined in technical economic terms as expressing a positive interdependence of utility functions, which contrasts with the usual assumption in economics of independent utility functions. The latter implies that people are indifferent to one another's well-being, whereas according to the former each friend considers his or her well-being to be increased or decreased according to the other's greater or diminished satisfaction/happiness.[15]

When people choose to care about each other's welfare, this generates a willingness to work harder and to work together, making sacrifices and innovating in order to accomplish things for the common good. We have seen many examples of social energy being mobilized and channelled in rural development programs, documented in Krishna et al. (1997).[16] Material resources are involved in these enterprises, but what makes them efficient and effective is the human factor that utilizes resources mobilized externally and internally carefully, creatively, and equitably. Although what Leibenstein (1976) called 'X-efficiency' has not been brought into the evaluation of such development efforts, its focus on the productivity-multiplying effects of morale, attention to detail, and cooperative behaviour is well-suited to help us understand how intangible factors of production can complement and make more beneficial the tangible factors we are accustomed to analysing.[17]

Unfortunately, attempts to analyse intangible factors are hindered by a lack of good tools for measurement. Comparison and explanation are handicapped. Much has to be understood by inference or indirect methods. In our Sri Lankan work, we concluded that the nonmaterial factors of ideas, ideals, and friendship had powerful and beneficial influences on the operation of our program, leading to impressive material results (Uphoff, 1996: 357–87). An idea like the distinction between 'wholesaling' and 'retailing,' discussed above, could contribute to quite different and better performance by the engineering staff, rationalizing and legitimating new modes of management. Similarly, engineers and officials according respect to farmers could have strong motivating effects on the latter, encouraging substantial physical labour and material improvements that would not otherwise have been forthcoming (ibid.: 94–7).

We still find it difficult to deal with such questions within standard social science ways of thinking. Though Karl Popper, one of the leading contributors to social science theory in this century, urged us twenty-five years ago to consider how nonmaterial causes could have material effects, this challenge has gone largely unheeded. Positivist methodologies and ontological assumptions do not readily accommodate such constructions of reality. Behaviouralist social science has been willing to 'measure' attitudes and values through survey instruments and to infer actions from beliefs. But this line of reasoning gets attenuated when it comes to explaining collective rather than individual phenomena. The collective action in Sri Lanka, which is observable in many other countries, as well has its origins in the thinking of people, both program planners and implementers and program participants.

More is involved than just ideas, ideals, and friendship, though these are relatively specific nonmaterial phenomena that can be studied. Some of these nonmaterial factors are beginning to be addressed under the rubric of 'social capital' (Coleman, 1988; Putnam et al., 1993). Things like obligations, trust, and social networks are surely energizing, although they cannot simply be lumped together; there are important distinctions to be made between, for example, structural and cognitive forms of social capital. The first is embodied in roles, whereas the latter are accumulated and expressed in values, norms, attitudes, and beliefs (Uphoff, 2000).

A start towards the integrated analysis of such factors has been made in an analytical framework that identifies the larger set of factors of political, economic, and social production, subsuming economics within a more encompassing social science scheme. This model of a new political economy identifies information, legitimacy, and status as factors of production alongside the more tangible factors of economic resources, physical force, and authority (Ilchman and Uphoff, 1997). Probably not coincidentally, the factors of information, legitimacy, and status, which depend on cognitive processes, parallel the set of ideas, ideals, and friendship noted above. What these factors have in common is that they are all positive-sum in important ways; that they are not diminished by use or exploitation so long as basic harmonization and convergence of interests is maintained.

Development itself must have some positive-sum features. Otherwise the proverbial 'pie' is not made larger; it is simply redistributed. This points to the genuinely transformative nature of development. In Schumpeter's terms (1934), development is spurred by drawing forth new supplies of inputs and uncovering new sources of inputs;

by inventing new outputs and finding new markets for existing ones; and most importantly, by devising new production processes and structures (technology and organization) that can convert inputs into outputs more efficiently and effectively. These are qualitative, not just quantitative changes. They are redirective rather than redistributive.

New relationships are not merely physical but also social and mental. Gerry Helleiner's concept of ownership in Chapter 4 is a case in point: the inflow of resources into a developing economy is at once physical capital as well as the relationships entailed by those who manage it. Whereas the physical realm has some in-built constraints, the social realm (choosing with whom to interact and cooperate) and the mental realm (deciding what to think, value, and believe) are more amenable to modification.[18] The physical world cannot be remade simply by thinking about it. Subjective factors cannot eliminate objective ones or redefine them at will. On the other hand, there are ways in which the physical world can be recast and changed by the efforts stemming from social and mental processes; these realms are more interactive and interdependent than implied by the analytical dichotomy of material versus nonmaterial or the trichotomy of physical, social (interpersonal), and mental (intrapersonal).

We have for years lived with the distinction made between hard sciences, those dealing with physical and biological phenomena that can be measured and predicted relatively easily, and soft sciences, those dealing with people and ideas, the social sciences and humanities. By giving us a concrete distinction between hardware and software the computer age has to some extent reified this difference, but it has also revealed how interdependent these two kinds of tools really are. Just as induction and deduction are not really independent, neither ultimately are structure and function (Black, 1991).

Achieving real transformation in development involves moving not just from one physical form to another but changing physical production possibilities as a result of social reconstructions and mental reconfigurations. Once we can more actively and creatively bring social and mental dynamics to bear on physical constraints and needs, we will have a better chance of satisfying the latter. Recognizing the dialectic between 'soft' and 'hard' without giving priority to either should enable us to transform undesirable situations, as seen in the case of Gal Oya.

Notes

1 Development specialists would do well to engage themselves with the ideas coming from the natural sciences. 'Classical' physical sciences have shaped our thinking in the social sciences, as shown by Hirschman (1977). 'Post-Newtonian' social science can help us understand better the social universe in order to seek to make it more productive and benefi- cent (Uphoff, 1992). I will not elaborate those arguments here, but I will suggest some reading in the physical sciences that I have found helpful for thinking about development problems. Seminal books on self-organi- zation and chaos are Jantsch (1980) and Prigogine and Stengers (1984). Lewin (1992) and Waldrop (1992) make complexity theory accessible for everyone in the way that Gleick (1987) brought chaos theory to a wide readership. More advanced but still quite comprehensible guides to these bodies of theory include Cohen and Stewart (1994), Gell-Mann (1994), Goodwin (1994), and Coveney and Highfield (1995). Bailey (1996) pur- sues the implications of these new paradigms for mathematics. He argues that, thanks to enormous increases in computing power, new analytical and inductive methodologies, which he calls 'intermaths,' are supersed- ing the deductive mathematics of geometry and calculus. These new mathematical methods are better suited for identifying and analysing patterns, which are crucially important in both biology and the social sciences.

2 The failure of economists to pick up on the prescient ideas of Leibenstein, a member of the Harvard economics department, and thus very visible in the profession, is amazing. There is now some prospect that his thinking will be revived and extended (Weiermair and Perlman, 1990).

3 Officially the Left Bank system served only about 17,000 hectares, but addi- tional area had been brought under cultivation without permission or pro- vision for legal access to water. Nobody knew exactly how many acres were actually being cultivated with the Left Bank's inadequate water sup- ply. The Right Bank system, served by a separate main canal, covered a similar area, and the River Division, that part of the system which had tra- ditionally been irrigated by diversion canals from the Gal Oya River, was about 8,000 hectares.

4 Because not all farmers using irrigation water, being tenants, leaseholders, labourers or the children of original settlers, have title to the land they culti- vate, not all can be official members. About half of this number are legally recognized members, but all participate in the decision making at the field channel level. The lowest level of organization is informal by design, to

avoid the need to exclude any water users from planning and implementing water use.

5 An indication of how much efficiency gain was possible with careful and cooperative investment of labour, the reservoir was even lower at the start of the 1982 dry season – only 20 per cent full. The Irrigation Department was willing to authorize planting of 2,000 hectares on the Left Bank. Farmers naturally objected. Through their representatives, a role created by our program, they promised to use water much more efficiently and eventually persuaded the government to authorize planting of 5,000 hectares. In fact, almost 7,000 hectares were planted, and by careful distribution of water, cutting all waste, a satisfactory crop was obtained with the amount of water that the Irrigation Department had thought could supply only 2,000 hectares.

6 The Irrigation Department's deputy director for the district claimed that he used to get hundreds of complaints each season sent by registered letters that had to be answered. 'Such letters are reduced to a handful,' he said, once the organizations were functioning. The top civil servant in the district told a newspaper that before the project, on the days when his office was open for public complaints, he would have a hundred persons coming to him about irrigation. 'Now not a single farmer comes to complain to me about water problems,' he said. Even if this is an exaggeration, there was a huge drop-off in complaints. The district minister made a similar comment to me: 'Before there were farmer organizations, out of every ten farmers I talked with, eight had problems getting water. Now I hear practically no complaints about irrigation distribution' (Uphoff, 1996: 8–9).

7 My colleague Anirudh Krishna interprets this as meaning that the space for individuals' decision making regarding irrigation was transferred from the private to the public sphere, making visible the nexus between individual decisions and collective outcomes. The blame for inferior outcomes could relatively easily be traced to specific individuals' actions, making it more likely that collective agreements could be sustained.

8 Although the delivery schedule throughout the system was officially one where each area would receive water for five days and then not for the following five days, in practice deliveries were quite erratic: five days on, seven days off; four days on, three days off; six days on, ten days off. One of the most remarkable things about the change in behaviour once organizations were created was that during that first, very water-short season, all of the changes that were made, by consensus, in water delivery rotations were from head-end-first schedules to tail-end-first schedules.

9 As far as we could determine, payments collected at lower levels were not shared up the line as they are in India (Wade, 1985). Also, from 1981 on, the

leader of the Irrigation Department in the district was scrupulous in his behaviour and set a good example for others.

10 Once a farmer commented to C.M. Wijayaratna, the ARTI coordinator for the program during its first three years, that it was too bad that we had young women as organizers. When asked why, he acknowledged that the women were doing a very good job. After some pressing, he finally said that the farmers were sad to see such fine young women spending so much time in the field, because they were losing their fair complexions (something much prized in Sri Lanka, which even affected marriageability). That the female organizers were willing to make a sacrifice in personal appearance was an indication of their commitment to their work and to the farmers' advancement, which created a sense of obligation among the latter to make sure that the effort succeeded.

11 The second year, when the reservoir was only 20 per cent full at the start of the dry season, when the next batch of organizers moved into more disadvantaged areas, in one particularly dry location no households would rent them rooms because they did not have enough water for family needs, let alone boarders. So seven organizers set up housekeeping in an empty cooperative warehouse. They biked three miles or more even to get food to cook for themselves, yet their morale was about the highest in the program and they catalysed remarkable cooperation, including between Sinhalese and Tamil farmers in an area were only eighteen months earlier there had been violent ethnic conflicts, resulting in some families being burned out of their homes (Uphoff, 1996: 119–23).

12 When twenty-four organizers left to join the teaching cadre, I was told that in the massive training camp for two thousand new teachers, when a representative council of twenty was chosen, sixteen of these were from our organizer cadre. Leadership skills, confidence, and maturity were all gained.

13 After only two weeks of training, the third batch of organizers, planning a party to conclude the training session, phrased their invitation in powerful and evocative language: 'We'll disperse tomorrow; We are going to a zone where some people are sweating blood to build a nation, and we will live with them. The friendship that has grown among us over the past few days causes our hearts to feel sorrow as we disperse tomorrow. But we endure it for the sake of greater friendship in the future. Colleagues, we invite you to join us in our farewell event' (Uphoff, 1996: 134). The training programs were all designed with a high degree of self-management by the trainees, to start them assuming responsibility for themselves from day one.

14 See, for example, Uphoff (1996: 68). The role of institutional organizer was patterned after that of community organizers with the National Irrigation

Administration in the Philippines (Korten and Siy, 1988) and of group organizers with the Small Farmer Development Program in Nepal (Ghai and Rahman, 1981). On the catalyst role in various programs, see Uphoff (1986: 207–9). One of the most remarkable programs using catalysts (social organizers) is the Orangi Pilot Project working in squatter settlements outside Karachi, Pakistan (Khan, 1996). The resource mobilizing dynamic of this participatory effort to improve quality of life in periurban slums has been remarkable, with seventeen rupees' worth of local resources contributed for every rupee of external resources utilized. The work of organizers in Gal Oya is reported and assessed in some detail in Uphoff (1996: 54–273).

15 These issues are discussed and analysed in more detail in Uphoff (1996: 284–9, 336–81).

16 This book contains case studies, including Gal Oya, written by the protagonists of eighteen innovative, (eventually) large-scale programs such as the Grameen Bank in Bangladesh, the AMUL dairy cooperatives in India, the Orangi Pilot Project in Pakistan, the Population and Development Association in Thailand, the Six-S Movement in the West African Sahel, and Plan Puebla in Mexico. These initiatives have benefitted hundreds of thousands, even millions of persons who bought into the participatory strategies of assisted self-reliance being pursued. These and other case experiences are analysed in Uphoff et al. (1998).

17 In his initial presentation of X-efficiency, Leibenstein (1965) reported that detailed quantitative analysis of intercountry differences in economic productivity showed output being only partly accounted for by the amount and allocation (allocative efficiency) of economists' standard inputs: land, labour, and capital. These factors explained much less than half of the variance in productivity observed. The remaining variation was accounted for by factors like the way in which production was organized, motivated, improved, and monitored.

18 In Gal Oya, people evidently had certain propensities for other-regarding behaviour (such as that encouraged by the remembered tradition of *shramadana*, voluntary group labour), which were stimulated by the organizers. Positive results reinforced these attitudes, resulting in the development of explicit rules and roles that carried forward and institutionalized the expression of other-regarding behaviour. The 'mental repertoire' from which such behaviour is drawn may itself be based on fairly long, historic, collective experience, such as suggested by Putnam et al. (1993). Anirudh Krishna suggests that what is modified in the short run is not the repertoire but rather the behaviour that is rationalized and motivated from it (personal communication).

10

A Case for Equity

JIM FREEDMAN

When an investment is made in an economy, the question of who gets what largely determines its consequences. Whether it amplifies the holdings of the well-to-do, the middle class, or the lower class makes a difference in its overall effect. An investment that narrows the income gap between the rich and the poor will also narrow the political divide separating the more and less powerful, and as political participation increases so will the economic confidence of those otherwise disenfranchised. Conversely, an investment that intensifies the differences between rich and poor is likely to stand in the way of democratization. It may in the end also reduce long-term possibilities for economic growth.

Oddly enough, equity enters the scripting of development projects and programs on the margins of planning and only rarely in the middle, where it matters. In a project's early stages, planners may make vaunted claims for its capacity to benefit everyone equally. Then follows a long silence. The matter may not surface again until a retrospective stage, at the moment of renewal or evaluation, for instance. If at this time the project is seen to have fallen short of its goals, the question of equity emerges as a lesson to be learned – just as the books are closed on the project for good. Why are the best of intentions abandoned once projects get underway? This is in part due to convenience. Project personnel are too busy to incorporate this complex ideal, which requires considerable sensitivity to a social environment, and hence takes time. Nor is there any quick fix that provides a guarantee of equity. Development programs already burdened with thorny logistical problems presume that if they have met the conditions for gender equity and satisfied basic ecological conditions they have satisfied the conditions for socio-economic equity writ large. Ignorance is also a factor: some planners come to the hasty conclusion that socio-economic equity does not much matter in the long run.

But equity and growth are in fact compatible, indeed, interdependent. Recognition of this transformative idea will allow development to achieve congruence between its humane aspirations and its material accomplishments.

A Paradox of Growth

Aesop told a fable about a farmer and a fox in which the fox had been enjoying himself in the farmer's fields, eating grapes and ripe corn. The farmer resolved to put an end to the fox's thieving and when, at long last, he caught the fox, he bound its tail with cloth and string and set it afire. The fox panicked and ran wildly through the farmer's mature crops, his flaming tail twisting this way and that, and in the end little was left of them.

In his earnest strategy to maximize his harvest the farmer failed to consider either the vanity of his aspirations or their complexity. In its quest for riches society often makes the same mistake. Some aspect of the quest itself makes the object sought elusive. Accumulating a surplus and placing it at the service of an economy to allow that economy to expand contains a consequence which, if ignored, jeopardizes the quest itself. Occasionally ignored by experts, lurking within the process of surplus accumulation is the tendency for growing economies to promote the enrichment of a small segment of society at the expense of others. Some of the consequences of this imbalance inhibit overall growth. This is why the matter of social fairness, or social equity, is crucial to a society's aspirations to accumulate wealth; social equity seems to be an important condition of success. Unless a society checks the differences that inevitably emerge among economic actors, inequities may thwart its goal of improving the well-being of its members as a whole.

Such was the lesson that emerged over a twenty-year period in a study of an irrigation scheme in northern Pakistan. The project was known as SCARP Mardan – 'salinity control and reclamation project' – and it was undertaken to the west of the Northwest Frontier Province city of Mardan. Inequities flourished in the wake of gains in farm production brought about by irrigation improvements. As they continued to grow, these inequities plagued the potential for income increases.

What happened in northern Pakistan is a version of a story that is remarkably common in the annals of development.

The SCARP plan to renovate an irrigation system assumed a simple and straightforward link between providing a better water delivery system and higher incomes for the people in the area. Salinization of soils caused by rising water tables would be controlled by installing an underground drainage system, while the quantity of water delivery would be increased by widening the channels. The theory of project effects was simple: better soils and more water would expand production of foodstuffs for consumption and for export. The incomes of those who owned land would rise and the benefits would spread to tenant farmers, nonfarmers, shopkeepers, and labourers as employment increased and underemployed labour was absorbed.

Once these ideals were inscribed in project documents, the arduous task of digging out surface drains, laying down pipes, and putting in new irrigation structures so consumed everyone's attention that the matter of equity was soon overshadowed. Project workers raised the issue from time to time, since it was obvious that small and tenant farmers were being adversely affected in the course of project works. A few workers proposed concrete steps to protect tenant farmers from the temporary losses caused by the installations. For the most part, however, advisers and designers accepted the costs to small farmers as the inevitable price to be paid for the value brought by technology to the more productive ones. That poor farmers become poorer and go to the cities, where they disappear in shanties, was the bitter pill to be swallowed in the interest of growth.

The study[1] of the project followed the fate of equity in the region from the planning stage in 1979 through the contentious negotiations among donors (the Canadian International Development Agency, the World Bank, and the Government of Pakistan) to the installation of drainage pipes and the widening of canals between 1984 and 1992. The final survey was conducted four years after installation, in 1996. The inquiry observed carefully the link between new technology, increased production, and higher incomes, paying particular attention to how and whose incomes grew.

As technology fell in place and better farm land yielded more sugarcane and wheat than before, incomes increased, though nowhere near to the extent expected. This South Asian experiment revealed a curious interplay between growth and equity, demonstrating how they fit together, how they don't, and the consequences of this relationship.

Four conclusions, each examined in some detail in the discussion below, may be drawn from the example of the project in northern Pakistan and its implications.

1 Prosperity and democracy are so closely linked that it is hard to have one without the other.
2 Economic growth typically undermines social equity, the condition for democracy.
3 Social and economic inequities brought about by economic growth probably compromise economic growth itself.
4 Without explicit controls on the concentration of wealth and power, neither development projects nor national economies will favour prosperity.

Prosperity and Democracy

From Marx to Rostow there seems to be a broad consensus that democracy and prosperity go together, even though opinions with respect to the obstacles faced may vary. For Rostow enthusiasts, it is loyalty to family or tribe that inhibits the participants in an economy from taking the initiative to enter a modern economy. A good dose of rationality is required to dissolve cultural rigidities. For Marxists, the bonds of the lower orders of society to a landed aristocracy have the same effect, until a revolution shatters those bonds. Modernizationists and Marxists agree that the individual freedom inherent in democracy's promise of equity is the progenitor of prosperity, and vice versa. The affluence of independent entrepreneurs contains the germ from which democracy springs. This is why townspeople emerge as the unlikely progenitors of modern economies, the missing link between feudalism and capitalism, for they simultaneously defy both rural roots and local aristocracy. Barrington Moore made this point particularly well in *The Social Origin of Dictatorship and Democracy*: '... A vigorous and independent class of town dwellers has been an indispensable element in the growth of parliamentary democracy. No bourgeois, no democracy' (1966: 418).

Setting poor people free from family bonds and the firm hand of landlords would seem, straightforwardly enough, to set development's agenda. But the path towards economic growth is not so simple as one might suspect. The most obvious itinerary in fact serves to undermine the very conditions for attaining it.

Two Economic Growth and Inequality

Consider a hypothetical society comprised of five households on an island. These households might choose to preserve an ideal of social fairness among themselves and ensure that no one of them achieves greater affluence than another. One collects coconuts and another palm fronds, one fishes, another builds shelters, and the remaining household assembles tools needed by the others. In this way, their affluence is complementary. But they soon reach the limits of the prosperity to be enjoyed within their terms of social fairness. They cannot become any better off without a greater specialization and this, whether they like it or not, threatens to undermine the equity the members of this society are committed to preserving. To expand its economy, the society will have to trade with a neighbouring island, and one or two of the households will therefore have to produce a surplus. The affluence of these one or two households *vis-à-vis* the others will increase. At some point, inevitably perhaps, prosperity, or the accumulation of a surplus, entails increased production by a minority of households, made possible by a transfer of wealth in some way from the others. The cherished complementarity and the equity they sought to preserve in the first place have to go. They may wish that the surplus enjoyed by the one or two newly affluent households will somehow make its way around to all the others, but this rarely happens.

The conundrum for these hypothetical households is that prosperity, which societies as a whole desire, will at some point involve some households doing better than others. The affluence of these few may actually require sacrifices from the others. Simon Kuznets, while by no means the first to describe it, enshrined this principle of economic growth in the proposition of the inverted U-curve, which graphically describes the scenario of the five households on the island (Kuznets, 1955: 1963). In the early stages of economic growth, the distribution of income or wealth among any group of households or individuals will become more concentrated for a while. Eventually, the curve should bend downward again as the original (and necessary) accumulations by the few households are spread around to the others and the relative inequality among them diminishes. This is easy to plot on a graph, with some measure of inequality on the vertical axis, such as the gini coefficient, and a measure of growth on the horizontal axis. The line begins low, where economic growth is low, peaks in the middle, and then descends, making an upside down U. The social costs that an economy will have to bear as differences among citizens increase sharply in the early years will presumably abate as some semblance of equity returns to society. Development planners have taken solace in the belief that the unpopular transfer of resources from the poor to the wealthy is only temporary.

Fifty years of deliberate development efforts have now passed, and the first part of Kuznets' prediction turns out to be true: inequalities increase in the course of economic growth, in some cases rather dramatically. But the second half of his proposition has been proven wrong. With some exceptions and some ambiguous cases, the social cost of development – increased inequities and the injustice that accompanies them – remains. The tail end of the upside down U- curve does not bend down.

The extent to which economic growth is blamed depends on the ideological disposition of the researchers and the techniques used for measuring and linking growth and inequality. Few would dispute the overall increase in relative inequality among households within developing economies since the 1960s or the intractability of the incidence of poverty, which has failed to drop significantly in recent years (Chen, Datt, and Ravallion, 1994: 375). But opinion does differ as to its extent and how closely the increase in social inequality can be associated with standard growth indicators. Irma Adelman, for one, seems unequivocal in her views on the relationship between economic growth and social inequity (1991: 135). Her study observes what happens to the portion of total income that accrues to the poorest groups of a population when the rate of per capita income growth increases, and in order to cover more than one year at a time she links the change in the percentage share of total income to the rate of growth of per capita income over the same time period. Adelman concludes that growth rarely benefits the poor; only if growth is remarkably rapid do any benefits spread to the poorer portions of the population. In other words, a country's economy would have to grow rapidly to avoid the social cost to the poor and the instances in which this happens are few and far between.

Gary Fields (1991: 3), like Adelman, links a measure of inequality – gini coefficients in most cases – with rates of growth, and does so only after a very scrupulous examination of the data available. The poor quality of data in transitional economies obliges him to eliminate a number of key countries, particularly those in which poverty is most severe and where, paradoxically, the process of immiserizing growth may be most pronounced. Among those countries with reliable data, he concludes that inequality increases with growth in only about half of the cases and therefore, unlike Adelman, he is reluctant to suggest a relationship. Fields is the more sceptical of authors on the subject, but taken as a whole, and accounting for a range of variation, most authors now accept the tendency for growing economies to shift wealth from the less affluent to the more affluent. The big question is what happens once the trend towards inequities is set in motion.

Social Inequities and Economic Growth

Consider the same five households on the island, at the point we left them, where one of the five households was producing a surplus for trade with a neighbouring island. The island's economy was prospering with the trade surplus, thanks in large part to the provision of raw materials and labour from other households at prices that made the export profitable. Soon, cracks began to appear in the island's equity compact as the exporting household began to take pride in its accumulations and even to enjoy a growing reputation. The affluent household easily convinced itself that its wealth was a measure of its political importance, and before long the members of that household took to riding in limousines. The affluent household soon ruled the other four and its rise to power became the stuff of legend, as tales recounted how local deities bestowed the mantle of power on the ruling junta. The affluent household then imposed its will even more on the other households, requiring them to work for wealth that was enjoyed disproportionately by the ruling household. Its wealth was matched by the others' deprivation. Discontent brewed. The poor households complained that the wealth of the ruling household was the cause of their penury, but their complaints moved the wealthy household to tighten even further its grip on the island's economy. The louder the complaints became, the more the rulers exerted their power and the more the other households were marginalized. Affluence bred discontent.

In this island microcosm lies a scenario familiar to many transitional economies, be they nations, regions, or villages. Powerful factions tend to grow even more powerful while the powerless suffer, and the consolidation of power by the one evokes resentment in the other. Fear of being overthrown drives the powerful to tighten their reign, which, in turn, heightens the determination of the powerless to resist. In this way the polarization perpetuates itself. There is a trade-off between social fairness, or equity, on the one hand, and economic growth on the other. In the absence of explicit constraints, economic growth intensifies economic differentiation as well as the political antagonism that typically ensues.

At local levels, landlords or politicians rule their tenants or constituents harshly. In competing among themselves for control over followers, landlords and local politicians typically drive the majority of village households to seek protection or access to land through alliances that splinter villages not only into rich and poor but also into antagonistic factions. At the national level, the same forces lead to social unrest, political instability, and an ineffective public sector. Political instability prevents governments from making necessary but unpopular decisions regarding taxation and this, in turn, worsens a nation's investment climate.

This scenario raises the original question of how economic growth affects inequities, except now it is re-posed with an interesting twist. The original question about the social costs, the inequalities and social tensions, that occur in the wake of economic growth is turned around to ask how these inequities, in their turn, affect a country's level of economic productivity. To what extent do social and economic inequities compromise a society's capacity for prosperity? The argument is brought full circle: if economic growth produces social inequities and these, in turn, inhibit economic growth, then the role of social inequities in this succession of causes and consequences would appear to undermine the search for prosperity.

The question of how inequities affect economic performance is posed in much the same way in North American business. Employees work well in some environments and less well in others, and the critical question for managers and owners is what kind of social environment works best. In one of many studies, salespeople in a North American department store were more loyal, worked harder, and were happier with their job when they perceived their pay and job assignments to be fair relative to others (Dubinsky and Levy, 1989). Similarly, the productivity of a sample of employees in an insurance firm worked harder when they were re-assigned, even temporarily, to offices with nice chairs and big windows; by contrast, the productivity of a comparison sample dropped when employees were assigned to dingier quarters (Greenberg, 1988). Applied psychologists have enshrined this principle in 'equity theory' (Adams, 1963, 1965), the central tenet of which is that employee motivation correlates neatly with employees' perception of equity. In other words, those who think they are treated unfairly perform poorly and those who think they are treated well out-perform others.

The principle applies in a national economy, a hair salon or, as Jonathan Barker indicates in Chapter 8, in village economies; his comparison of two villages in northern Nigeria shows that the hierarchical one was more reluctant to participate in development initiatives. Political instability at the national level, which grows out of demands by the underprivileged, makes economic actors nervous. Investors are reluctant to place their assets in a risky environment and will either hoard their wealth or send it out of the country. In either case, their reluctance to participate fully in the economy represents a net loss to that economy (Gupta, 1990: 254). Labourers and farmers have less to invest, and the precariousness of their social environment and the rigid constraints that make prosperity so unlikely lead them to maximize their security in lieu of productivity; risk aversion is a classic symptom of poor household behaviour. They too withhold resources from the economy, albeit to a lesser degree. Disenfranchised people, particularly the poor, are 'ill equipped to become actively engaged in their own development' (Salmen, 1992: 7).

Political unrest itself takes its toll on an economy, closing down factories and mines, sweeping farmers into opposing sides of active conflict, and alienating intellectuals and skilled labourers, who find refuge elsewhere (Gupta, 1990: 256; Alesina and Perotti, 1994: 362). Finally, there is what Alesina and Perotti call 'the fiscal channel'; voters in a country where income distribution is sharply skewed towards the rich will naturally vote for higher taxation, which taxes most those most likely to invest in capital projects (Alesina and Perotti, 1994: 362).

When inequalities increase economic growth suffers. Portions of the population, for various reasons, become increasingly disenfranchised, politically or economically, and this in turn deprives them of the entrepreneurial initiative that motivates economic actors in more equitable circumstances.

Projects and Prosperity

On the SCARP Mardan project, the average increase in household income (in constant rupees) for those households in the project area over the eleven-year period 1986–96 was surprisingly low, hardly more than 5 per cent (Freedman and Akram-Lodhi, 1997: 19). This period covered not only the time spent on installation of the new irrigation system but also a further four years in which it might be expected to have had effect. The modest growth in real income made a welcome difference to a number of households in the project area, particularly when compared with the stagnating incomes of those households outside the project's reach, but this slight increase was insufficient to generate real prosperity. The disappointing results undermined the wisdom of spending US$169 million to improve 123,600 acres in a valley at the foot of the Hindu Kush. They also raised the question of what pieces were missing in the puzzle of growth that the project pretended to solve.

One missing piece, perhaps the most crucial, was the effect of widening income differentials, compounded by shifts in power relations within project villages. The people in the project area are Pathans, whose ancestral roots lie in stateless, semi-nomadic regions of Southwest Asia. The Pathans harbour a marked antipathy to subservience; subservience is the antithesis of freedom and Pathans cherish personal freedom to such an extent that orthodox Pathans question the tribal pedigree of anyone who accepts political dependence on another. Pathans can fully realize their noble tribal heritage only if they are political equals. But colonialism, national governments, and development projects have stratified the Pathans in one way or another. Modern villages bear shameful witness to this development. In almost every one of them, there are those who own land and those who do not, those with valuable assets and those without. These differences in wealth have obvious consequences: most Pathans have to swallow their pride and the mandate of their heritage and become hired men and tenants.

Stark contrasts between rich and poor characterize most Pathan villages in irrigated areas, with dung-wattle tenant shacks on the periphery of sprawling manors. The villagers are loathe to acknowledge evident differences in status. Shopkeepers with paltry wares and tenants with hardly an eighth of an acre proudly stand up to men with hundreds of jareebs of land and speak their minds. The effect is a veneer of democracy, underneath which lies the anti-Pathan fact of feudal-like differences in rank. An outsider might expect the ideal of equality to temper the tendency towards extremes of privilege, yet the opposite is the case. Inequities may be a public shame, and Pathans may indeed prefer to deny them rather than make an issue of them, but since there is no socially acceptable form of privilege and no public sanction to say what is right and wrong about inequities, they continue to flourish.

When outsiders turn a blind eye to these inequalities, as Pathans are wont to do, they relegate them to the same dark corners as those who practice them. There is a difference, however. When planners ignore these inequalities the effect of their fiction is much worse since, in denying them, they ignore this society's profound internal contradiction, something Pathans themselves never do.

With rare exceptions, every village has its landlords. The power of landlords issues from their control over land needed by other villagers. Rental of land is never just an economic exchange. Controlling land in a village gives local landlords more power than the actual value of land might suggest, since the market in land, or tenancy contracts, is inflexible. Prospective tenants give more than a fixed rent or a share to the owners; they are also expected to give their political loyalty. Tenants become members of the landlord's village faction and one of his coterie of dependents. They vote for his choice of political candidates and they accept his terms when they borrow money. Usually there is more than one landlord in a village and more than one faction. Rivalry between factions renders the condition of unprotected households more precarious, and the increased dependence of faction members on the landlords increases in turn the power the landlord can exercise.

The effect of the SCARP Mardan project was to nourish this self-reinforcing process binding landlords and followers. As clients gather in factions to support the private interests of a patron they intensify the conflicts among factions and increase the need of all villagers for the protection they offer. The likelihood of project benefits spreading beyond owners depended on the project's ability to dilute the strength of these patron-client bonds. But by increasing the income of landlords and making them the main beneficiaries, the project served only to strengthen these bonds and to reinforce the subservience of tenants and other followers to the landowners. In one of the studies to determine project impacts, researchers asked tenant farmers whether their relations with landlords had changed following the project. Their answers were telling. The majority said tenancy meant, more than before, performing social services for the patron, voting for his candidates, coming to his aid in court cases, or attending social occasions. Tenancy contracts became an expression of broad political subservience instead of an economic exchange.

From Crop Yields to Cash Income

Per acre yields of the main crops – wheat, maize, and sugarcane – all experienced decent, if sporadic percentage increases following the project's installations. Farmers were particularly delighted with maize yields, which were on average five times higher than before, and wheat yields, which were on average 50 per cent higher. Nominal cash income (measured in current rupees) also increased. On superficial inspection, there had been respectable economic growth, since gross income per household increased, on average, two and a half times. But on closer inspection, once incomes had been adjusted for rupee inflation, income growth was minimal.

One of the most conspicuous changes over the course of the project was the shift in income distribution. Obviously, the income gains had occurred differentially. Some households had done very well, some had done only modestly well, and large numbers of households had become worse off. The pattern of changes summarized in Table 10.1 is reminiscent of the growth scenarios described in the parable of the five island households, except here the effects are more dramatic since differences already existed between powerful and dependent households. Changes in income distributions were calculated for six sample villages in the project area. The breakdown by village is especially important, because the extent of the changes depends very much on the distribution of power and wealth that existed beforehand. The six sample villages are ordered from top to bottom according to increasing concentration of income, village 1 being the most egalitarian and village 6 the least. The concentration of income is given as the ratio between the percentage of total income earned by those 20 per cent of households with the most income and that earned by those 40 per cent with the least.

Differences between rich and poor households increased in every village. In villages 1 and 2, where originally the differences were slighter, the increase in disparities was also slight. Where there was already a skewed distribution of income beforehand, as in villages 4 or 6, the increase in disparities was greater, in some cases dramatically so. In one village disparities doubled; in another they tripled. Increasing the concentration of income among village households augments the power exercised by privileged families. Local government becomes less democratic when the terms for poorer households to participate in the farm economy become less favourable, a process that ultimately

TABLE 10.1
Income distribution within villages for pre-project and post-project years

Villages in order of increasing inequality	Ratio of income earned by highest 20% to lowest 40% 1986 (pre-project)	Ratio of income earned by highest 20% to lowest 40% 1996 (post-project)
Village 1	2.3	2.7
Village 2	2.5	3.0
Village 3	2.9	3.2
Village 4	2.6	3.3
Village 5	2.3	5.9
Village 6	3.4	8.9

Note: Income includes cash plus own-produced non-cash income.

increases the number of disenfranchised households. One would expect a greater number of families to fall below a fixed poverty line, and by all appearances this, too, has happened. In 1986, 40.6 per cent of the population in Pakistan's Northwest Frontier province fell below a fixed poverty line (World Bank, 1995a); by 1996 in the smaller (and incidentally, wealthier) region of the project area, 44.9 per cent of the population fell below the same fixed poverty line.

More than a third of all households in 1996 earned an income, in whole or in part, as simple tenant farmers (they owned no land) and paid rent to landlords. Their numbers increased following the irrigation renovations because yields became higher; households that did not bother to farm before now believed that renting in land was worthwhile. At the same time, obtaining access to land became more difficult, since landlords used their increased power and wealth to demand higher rents from prospective tenants. For a few households, especially those that had equipment and could put fragments of owned land and rented land together to make a viable holding, the extra payments were worth it, but these were the exceptions. Most tenants are bound to their village for a myriad of extra-economic reasons and rely on farming small parcels of rented lands, and for most of these, their rents rose higher than their income. While their production was greater, their income (in constant rupees) was typically less. It was the landlords who captured, through their own production and through the rents they received, the lion's share of the income benefits. Of course there are other explanations for the shift in distribution. Access to productive inputs, access to markets, the flexibility to use markets to best advantage – all of these advantages accrue only to landlords. Did the landlords, in their turn, hire more villagers; did they invest in other ways in village economies? Did their increased wealth translate, in any way, into increased well-being for the area as a whole?

In most instances, probably not. Real incomes had not risen by 1996 commensurate with the rise in yields. Something happened between the production of crops in the fields and the conversion of these yields into the kind of economic growth that shows up in average constant household income. Markets did not cooperate, since the rise in output prices was matched by an equal rise in the price of inputs, due to the liberalization of input markets. The more essential a commodity has been for generating farmers' cash incomes, the more monopolistic the markets have become and the less favourable they have been to small farmers (Akram-Lodhi, 1997). The intensification of inequalities has had a similar though indirect effect. Powerful landowners used the increasing value of land to magnify their influence over others, altering the commitment of both landlords and tenants to the economy.

The Burden of Inequities on Village Economies

Well-endowed households use their power to extract resources from their dependents to fuel their own financial position, presumably producing growth through a transfer of resources from the poor to the wealthy. Social power is the mechanism that facilitates the transfer. A similar process is described by Arthur Lewis in his dual sector model, where low wages make industrial expansion possible. The difference in rural northern Pakistan is that labour does not move to the urban areas and the social effect of the transfer is not to free those who labour in the rural areas from traditional bonds of dependency but rather to reinforce them. Two things happen when participating in the farm economy means accepting increased subservience. Those households with the option will minimize their reliance on farming and look for alternative ways of generating income, ways that allow them more freedom. Those lacking this option, because they inhabit villages dominated by patron landlords, will continue to participate in the farming economy but the political homage they pay in order to farm detracts from the initiative required to maximize their income.

These two tendencies pull households in opposite directions: either away from farming, whereby they become less dependent on the local economy, and towards greater participation in far-flung economies or alternative occupations; or more inexorably into the orbit of landlords, where they are increasingly implicated in the factional obligations entailed by the necessary alignments. A few entrepreneurial farmers seek the best of both worlds, preserving their autonomy by farming some of their own land as well as rented land. These in-between farmers who simultaneously own and rent in land are a threatened species. They do well if they survive, but the number of these so-called owner-cum-tenants has declined noticeably in the wake of the irrigation project.

Farming in the project area has increasingly assumed a feudal social cast. As prominent farmers reap greater bounty from their land, they put less into it. The larger their operational holdings, the more they invest in nonfarm assets such as trucks, capital resources, or property. Following the project, 60 per cent of all assets for households operating more than twenty-five acres were nonfarm assets. Tenants or small farmers are likewise inclined to place their income, wherever it comes from, into nonfarm resources: sending a family member abroad, buying tools to become an artisan, or paying a local official to arrange the employment of a family member in government services.

One tell-tale consequence of these two tendencies is a decline in the relative importance of farming as a source of income. Farming slipped from being a primary source of income (56 per cent of total income in 1986) to being much less so (35.2 per cent of total income in 1996). The portion of total income generated from wage labour rose from 11 per cent in 1986 to 17 per cent in 1996. The portion of income derived from the sale of livestock, borrowing or lending money, and equipment sales, what one might call the liquidation of assets, jumped from 19 per cent to 29 per cent. More householders are working for a wage or selling off assets, and neither of these transactions indicate a growing economy. Paradoxically, the project has diminished the relative contribution of farming to the economy instead of augmenting it, as was intended. Crop yields may have increased, but farming is certainly not a booming business.

The social complexion of villages varies according to which of these two tendencies prevails. Where landlords are absent or ineffective and poorer households are less obliged to align with one of them, members of those households are free to choose other ways (than farming) for making a living. In these villages, households associate with each other more freely, usually in democratic villagewide organizations where the interests of the village as a whole take precedence over a household's need for landlord protection. Households are freer to align with local leaders, and this pattern of consociation, rather than subordination, more readily sets the stage for the kind of collective decision making that benefits a broader base of constituents. There may be better schools; there is more ready agreement to maintain irrigation facilities; intravillage conflicts decrease and their resolution requires less compromising intervention; more household resources are available for assembling collective resources. The labyrinth of village power politics is less inclined to discourage households from exercising entrepreneurial initiative.

Only one or two of the study's six sample villages moved in this direction, and this ratio, two out of six, is probably the portion of villages overall whose changing social complexion has favoured human development and a more liberal economic environment. The other two-thirds moved in the opposite direction. Not surprisingly, this two-thirds included the wealthiest villages, those most favourably endowed with good land and reliable water delivery. Here, the effect of improving the value of land was to reinforce the dominance of those whose power derived from controlling it. Households relied more on the power of landlords for their political welfare, for protection against rivalries with households of other factions or even with households within their own factions, and the price for this protection was fealty to a powerful patron. Patron landlords used this extra power to carve splinter groups out of previously cohesive villages, pulling them apart along factional seams.

The economic lives of the poorer client households became ever more precariousness and their dissatisfaction consequently increased. They responded, as do most households in such circumstances, by cultivating the fragile agreements that link them to their patrons instead of seeking alternative and no doubt more lucrative livelihood strategies. In the volatile social climate that results local landlords respond by committing as much concern and resources to their political control as they do to maximizing farm production. Whatever sense of collectivity a village may possess tends to evaporate in such a social climate.

These are the very conditions that compromise economic growth at a national level. Investors and politicians (typically the same persons) invest in their political power in lieu of committing whatever capital they have to economic growth. Small farmers and tenants cultivate relations with patrons with greater care than they cultivate their economic possibilities. And the capacity of the society as a whole to mobilize the economic resources of its citizens decreases as the result of persistent political conflict, leaving the society in economic stagnation.

There must be a place in the project cycle for assessing existing social and economic inequities and how they influence the growth equation. In Pakistan, over half of the total cultivable land is farmed by landlords owning fifty acres or more. This resource concentration inevitably affects the economic behaviour of economic actors, and it is the responsibility of planners to comprehend how asset concentration will compromise the goals by which a project is justified. Donor agencies will find such assessment onerous, since the way resource concentration factors into a growth equation is rarely straightforward. But the first step is to accept the validity of the interdependence between growth and equity. The second is to anticipate that asset concentrations will increase unless some form of redistribution occurs, or unless specific protection is given to the disenfranchised. The third step is to anticipate the social and fiscal channels by which the affluence of some and the deprivation of others actively diminish the potential for growth. The fourth step is to do something about it.

Protection of tenants' rights and the imposition of ceilings on land rents constitute a move in the right direction. But the real solution lies in structural reforms, such as land redistribution. Pakistan has made three attempts at land reform, in 1959, 1972, and 1977, none of which has had any lasting impact. Most of the distributed lands have moved within extended families; the acreages of redistributed land may appear respectable, but the reality is not. The link between power and land is crucial. Political power at the state and federal levels belongs to the landlords, who are unlikely to adopt legislation that would alter the political status they enjoy as large landowners. Unless development planners design programs that reduce prevailing concentrations, they will only reinforce the nexus between power and land that led to the crisis in the first place.

Note

1 Two documents comprise the complete study, one a baseline (Freedman, 1986) and the other an impact study (Freedman and Akram-Lodhi, 1997) conducted ten years later.

PART SIX

Democratizing Research

The remarkable success that the rhetoric of participatory development has enjoyed in academic and donor institutions is something
of a Cinderella story. In 1964, Paulo Freire was imprisoned for advocating social transformation through collective research activities, and he
was later exiled from his homeland in Brazil for fifteen years. The ideas
that rendered him subversive differ only modestly from those in the
numerous protocols that mainline donor agencies now hire consultants
to write for them. The irony is inescapable. Only a generation later,
Freire's rogue ideas as applied to social development have risen to
such esteem that the mandarins, who once dismissed radical pedagogy
as Marxist, now accept it wholeheartedly as the princeling of development credos. Paulo Freire himself was named secretary of education
for the city of Sao Paulo in 1989. It is almost as if the good people of
Nottingham were to ask Robin Hood to be their sheriff.

Participatory practice now seems capable of achieving anything
from raising social consciousness to increasing gender sensitivity, from
resolving the contradiction between growth and equity to acquiring
relevant data for project design. And to some extent it can: Saturn plant
workers, management wizards, radical pedagogues, and Filipino
women in sewing cooperatives all embrace the concept as if it were
their own elixir for promoting efficiency. There is little doubt that
investing local groups with the responsibility and authority to carry
out activities that experts or technicians might otherwise do has surprising pay-offs. Often the work is performed more reliably and the
social infrastructure that emerges to assume the responsibility almost
always moves communities in the direction of self-sufficiency.

Introducing an ethos of equity into the management of infrastructures, spreading the authority for something formerly controlled by experts, often makes things work better. It promotes a more even and reliable flow of water in irrigation systems when water users decide among themselves who will maintain the system instead of receiving orders from a central authority. It promotes a better use of money and a greater pay back rate in microcredit schemes. And in project design, it ensures access to a broader base of information and increases the likelihood that this information will be useful. In the article that follows Marie France Labrecque demonstrates how this innovation in acquiring information enhances the value of information and the likelihood that the beneficiaries will act on it. She describes how she passed the mantle of expertise in acquiring knowledge to farmers who had once been the subjects of study. The effect was dramatic.

And yet there is a downside. The popularity of participatory action has turned what was once a novel idea into a dogma of sorts. Participatory approaches have evolved from progressive empowerment techniques to become standard practice. Jane Parpart, in Chapter 12, asks whether the allure of participation neglects the subtleties of its application, especially whether its widespread endorsement has perhaps happened too quickly to allow for a measured assessment of some of its consequences. Participatory ap-proaches listen to those whose voices are heard, but those whose voices are typically submerged within gender and other social inequities continue to be ignored.

11

Social Research as an Agent of Social Transformation

MARIE FRANCE LABRECQUE

Introduction

On my first evaluation assignment in Colombia, I was surprised to discover that my sponsors had prepared business cards presenting me as a 'specialist in micro-projects' when they knew perfectly well that I was an anthropologist. My professional identity henceforth became vaguely identified with that of an economist, confirming the domination of economics in the field of international development, as Escobar (1995) has observed. Apparently, the title 'specialist in social relations' was unacceptable for an agency working in the field of savings and credit. And it goes without saying that ten years ago, it was still too soon to travel with the title 'specialist in women and development.'

But times change. The status of social research in the field of development is changing, as there is a growing interest in the significance of the social forces that stand in the way of the kinds of economic changes initiated by development schemes. There are, furthermore, innovative and even controversial approaches to acquiring information, that simultaneously obtain information on social dynamics and act on them. This chapter begins with a description of the circumstances of the research that constitutes its object, presenting the regional context in which it was conducted. I next examine the crucial distinction between conventional research and participatory action research, highlighting their different features. Some lessons to be learned from my Colombian experience then follow.

My primary intent in this chapter is to challenge conventions of expertise by showing how incorporating local expertise, even transferring the authority of research and policy development to local committees, can often succeed where conventional, academic expertise falters. This approach can not guarantee an equal voice for every household or every household member, as Jane Parpart reveals in the next chapter, but it can ensure a unique sensitivity to the tensions of local social hierarchies, hierarchies that always plague and often undermine development interventions. Furthermore, incorporating the study population into the social research process effects on its own a kind of social transformation capable of initiating resolution of otherwise intractable environmental and economic problems. Local expertise has the potential for enhanced social sensitivity and for effecting the kind of social transformation that foreign expertise lacks.

Participatory Research in the Colombian Andes[1]

My research in the Colombian Andes was carried out between 1989 and 1996. The population, generally considered peasant, engages in agricultural activities in tandem with other tasks such as making charcoal and small-scale trade. Small land holdings are the norm and a large proportion of young people emigrate to other regions and to the cities. The back country is controlled by guerilla forces, and the results of their actions can occasionally be seen in some of the villages (bullets embedded in a wall, slogans scratched on a building, or a destroyed police headquarters, for example). However, people's daily lives are not particularly affected by a guerilla presence.

Although each of the studies discussed below dealt with different themes, they were all carried out within an applied anthropology perspective that sought to bring an anthropological sensitivity to the dislocations of economic change among a disenfranchised population. The cultural institutions within which individuals' economic fates were conditioned were carefully dissected. The first study, which was exploratory, researched the impact that women's income-generating projects had on gender relations.[2] This study was carried out between 1992 and 1996 in collaboration with the peasant members of the *Asociación para el Desarrollo Campesino* (ADC), a regional association for peasant development. The ADC was formed in 1980 and involved a core group of professionals from the city and peasant leaders. Both groups wished to improve the condition of the peasants in La Cocha region, located near the regional capital, where ruthless moneylenders routinely took advantage of the poorer inhabitants. The ADC sought economic alternatives that would enable the peasants to free themselves from these *gamonales*. As it happened, the ADC eventually received donor assistance, which helped it to consolidate its organization, to set up a consumer cooperative, and to fund small income-generating projects. The experience spread throughout the region and soon two cooperatives were united under the aegis of the ADC, then three, and finally, five.

The first study carried out in this region had the ultimate objective of informing the way the development initiative affected women. The practical objective and the contribution to the ADC was to provide specific demographic, economic, and social data for broadening its work in the region. In order to do so, the ADC invited peasant members and some of its employees to join our research team, which was made up of a professional researcher and graduate students in anthropology.

For over three months, these young men and women helped design the research strategy and techniques, tested them, and then used them with informants from selected hamlets. It stood to reason that the young Colombian men and women would participate in the research, given our partnership with the ADC and their previous experience either in the streets or in the poor neighbourhoods of Bogotá. Curiously, the inclusion of the ADC members was not viewed as a participatory research strategy at all, as it was in the later study. Instead, it was seen as a means of maintaining a critical distance from the sometimes rigid conventions of traditional anthropology (see Copans 1975 for a critique). At the end of the fieldwork, as we were preparing to leave, the young peasants asked if they would be able to conduct research by themselves after our departure.

This desire, while unexpected, was of course the logical next step to the peasants' integration in the research team. During the course of our stay, the researchers had often given the peasant participants responsibilities such as writing down observations and transcribing directed tape-recorded interviews. One of them had even done a life history with one of her parents. Though the question was logical enough, we were nonetheless amazed that we had not thought of it earlier. How indeed, in the country of Orlando Fals-Borda, one of the most prominent Latin American advocates of participatory action research, had we managed to overlook this approach?

The peasants' request set in motion a process of elaborating a project that focused deliberately on training peasants for social research. It was structured around the issue of gender and generational hierarchies funded by the International Development Research Centre (IDRC) over the period between 1992 and 1996.[3] It encouraged the members of the association for peasant development to participate in the research process, from determining the subject to 'returning' the data to the population who provided it. A research committee was added to the ADC's structure and three research teams were organized.

The teams included more than peasants. In order to accurately reflect the ADC's composition, each group included researchers with academic experience and Colombian employees of the ADC, specifically a social worker, an economist, and a psychologist. Each research team included at least five peasants and only one ADC employee. While the peasants and the professionals both participated in all stages of the research, from conceptualization to sharing the findings, the academic researchers participated only in periodic supervision and selective assistance. Workshops for placing everyone on the same footing were organized, as the need was expressed, on data collection and on methods of analysis.

Most of the peasants who were part of the research teams had participated in the first study I had carried out in the region and had learned some research vocabulary and concepts.[4] They were the same peasants who had received funding for small income-generating projects, which they continued to develop alongside their research and other activities. The ADC committee which had set up the research training project had agreed from the outset that relations of power and economic privilege would figure significantly in the studies carried out by the various groups, including gender relations, intergenerational relations, and ones based on differential access to land and market. Moreover, each team had to include both men and women, younger and older people.[5] In each phase of the research, if a sample was needed, the team had to respect the same principle of representativity in selecting individuals.

Beyond these indications, any topic could be researched. It was agreed that the first research cycle would last six months (very part-time) and at the end of the cycle, the three initial research groups would become six groups composed of 'seniors' and new researchers recruited by them. During the third stage,[6] the six groups were to expand into twelve new groups.

To enable relatively uneducated peasants[7] to use the research methodology, we used the *minga* model developed by the *Instituto Mayor Campesino*, a Jesuit organization. The concept of *minga* is devoted to experimenting with alternative forms of agricultural production and with participatory research (IMCA, 1990). *Minga* comes from the

Andean region and is based on an ancestral custom dating back to the Incas, referring to a type of communal work used to solve material problems such as repairing paths or building infrastructures for collective use (Elias Ortiz, 1946). To organize a *minga*, a problem must first be identified. Then a *minga* committee is formed. This committee is responsible for recruiting *mingueros*, or participants; it also decides on the place and time of the *minga*, determines what type of work will be done and what tools are needed, and it raises funds for the food and drink to be distributed on the day of the *minga*. During the course of the *minga* it divides up the work and oversees operations. At the end of the day, the committee assesses the results with the participants and determines whether more work will be needed.

The research *minga* involves more or less the same stages. First a research topic or theme related to a concern among the population is identified. A research group is then instituted to formulate a research question; it must agree on the population with whom the research will be carried out and the tools to be used; it does the work (data collection), analyses the data, assesses the results (in this case, shares the findings with ADC members), and looks at how the findings can be applied in practice.

The topics chosen by the various groups reflect local concerns and the willingness to find solutions to problems experienced by the population. The research *mingas* that were carried out during the course of the project dealt with

1 decreasing water supply, its causes and its connection to living conditions;
2 woodcutting for energy consumption;
3 low agricultural productivity;
4 historic transformations in land tenure;
5 the population's participation in the cooperative;
6 continuity and change in local eating habits;
7 family and community conflicts created by charcoal production;
8 corn growing as a sustainable system; and
9 the environmental history of one of the region's farms.

The study region is made up of a number of natural environments, all of which are threatened both by climatic changes and by human activity. It includes the La Cocha drainage basin, located at an altitude of nearly 3,000 metres which contains a lake 17 kilometres long and

5 kilometres wide. The lake drains into the Putamayo River, a tributary of the Amazon. Until about fifty years ago the hills surrounding the lake were covered with thick virgin forest. Part of an indigenous reserve, it had remained virgin because the indigenous people pre-ferred the more hospitable neighbouring valley of Sibundoy, which is better suited to growing corn (Bonilla, 1972).

La Cocha was opened for settlement at a time when *minifundismo* and violence were rampant in the department of Nariño. Peasants were being driven away from their communities both by the political violence and through the concentration of land tenure (Ceron, 1985). When settlers arrived in La Cocha, they immediately cleared the trees in order to take possession of the land and to take advantage of the income generated by charcoal production. In principle, the settlers were supposed to practice agriculture on the cleared land, but some people continue to produce charcoal. The peasants involved in char-coal production have no alternative, but it is an obvious factor in envi-ronmental deterioration. With the exception of a few scattered patches the hills surrounding the lake are now devoid of their original vegeta-tion. From its beginnings the ADC has heightened public awareness of the consequences of this deterioration, and conspicuous landslides have provided even more dramatic testimony. All families are affected directly or indirectly by deforestation.

The other natural environment in which the research was carried out is located at an altitude of approximately 1,500 metres. It too has been affected by deforestation, but unlike the La Cocha region, this area is becoming increasingly dry. As a result, and given the current interest in 'sustainable development,' it is not surprising that each of the research teams in the region focused on issues that were closely related to the environment.

Research and the Different Dimensions of Social Transformation

How can training peasants to work as researchers make a difference to the communities involved? The link between inquiry and social change relies on the effect of producing knowledge on the initiative of a com-munity. Paulo Freire is one of the foremost advocates of approaching social change through self-generated knowledge; his book, *Pedagogy of the Oppressed*, and his philosophy of consciousness-raising are now well known (Anyanwu, 1988: 12). This approach can take different forms, each of which has been applied in diverse contexts, including participatory research. Since the 1980s, the participatory approach has become an integral part of both discourse and practice in the field of development. The World Bank, universities, non-governmental organizations, religious groups, and bilateral development agencies now all speak the language of participation (Slocum and Thomas-Slayter, 1995: 3). But in absorbing the participatory approach bureaucracies have stripped it of its epistemological implications, reducing it to a mere methodology. Rapid rural appraisal is the result of this absorption (Sabelli, 1993: 81–7) and the populist version of participation is far from benign. Escobar noted for the specific case of Colombia that the widespread rhetoric of participation 'must be seen as a counter proposal to increased peasant mobilization' (Escobar, 1995: 141). But the participatory approach is capable of challenging traditional practices both in the field of development and in social research (Rahman and Fals-Borda, 1991: 43).

The research conducted in the Colombian Andes was participatory action research (PAR), which has much in common with the approach advocated by Colombian sociologist Orlando Fals-Borda. Fals-Borda and Rahman have traced the lineage of this approach, recalling that one of its theoretical mentors was Antonio Gramsci, with his notion of the organic intellectual. While contradictory tendencies have emerged over the past thirty years, the central idea is to grant control over the production, accumulation, and use of knowledge to marginalized populations (in economic, political, and ideological terms). Inevitably, research and its technical tools must be demystified for this to occur (Rahman and Fals-Borda, 1991: 45, 47).

In most of the cases reported by Rahman and Fals-Borda, participatory research recruited outside agents to organize people. In our research, the population was already organized under the auspices of the ADC. Their affiliation with participatory research was evident in the name chosen to designate the process – research *minga* – which highlights its Andean identity. What is most distinctive of the research *minga* is not that it resolves the contradiction between 'those who know' and 'those who do not know,' but that it acknowledges the inescapable reality of this social hierarchy. This hierarchy is not, however, immutable; it is shaped by circumstances and as such is neither constant nor absolute. In other words, persons are not always ignorant, nor are they always knowledgeable. They may be both at the same time or successively one or the other, or one and the other. For instance, each team of *mingueros* was made up of peasants, technicians, and intellectuals, men and women, youths and seniors, Colombians and foreigners, all of whom were placed in circumstances that affected their relation to knowledge and its production. The efficacy of the research *minga* lies precisely in the composition of the research teams. The researchers trained in traditional research methods did not simply play the role of leaders; they too were true actors in the research (see Sabelli, 1993: 79–80).[8]

One of the important features of the research *minga* was its capacity to reform practices affecting forests and soils. Through discussions with people on history, botany, geography, and hydrography, the *mingueros* revived knowledge they thought had died. The solution to the deterioration of plant cover and the decrease in soil productivity involved complementing technical knowledge with multidisciplinary projects incorporating a particular sensitivity to social relations. The ADC began to turn its attention away from small income-generating projects to focus on alternative agricultural production and environmental education, owing to the research undertaken by *mingas*. For example, those who were most active in the income-generating projects, and later in the participatory research, gradually became involved in establishing private natural reserves created by removing a part of the land from agricultural production and making a commitment to regenerate it. The project did not necessarily generate income, but the prospect of leaving a regenerated heritage to their heirs appealed to the region's peasants.

The research process enabled the peasants to gain confidence in their own capacity to address problems. One of the teams from Yacuanquer (one of the municipalities in which the ADC is involved) carried out research on water scarcity and its effects on the quality of life among the local population. As they interviewed elders and carried out surveys, team members discovered to their surprise that only twenty years ago there was an abundance of springs and streams throughout the territory. At first convinced that their disappearance resulted from 'natural' causes, after the research was completed they discovered the importance of social relations. A chain of negligence had reduced the water supply, beginning with the Department of Health and trickling down through the municipal employees in charge of maintaining the aqueduct, eventually reaching the users. They also realized that the former *hacendados* (large landowners) had diverted springs and streams from their natural beds for their own purposes and that agrarian reform, although it had expropriated some of the large holdings, had not been concerned with conserving the water heritage.

On the basis of its research the team successfully petitioned the town council to maintain the aqueduct properly. On a structural level, the research *minga* was able to challenge previous academic research on this matter, and in doing so it challenged local political power. Equally important was the impact of the research on the organizational capacity of those who conducted it. Those who participated in the process realized that differences of opinion are not necessarily due to antagonism; they often reflect the diversity of social relations at work. In this sense, research has proven itself a tool for mobilizing and democratizing participation in organizations. The leaders of the ADC came to consider the research *minga* as a fundamental instrument in grass-roots consciousness-raising and in identifying environmental and social issues in the region. At the end of the research process, the ADC was beginning to be invited by other organizations, both within the province and in the rest of Colombia, to present the research *minga* experience and to encourage other community work initiatives. The *minga* had become the association's 'passport.'

Today, the ADC is a regional federation of cooperatives which has managed to diversify its sources of funding and which has also become part of the national network for the defence of the environment and for advocating sustainable development. On the individual level, the research *minga* has allowed people with little or no prior contact with research to gain new self-confidence. (This was true not only of the peasants, but also of technicians with university degrees in their respective fields, who were often expected to guide the former.) A peasant who was asked to comment on the process stated: 'In the research *minga* the information we gathered has shed light on the situation and helped us reflect on how we can improve our lot. The *minga* is a wonderful experience for reflecting on the future. We have gained knowledge that will be useful all of our lives.'

Conclusion: Modernity and Development

The distinctiveness of the participating approach lies in the challenge it poses to the conventional duality between 'those who know' and 'those who do not know.' In this case, no distinction was made between Western and indigenous knowledge because everyone possessed both, albeit in differing degrees. Knowledge was acquired and utilized by several social categories; in this way, it simultaneously revealed and undermined the rigid social conventions that inhibit the usefulness of academic research.

Social research has become shackled, preventing it from becoming an agent of transformation. However, any institution of modernity has a dual character (Cassells, 1993: 288). While research contributes to the domination of institutions over social agents, it can at the same time be used to question this domination, by viewing human beings as agents of knowledge and by helping them become aware of their historical destiny.

Notes

1 For a more in-depth presentation of the study region, see Labrecque (1996 and 1997).

2 The title of the research project was *Rural development, peasantry and women in development: the case of the provinces of Nariño and Santander in Colombia*. It received funding from SSHRCC.

3 The research project was carried out in collaboration with Université Laval and the Asociación para el Desarrollo Campesino, and was entitled *Peasantry and Hierarchical Relations*.

4 This later gave rise to questions from other researchers regarding the authenticity of the peasant approach. I do not consider this issue relevant, since I believe that all actors, whether from the North or the South, are actively involved in the process of change.

5 In a subsequent stage, this principle was expressed through the organization of a team composed entirely of children between ten and fourteen years of age guided by the youngest ADC employee.

6 We never reached the third stage. The peasant, professional, and academic researchers had much less time than anticipated and the research process became much longer than expected. As a result, the research conditions and interests had changed. In addition, the funds that had enabled the peasant researchers to get together and to pay agricultural workers for the days they were busy doing research ran out. The fact that the research process slowed down or ended once the funds dried up may appear to suggest that the commitment to research was not strong enough. However, it is important to keep in mind that research is not volunteer work, it is a job, and like all jobs, it must be remunerated.

7 The peasant researchers, in general, had not finished primary school. Several of them, especially the older ones, had to learn to read and write again during the course of the process described here.

8 Sabelli in fact denies that action research is research. He may be correct in the case of PAR, although this article shows, in my opinion, that distinctions need to made between the different types of action research. In the research *minga* for instance, all actors were researchers. Each of them, however, was at a different stage with regards to the mastery of basic skills.

12

Rethinking Participation, Empowerment, and Development from a Gender Perspective

JANE L. PARPART

Participation and empowerment are the current watchwords of such disparate institutions as the World Bank, Oxfam, and many small non-governmental organizations (NGOs). The expectations of this approach vary. Mainstream development agencies tend to look to participation for increased efficiency and productivity, for economic empowerment of the poor within the established structures of governance and order. More alternative development stresses the role of participatory empowerment techniques in social transformation. Yet both mainstream and alternative development institutions have found the methodologies and techniques of participatory rural appraisal (PRA) appropriate and useful. This chapter will explore the apparent contradiction of such widespread popularity for PRA and participatory empowerment approaches and explore both the strengths and weaknesses of this approach from the vantage point of women. Women constitute one of the groups most often acknowledged to be left out of development decisions and activities and thus most in need of participation and empowerment. The chapter will focus on the PRA approach developed by Robert Chambers; it will also consider the possibility that the 'practical,' experiential focus of this perspective could benefit from the introduction of some theoretical analysis, particularly the conceptual tools provided by political economy, with its focus on material structures, and current debates about the discursive/cultural nature of power.

The Participatory Empowerment Approach

The development enterprise was initially introduced in the 1940s as a very top-down affair. The less developed regions of the world were regarded as underdeveloped because they lacked modern, Western knowledge and technology. Development was seen largely as a technical problem, wherein experts from the North would provide the information and skills needed to transform the South. This required cooperation, but neither direction nor knowledge from the South (Crush, 1995). While colonial subjects sometimes used development discourse to legitimate their struggles for independence (Cooper and Packard, 1997), since independence the language of development has more often been used by Third World politicians and bureaucrats to legitimate the extension of state power. This public commit-ment to development by Third World elites has sometimes led to conflicts with mainstream development agencies; more often, however, it has provided comfortable partners for these agencies, which generally regard Third World states as their natural, if subordinate, allies in the development enterprise (Ferguson, 1991).

The failure of development institutions to alleviate poverty, much less to eradicate it, led to various external and internal critiques. Alternative approaches to development emerged in the 1970s, arguing that Northern expertise and capital was the cause of rather than the cure for developmental problems. These dependency analysts castigated the Third World allies of Northern development agencies as sell-outs who put their own interests above those of their societies, especially above the interests of the poor (Schuurman, 1993). More recent critiques have maintained this critical stance towards both development specialists in the North and their Southern collaborators, but the focus has shifted to the way development discourse/language has been able to define development 'problems' and 'solutions,' and to silence the voices and knowledge of indigenous peoples (Crush, 1995; Parpart, 1993).

While rejecting many of these criticisms, mainstream development agencies gradually evolved their own critique of Third World states and their bureaucratic elites. The failure of state-led development projects gradually undermined the easy belief in Third World states as allies in development. In the 1970s, a focus on basic human needs promised to address poverty issues ignored by the state, but by the 1980s the dramatic decline of most Third World economies cast doubt on earlier state-led development strategies and provided ammunition for an increasing focus on the invisible hand of the market. Neoclassical economists argued for the reduction of state size and functions in the North and South, leaving development to the wisdom of the market. While some collaboration with state actors was seen as inevitable, mainstream development agencies increasingly turned to structural adjustment policies and a new emphasis on non-state social actors and institutions, particularly NGOs (Schuurman, 1993).

Thus, by the mid-1980s, both alternative and mainstream development practitioners shared a common scepticism towards Third World states and their bureaucratic elites. Both increasingly called for more interventions directed at the poor, for greater participation by the poor and the marginalized in the development process, and for their empowerment 'through shared knowledge and the experience of action' (Thomas-Slayter et al., 1995: 9). While the mainstream development community generally saw participation and empowerment as a way to improve the efficiency and productivity of the poor without challenging the status quo (World Bank, 1995b), alternative development practitioners wanted to foster societal transformation (Craig and Mayo 1995; Friedmann, 1992; Mayoux, 1995). However, both schools of thought have been deeply influenced by the work of Robert Chambers, whose thinking thus provides a lens into the world of participatory empowerment approaches used by both mainstream and alternative development practitioners and an entry point for critically assessing this approach from a gender perspective (White, 1996; Mayoux, 1995).

Chambers' ideas and methodologies, developed over the last fifteen years, have had an enormous impact on the field of participatory development. His approach builds on the work of rural development specialists and the evolution of rapid rural appraisal (RRA), which emerged in the late 1970s. RRA called for greater attention to local people's knowledge but continued to rely on the expert to obtain and organize this knowledge. Participatory rural appraisal, which emerged in the late 1980s and is still evolving, shifted the focus from gathering indigenous people's knowledge to encouraging their analytical skills. Western development experts are no longer in charge; rather, they aim to empower local peoples so they can analyse and solve problems in ways that lead to sustainable development practices. This approach is highly critical of Western experts, emphasizes the need for less top-down approaches to development, and assumes that the knowledge and analytical skills of the poor, regardless of their education, can be brought to light and strengthened through participatory methods that will lead to true empowerment and development (Chambers, 1994c: 1254).

PRA is primarily a methodology, emphasizing experiential innovation rather than theories and abstractions (Chambers, 1994b: 1263).

Part of its appeal lies in the various techniques that it has developed, usually involving groups rather than individuals. In one group activity called 'do it yourself,' the PRA team learns a local skill and then participates in the activity; 'they do it' has villagers interviewing, collecting, and analysing data (very much as Marie France Labrecque describes in Chapter 11). In participatory 'analysis of secondary sources' groups evaluate information such as aerial photographs, maps of resource types, and so forth; participatory 'mapping and modelling' has local people draw maps and create models of social, demographic, and health patterns and natural resources, among other things. 'Transect walks' engage local people with PRA facilitators in walking around an area identifying local resources while their participation in 'time lines, trends, and change analysis' involves making chronological lists of events in their history, especially on subjects normally left out of historical discussions, such as ecology and education. 'Well-being and wealth groups and rankings' asks for group identification of wealth rankings of groups or households and for key indicators of well-being; the 'analysis of difference' explores contrasts, problems, and preferences by gender, age, social group, and wealth. 'Story telling' and 'presentations' of findings are also important. This cluster of methodologies (and others) is often used in particular sequences in order to maximize knowledge production and inclusiveness, especially among the most marginalized. Triangulation also encourages feedback by cross-checking sources of information at regular intervals. These methodologies are designed to facilitate participatory data collection, analysis, planning, implementation, report writing, and monitoring in order to empower broad-based participation in development (Chambers, 1994a; 1994b).

Above all, PRA is designed to bring the least privileged members of society into the development process. Inclusiveness is thus a central pillar of this approach. In order to include those with poor verbal skills, many techniques emphasize visual as well as verbal participation. While local power structures are recognized as a potential problem, the PRA approach assumes that inclusiveness will solve that problem – that giving voice, whether verbal or through visual inputs, and bringing the poor and better off together to discuss differences and identify problems will empower the disadvantaged and resolve conflicts (Chambers, 1994c: 1445). While acknowledging the possibility that local knowledge could be used in unsavory ways, Chambers argues that highly trained PRA experts can stop potential abuses. They will take the time and care 'to find the poorest, to learn from them, and to empower them' (Chambers, 1994c: 1441).

While Chambers openly worries about the current popularity of PRA, warning that formalism and practitioners with little understanding of the methodology could make a mockery of this approach, he places considerable faith in PRA techniques for overcoming this problem, outlining various methods for neutralizing development practitioners' preference for top-down development and for maintaining awareness and sensitivity to power imbalances between development experts and the people (Chambers, 1994b: 1256–7). While calling for more research on the 'shortcomings and strengths,' most reports of PRA, according to Chambers, have been positive (Chambers, 1994a: 963).

Participation, Empowerment, and PRA: A Gender Perspective

Research on PRA has grown considerably since 1994, and we now have a better idea of both the successes and pitfalls of this methodology and approach. The World Bank has formalized its interest in participatory approaches and established a working group on the subject, although PRA is still hardly mainstream Bank policy. A 1990 study of fifty-two USAID projects discovered a clear correlation between participation and success (Weekes-Vagliani, 1994: 31–2). Several scholars have reported considerable enthusiasm for participatory techniques in villages, especially mapping and transect walks (Kelly and Armstrong, 1996; Tiessen, 1996). The visual mapping techniques seem to be particularly popular, as they transcend the barrier of illiteracy that so often impedes participation by the most marginalized groups. Group activities are quite popular, although attendance often seems to drop over time (Mayoux, 1995; Wieringa, 1994).

Certain problems, however, keep surfacing in reports from the field, and they raise some difficult questions about some of the methods and assumptions of this approach, particularly for women. For instance, most development projects have to deal with government structures and officials at one point or another and these dealings are often problematic. While there has been a move to bring participatory practices into government bureaucracies, most government officials have little understanding or empathy for PRA techniques, nor do they tend to believe that the poor (especially women) should have a say in policy making or program development (Thompson, 1995). Moreover, even sympathetic bureaucrats are frequently constrained by political and economic factors, such as structural adjustment programs or male-dominated political structures. More broad-based representation on government boards and committees has done little to change challenge national and regional power structures. For example, an Oxfam project in Burkina Faso that placed members of peasant organizations on a government/NGO participatory planning board discovered that this had no observable impact on the board's planning agendas (Ashby and Sperling, 1995:757). Indeed, the poor are rarely able to challenge national elites and often require intervention by outside 'experts' who can insist on participatory methods and processes (interview, CIDA consultant, Makassar, Indonesia, 20 September 1997). This is particularly true in regard to women, as government officials often operate within a cultural context that undervalues women's opinions and contributions to public discussions (Mosse, 1994: 498–9). Participation in bureaucratic structures by women, unless it addresses these rather intractable and often unrecognized assumptions, can do little to alter the gendered context in which participation occurs (Mayoux, 1995).

Despite the increasing popularity of participatory approaches and gender equity, development practitioners often have deeply held reservations about the knowledge and capacities of the poor, especially women. Kelly and Armstrong, reporting on a food systems development research project between McGill University and the University of the Visayas, in the Philippines, discovered that the initial Canadian and Philippine research teams had little real understanding of participatory research. Initially the project was in fact very hierarchical, and the effort to create a more participatory approach led to the disbandment of the initial teams at both universities (1996: 250–1). Moreover, some of the more committed participatory development practitioners find it difficult to relinquish their authority over the poor. They want to empower the poor, but on their terms. This heavy-handed approach is particularly apt to happen with women, as most development practitioners come from cultures where women's subordination and need for direction is taken for granted (Rahnema, 1990: 206–7).

Power structures exist at the local level as well. Indeed, even the smallest village has its own power brokers. Chamber's belief that these inequities can be transcended through the powers of persuasion, discussion, and inclusion is frequently contradicted by reports from the field. Jesse Ribot, for example, discovered that local elites involved in participatory forestry projects in French West Africa had neither support from villagers nor an interest in participatory practices (1996a; 1996b). Local officials often reflect and support a gendered social context that dismisses women's contributions to public discussions. In such a context, simply placing women on project committees can do little to make them heard or to bring them into committee activities in a meaningful way (White, 1996). Mayoux points out that 'statistics on co-operative and peasant movements indicate a continuing marginalization of women in mixed-sex participatory organizations' (1995: 240). Moreover, some female committee members may support the status quo, because it legitimates their superior position *vis-à-vis* other women. A Zimbabwean participatory ecology project, for example, was initially captured by the local elites, and the presence of women did nothing to challenge their control. When the team leader disbanded the committee and set up a more representational one, the project stalled for lack of support from the more powerful members of the community (Robinson, 1996).

This example raises the issue of the relationship between the PRA team and the villages/region in which they are working. Lack of familiarity with the community's power structure and cultural context may lead to problems such as those described above. In the early stages of participatory projects, lack of familiarity with village structures and culture(s) can lead to fatal mistakes. David Mosse describes a participatory project in India that fell afoul of such a situation. He points out that villagers often react to a development team on the basis of previous experience rather than on the quality of the existing project. Indeed, the norm is more often deep scepticism rather than open acceptance. The participatory empowerment approach, with its emphasis on collective data gathering, offers few guidelines for these problems. Mosse argues that 'where deeply entrenched suspicion of the motivation of outsider's development intentions exists, participatory styles of interaction often do not have the effect of allaying fears and suspicions' (1994: 505). The informal and public nature of PRA techniques can be very off-putting to people accustomed to more formal patterns of communication. Non-directive, consultative approaches can be misconstrued, as can mapping, transect walks, and wealth measurements when they suggest all-too-familiar interventions by government officials. These practices, when combined with ignorance of the local and national power structures, can undermine the potential for participatory work (Mosse, 1994: 506–7).

The collection of local knowledge and the fostering of local analytical and planning skills also turns out to be a rather more complicated process than anticipated by PRA methodologies. Knowledge is not something that simply exists, ready to be discovered and used; it is embedded in social contexts and attached to different power positions. Control over knowledge is often an essential element of local power structures, and thus not something local elites are willing to discuss. Moreover, controlling knowledge, even through silence, may be an essential survival strategy for marginalized people (Suski, 1997; Mahoney, 1996). The public group discussions so central to PRA methods may thus be both disempowering and threatening for many different groups and individuals. Women are often in this position. The collection of knowledge is thus not a purely technical business; it is deeply implicated in power structures and struggles, particularly in regions where development activities are well established and community leaders have learned the importance of presenting foreigners (or government bureaucrats) with the 'right' kind of information. The public nature of these transactions makes it all the more plausible that certain knowledge will be suppressed and groups will be silenced (or forced to speak) by those leaders most able to control community discourse. The groups most apt to be silenced, or pushed into public disclosures, are the poor and women (Mosse, 1994: 508–9).

Moreover, PRA activities do not always fit women's schedules or agendas. Mosse discovered that projects in India often assumed that women would be available at central locations (away from fields and home) for lengthy periods of time. These requirements were incompatible with female work structures, leading to poor participation by women in project activities. Collective activities often took place in spaces that were forbidden to women, making their participation impossible. This lack of participation was often explained as 'natural' and so unremarkable. Indeed, at a participatory project in India, Mosse discovered that women's presence at activities caused comments while their absence went unremarked (1994: 512). Mapping and transect walks are often seen as men's work. The emphasis on spatial mapping in a Sierra Leone project, for example, did not fit women's concerns – they argued that 'the changes we need cannot be drawn.' Gender issues such as relations between men and women or violence against women were of no interest to men (Welbourn, 1991). Nor do women always share common interests. Even in a small community, women often have different, sometimes interrelated, but sometimes conflicting needs. Inequalities between women can create serious divisions that participation cannot overcome. Many women have internalized ideas of appropriate behaviour that go against participatory methods and undermine any pressure for gender equity. The degree to which women wish to openly discuss sensitive issues like domestic violence varies by culture and class. Indeed, consensus among women is highly problematic; many cross-cutting issues divide them (Mayoux, 1995: 242–5). Sharing thoughts and dreams will not necessarily overcome these divisions, and the fact that these kinds of issues keep coming up in the literature on PRA suggest they are not yet being adequately addressed.

The need for specific skills training is also rarely discussed in the PRA literature. Yet we know that women, especially poor women, often need specific skills if they are going to challenge existing stereotypes about their inability to plan and monitor activities. While gender planning has become more accepted in the literature on development planning (Moser, 1993; Kabeer, 1995), this literature is generally aimed at Northern experts or Southern experts trained in the North. Participatory approaches call for full participation in all phases of development projects, but they often underestimate the skills needed for such participation, especially report writing and evaluation – skills that poor women rarely have. Participatory projects, like all development projects, must submit frequent reports and budgets. These requirements, daunting as they are for local people, have been made more difficult by the current emphasis on results-based management (Wieringa, 1994). This approach locks project managers into the need to obtain base-line data and then to measure, frequently, the project's advance against these measurements. This process runs counter to more participatory development practices, as it requires highly skilled experts on indicators, the ability to handle figures, and both numeracy and literacy. Thus while the language of participation and empowerment spreads, some of the practices of development on the ground undermine the possibility for participatory empowerment. Poor people are left outside the discussions; measurement and evaluations are once again the purview of the development 'expert' rather than local people, and women, with their lack of skills, remain outside the loop.

Conclusion

This brief overview of participatory empowerment approaches to development, especially the use of PRA, is not exhaustive. The successes of participatory empowerment approaches are undoubted, and they are important. However, the failures are also apparent and may go some way to explaining why these concepts and practices can be comfortably advocated by what appear to be conflicting perspectives on development. Mainstream development agencies have been committed to the market and to reduction of the state; any policies that shift state functions onto society without upsetting the status quo fit that mandate. Participatory empowerment approaches, with their emphasis on the local and their tendency to ignore larger political and economic structures, actually do little to challenge national power structures. Participation, as Rahnema (1990) points out, is no longer perceived as a threat.

This rather cynical assessment should not lead us to underestimate the very real importance of participatory empowerment approaches. Bringing the marginalized and the poor into discussions, encouraging and facilitating local knowledge and analytical skills is crucial to both development as an economic activity and as a personal and societal goal. However, the research described above clearly warns that gender inequalities will not disappear through giving voice to women or simply including them in development activities. The same is true for many other inequalities. The challenge is to think in new ways about participation and empowerment, particularly for women, and to use theoretical tools to help design new methods and techniques that will enhance both women's ability to fully participate in development and their capacity to transform cultural and material practices that contribute to gender inequalities.

This rather daunting task will require melding theory with practice in ways that address fundamental impediments to participation and empowerment while maintaining the accessibility and practicality of PRA techniques and methodologies. The challenge, it seems to me, is to develop a more nuanced and sophisticated analysis of power.

Participatory empowerment techniques will have to pay more attention to the way in which national and global power structures constrain and define the possibilities for change at the local level. Structural adjustment programs, for example, have often hampered local and national development efforts. The participatory approach needs to develop techniques for analysing the way in which global and national political and economic structures and practices intersect with and affect local power structures. This will require more explicit methods for identifying these structures and their relationships with local communities. Interviews with key elites will be necessary, and these cannot always be fully participatory. However, the increasingly global-ized world in which we live leaves no doubt that these elements must be incorporated into our analysis (Hettne 1985; Mittelman 1997). The gendered character of these political and economic structures also requires specific attention in order to understand their differential impact on the sexes (Staudt, 1990).

Local power structures require more explicit analysis as well. One of the strengths of the participatory empowerment approach to develop-ment has been its focus on the local and its belief that even the poorest communities can understand and solve their own development prob-lems. The participatory approach is based on the assumption that divi-sions in society can be overcome by full and frank discussion by all parties. This rather liberal belief in democratic processes underesti-mates the intractable nature of many local economic and political structures. Moreover, sensitivity to existing social arrangements has often led to the uncritical acceptance of traditional inequities, espe-cially those based on gender, which are regarded as private and thus outside the realm of economic development and challenges to the sta-tus quo (Fals Borda and Rahman, 1991). The wealth and status rank-ings and the time-line techniques of PRA reveal the differential access to power and resources of men and women but offer little explanation for how these differences come about. To understand the forces at play, we need a more detailed exploration of the relationship between gen-der and local political and economic structures. We need to know how women and men participate in these structures, and whether some women are able to use them to their advantage while others are silenced and marginalized. The conceptual tools of materialist femi-nists (Hennessy, 1993) and gender and development scholars (Kabeer, 1995; Moser, 1993) offer some insights for this endeavour.

However, a focus on the material elements of power is not sufficient in itself. We need to understand how belief systems and cultural prac-tices legitimize and reinforce material structures. The link between lan-guage/knowledge and power is increasingly recognized as a central factor in development activities, particularly the power of develop-ment practitioners to define developmental 'problems' and 'solutions' (Crush, 1995; Marchand and Parpart, 1995; Escobar, 1995). PRA tech-niques pick up on this critique with their rejection of top-down devel-opment practices and their desire to bring the marginalized into development discussions and plans. This is an important first step, but it is based on the assumption that giving voice to the voiceless will solve power inequities. We know that the marginalized, especially women, can speak but not be heard. And speaking is not always a source of power: speaking can disempower if it removes the ability to control the dissemination of knowledge. To address these issues, PRA techniques need a much more sophisticated analysis of voice, of the link between language/knowledge and power. This is particularly true in matters of gender, which are deeply embedded in the unconscious and often presented as naturalized, unchanging cultural practices and symbols.

Finally, the current interest in identity politics and shifting and multiple subjectivities offers some insight into the analysis of individual behaviour, and thus to empowerment. PRA techniques are sensitive to the complexity of local conditions and the need to bring the marginalized into the centre. But they fail to theorize the subject. Individuals are generally assumed to play a particular role in the community, when in fact they may play several, sometimes conflicting roles. These conflicts can offer entry points for otherwise unexpected alliances. For example, women from the wealthier groups in a community may align primarily with their class rather than their sex, and thus possess little empathy for their poorer sisters. But some women from this class may resent their treatment as women and could thus conceivably align themselves with poor women over certain gender issues. PRA techniques, with their multiple data sets, have the potential to reveal such complexities, but to do so they must move beyond description to analysis – something that requires attention to theory as well as technique.

These rather preliminary ruminations on PRA and participatory empowerment methodologies are, of necessity, more an opening salvo for future discussions than a set of prescriptions. However, I believe PRA techniques, particularly as outlined by Robert Chambers, are undertheorized, especially in relation to power. They too readily assume that participation can overcome deeply embedded material and cultural practices that legitimate and maintain social inequities. At the same time, the goals of PRA techniques are laudable and important. They have contributed a grounded grass-roots perspective on women's experiences and have sensitized conventional accountability exercises to the gendered nature of daily life among the poor. If these techniques are going to effectively challenge established power divisions, especially along gender lines, they will have to incorporate more nuanced understandings of power, particularly the connection between power, voice/silence, and gender. The challenge is to develop techniques that retain the accessibility and practicality of PRA while incorporating the insights of current thinking on the material and discursive nature of power. This will require time, effort, and considerable experimentation. Some important efforts in this direction have been taking place (Fals Borda 1991; Jackson, 1997; Goetz, 1995). More will be needed. However, one thing is clear: if PRA and participatory empowerment approaches do succeed in melding theory and practice in ways that successfully destabilize established power structures, they will certainly no longer be the darling of all participants in the development enterprise.

PART SEVEN

Food and Information

The focus in this book is on the broad issues of compassion, comparative advantage, globalization, equity, and conditionality rather than on specific projects in one continent or another, or specific sectors such as agriculture, energy, or the environment. These two final chapters constitute something of an exception, and this is because they deal with exceptional issues: the controversy that surrounds providing commodity food aid in emergency situations and the allure of telecommunications technology. When aid budgets are cut, debates rage between proponents and detractors over the need to preserve emergency assistance and when development fatigue seems to make even its most ardent advocates flag, everyone is revived by the promise of reaching the remotest peasants with the magic of telecommunications. These two topics figure significantly in any discussion about the transformation of aid.

Outright gifts of food are thought to compromise local agricultural production by depressing the prices of local crops, and food aid programs have consequently been discredited. Some donors have avoided this kind of criticism by making food available for sale on the open market in recipient countries, with the understanding that the proceeds of the sale will go to support other viable development efforts. These counterpart funds, however, have frequently been poorly managed. Since most food aid programs are driven by surpluses of food in donor countries, they also bear the stigma of tying aid to the sale of donor country commodities. Food aid has thus become the bad boy of the aid regime and a victim in recent rounds of cuts to aid. Is this warranted?

Nutrition remains a pressing global concern, especially in emergencies. In fact, the incidence of new emergencies, of famines and conflict and refugees and displacements, has quadrupled in the latter half of this decade. Food is the stuff of emergency relief and the propriety of food aid is left stretched awkwardly between the views of its detractors and its advocates. Detractors of food aid fear its long-term effect on economic growth, while its advocates argue that this criticism misses the point, for it is in short-term, emergency situations that food is most needed. Sue Horton deciphers these complex issues to make a case for the redemption of food aid.

Just as food aid's precipitous downward slide has made it the subject of contentious debate, so the over-inflated allure of information technology has raised the question of whether its promises are false or not. Can the communication capacity of computers provide the salvation of poor countries? Einsiedel and Innes chasten those who too precipitously embrace this new technology while appraising, point by point, what it has to offer. Information technologies may hold great promise – they may mobilize villages, build bridges to other worlds, even integrate a nation – but the magic of electronic linkages cannot cure people nor can it give them greater political representation. Information technology is only a technology, and it can be used just as readily to buttress an irresponsible authority as to promote a responsible one.

13

The Decline and Possible Redemption of Food Aid

SUSAN HORTON AND ANNE GERMAIN

Food aid has been a component of modern development assistance programs for almost fifty years. The United States included food aid in the Marshall Plan to Europe immediately following the Second World War and enacted the Agricultural Trade and Development Assistance Act (PL-480), which sends food aid to developing countries, in 1954. Canada sent its first food aid as part of the Colombo plan in 1951 and began a separate food aid program in 1964/5, a few years after the forming of the World Food Program (WFP), administered by the Food and Agriculture Organisation of the United Nations (FAO) 1961.

Food aid has been important, especially for low-income, food-deficit countries. Although food aid in cereals accounted for less than 1 per cent of world food production in the 1990s (WFP, 1995: averages for 1991–5), it accounted for nearly 6 per cent of world cereal imports over the same period (WFP, 1995) and an even higher share of the cereal imports of low-income, food-deficit countries (on average 25 per cent in the 1970s, 18 per cent in the 1980s, and 15 per cent in the 1990s: FAO, various years). For forty very food-dependent countries, food aid exceeded 40 per cent of cereal imports in recent years (FAO, 1996). We may now be witnessing the unremarked decline of food aid. Food aid shipments are currently at levels below that of any year since 1971, with the exception of the 'food crisis' years 1973–4. Food aid commitments by donors under the Food Aid Convention are currently at their lowest levels since 1980/1. Unfortunately, the decline in food aid has not occurred because aid donors have decided to 'untie' their assistance and provide more cash: food aid is declining along with overall development assistance to developing countries, although it is declining faster. The developed countries are moving further and further away from their aid commitments. The Nordic countries and the Dutch are the only donors to achieve the target of sending 0.7 per cent of their gross domestic product (GDP) as official development assistance (ODA). And the 1974 World Food Conference target of 10 million tons of food aid commitments has never been met (although actual shipments exceeded this level throughout much of the 1970s and 1980s).

Part of the reason for the decline in food aid may be the considerable controversy which it has aroused. Food aid has been criticized for depressing domestic agricultural production, for creating dependency on exotic foreign food, and for hindering necessary domestic policy changes. One food policy expert argues that '(t)he greatest development disappointment of the last 20 years is the growing irrelevance of food aid for development purposes' (Falcon, 1995). These criticisms have combined with a growing 'aid fatigue' – chronicled for the Canadian context by David Morrison in Chapter 1 – to undermine support for food aid, and a recent important development has been the sharp decline in agricultural surpluses following the most recent round of GATT negotiations which, for the first time, included agricultural trade.

At the same time, the need for food aid has grown, with the increase of humanitarian emergencies involving refugees in recent years. In 1997, it was estimated that there were twelve million refugees in Africa and four million in Asia (ACC/SCN, 1997). With experience, food aid has evolved to become more effective at improving nutrition and reaching vulnerable groups, while having fewer adverse effects on domestic agriculture. Canada has played a leadership role in promoting the fortification of food aid with micronutrients. Is it possible that, just as we have finally learned how to use food aid relatively well, it will disappear?

Food Aid Past and Present

A DEFINITION OF FOOD AID

At first sight, food aid might seem easy to define. The images highlighted in the press – hungry people facing some kind of natural disaster or man-made emergency receiving food shipments from a food-surplus country – are clearly of food aid. However, there is also a grey area between outright gifts and commercial sales. Consider grain sales at prices below the world price and export credits or loans at concessional interest rates: at what point do these cease to be simply aggressive export subsidies and become food aid? Or what about the case of food sold to a developing country, but for local currency and not hard currency? In practice, the (arbitrary) dividing line between commercial sales at a discount and food aid is where there is a grant element of at least 25 per cent of the commercial price. This can be achieved by below market prices, soft loans, or some combination of the two. According to Singer (1995) the grey area is large: over half of total food trade in 1995 was covered by bilateral agreements providing discounts from commercial prices, overhanging surpluses providing the incentive for the exporter. Singer also argues that these surpluses in any case depress the traded price from the hypothetical equilibrium price, forcing the (relatively few) developing country exporters to receive lower prices for their exports. Thus he argues that the whole concept of food aid is somewhat nebulous. At the same time, it is fairly clear that food aid tends disproportionately to reach poorer, food-deficit countries than do commercial sales.

HOW MUCH FOOD AID IS GIVEN?

Food aid programs have changed over the course of their post-war history. Food aid has fluctuated over time, usually in the opposite direction to needs, because a strong motive for food aid is its relation to surplus disposal. Following the Uruguay round of trade negotiations, which reduced domestic subsidies to agriculture, food surpluses have begun to decline and there has been a corresponding rapid decrease in food aid.

Table 13.1 provides an overview of developments between 1971 and 1996. Donor countries pledge a certain volume of aid under the Food Aid Convention, which is one component of the International Grains Agreement. International agreements in wheat date back at least to 1934 and have been in force continuously since 1949; the Food Aid Convention itself dates from 1967. The pledges are usually for two years at a time. At the World Food Conference in 1974 (following the world food crisis of 1973/4, when food prices rose dramatically) the goal of a minimum of 10 million tons of food aid pledges was set, a goal which has never been reached, although actual shipments have often exceeded the target. Pledged amounts increased from the original level of just over 4 million tons to 7.5–7.6 million tons throughout the 1980s. However, 1995 marked a critical divide, as pledges fell back to 5.4 million tons, and (even more worrying) actual shipments in 1996/7 fell almost to this floor level. (Note that in Table 13.1, as in others, most of the statistics for grains refer to the July–June year.)

TABLE 13.1
Global food aid commitments and shipments, 1971–1996

Year	Commitment grains*	Shipments grains*	Shipments other**	Food aid as % of ODA	% Food aid multilateral	% Food aid as grants
1971	4.0	12.5	0.6	15.0	4.2	51.8
1972	4.1	10.0	0.4	13.9	19.6	59.6
1973	4.2	5.8	0.2	13.1	16.3	62.9
1974	4.2	8.4	0.2	15.4	15.9	69.7
1975	4.2	6.8	0.3	12.9	16.8	62.2
1976	4.2	9.0	0.5	12.2	15.2	66.5
1977	4.2	9.2	0.5	10.2	19.3	63.4
1978	4.2	9.5	0.6	10.0	20.7	68.2
1979	4.2	8.9	0.5	9.6	21.0	63.6
1980	7.6	8.9	0.6	11.4	24.8	65.8
1981	7.6	9.1	0.5	8.4	21.4	66.0
1982	7.6	9.2	0.6	8.4	21.7	70.3
1983	7.6	9.8	0.7	9.0	23.0	69.6
1984	7.6	12.5	0.7	10.1	21.2	73.8
1985	7.6	10.9	1.0	10.7	15.4	70.8
1986	7.5	12.6	1.0	8.5	21.6	75.1
1987	7.5	13.5	1.2	7.5	19.4	80.3
1988	7.5	10.2	1.3	8.1	22.5	83.1
1989	7.5	11.3	1.1	7.1	22.9	84.3
1990	7.5	12.4	1.2	5.8	25.6	83.2
1991	7.5	13.1	1.2	6.1	24.7	80.7
1992	7.5	15.2	1.9	5.4	26.8	90.6
1993	7.5	15.1	1.8	n/a	22.0	n/a
1994	7.5	10.7	1.9	n/a	27.0	n/a
1995	5.4	7.5	1.2	n/a	30.0	n/a
1996	5.4	5.6	n/a	n/a	n/a	n/a

*Refers to 12-month period commencing July (thus 1971 data refer to July 1970 – June 1971). Amounts are in million tons.
**Provisional Commitments are made under the Food Aid Convention; shipments are in million tons; other includes non-grains (skim milk, canned fish, etc.)
Sources: FAO, *Food Aid Figures* (1985) for 1971–82, FAO, *Food Aid in Figures* (1993) for 1983–92; WFP (1995) for 1993–4; FAO/WFP (1997) for 1995; IGC (1997) for 1996.

Food aid is closely tied to food trade and food aid shipments are correlated with food surpluses. Developed country exporters have tended
to be more generous with aid when stocks were high and world prices
low, often with one motive being the development of future commercial markets. Thus food aid was at its scarcest in the food crisis year
1973/4, when developing country importers faced the highest prices.

Canada's food aid shipments have followed world patterns (Table 13.2) and surplus disposal has been for Canada, as for other donors, a major motivation. Hence Canadian food aid grew in the 1980s, when subsidy policies of competitors (primarily the European Community but also the United States) led to international surpluses. With the end of this competition following the Uruguay round, Canada's food aid has fallen dramatically.

HOW IS FOOD AID MANAGED?

Originally much food aid was provided through bilateral channels and administered by governments. Over time, there has been a steady increase in the proportion of food aid provided multilaterally, that is, through some intermediary international organization (see Table 13.1). Although donors prefer the political ties fostered by bilateral aid, recipient countries often prefer donations without political strings attached. Multilateral agencies tend to have more of the infrastructure and in-country expertise to manage food aid projects, which most donor governments (other than the United States) do not. Thus a substantial proportion of bilateral aid tends to be sold on the open market by the recipient government, with the donor often requiring that the 'counterpart funds' (the proceeds from the sale) be used for development purposes. Open market sales are a cheap way to dispose of food aid, but in practice the ability to ensure that the counterpart funds are used for development purposes is limited, and these sales pose the greatest danger of depressing domestic agricultural prices. Consequently donors have tried to move away from open market sales. In Canada for example 87.5 per cent of bilateral aid in 1971 was used for open market sales, but the proportion had fallen to 48.3 per cent in 1989, and bilateral aid was instead channelled to feeding programs and other programs directly distributing food to consumers (Charlton, 1992.)

The two main channels for multilateral food aid are the WFP, administered by FAO and the United Nations, and the European Commission's program. Of these, the WFP program is the larger, and accounted for about 29 per cent of global food aid in 1995 (WFP, 1995). The program began in 1961 on an experimental basis, and commenced continuous operation in 1965. The WFP receives pledges from members mainly in kind, but also in cash (those countries which are not net exporters tend to provide cash). The WFP monetizes a small fraction (less than 15%) of the in-kind donations to cover other costs, but the majority is used either for development projects or for humanitarian relief. As will be discussed below, the humanitarian role has increased very rapidly and threatens to dwarf the development role. The WFP has country officers in many countries and utilizes UNDP personnel elsewhere to propose development projects or humanitarian relief projects. Development projects include child feeding (at schools or maternal and child health (MCH) centres), food distribution (at MCH centres, for example), food-for-work (often labour-intensive infrastructure projects), and agricultural support (such as using food as an incentive for reforestation or environmental conservation). The WFP also plays a major role in coordinating food aid during emergencies (natural disasters and man-made disasters such as wars and refugee crises). The program was recently reviewed (CIDA et al., 1994a).

The European Commission's food aid program has been of increasing importance as surpluses began to grow in Europe. The definition of the commission's program varies between documents. Usually included are the bilateral contributions of members, which are channelled through the European Union, as well as food aid funded centrally by the European commission. The commission operates its own projects and also channels aid through other multilateral agencies, primarily the WFP, but also the European Association of NGOs for Food Aid and Emergency Relief (EURONAID), a confederation of NGOs primarily but not exclusively based in Europe. The situation is further complicated by the fact that there are three separate food aid programs operated by the European Commission: the development program operating through the Food Security and Food Aid Unit of the Directorate-General for Development (DG–VIII), the humanitarian relief program operated through the European Commission Humanitarian Office (ECHO), and a special program for Newly Independent States (in Europe).

Members of the European Union increasingly channel more of their ODA through the commission: 7 per cent of total ODA of members went through the commission in 1970 as compared to 17 per cent in 1994 (OECD, 1996b), and a similar trend is evident for food aid. According to the European Commission (undated) 70 per cent of food aid from the European Union is sent via the commission. One distinctive feature of the commission's program is the volume of triangular transactions and local purchases, which account for over 40 per cent of its resources (European Commission, 1996), a larger percentage than for other donors. (Canada permits only up to 10 per cent of its food aid to be purchased outside Canada, and this began only in 1995.) A triangular transaction occurs where, for example, European wheat is sold in Zimbabwe and the proceeds are used to purchase white maize to ship to Mozambique. In a local purchase cash is used, for example, to buy white maize in Zimbabwe to ship to Mozambique. These methods can be more flexible in terms of providing commodities suited to recipients' needs. The European Union recently evaluated the food aid program of its members and of the commission (Clay, Dhivi, and Benson, 1996, cited in CIDA, 1997b).

Another change is the increased proportion of food aid channelled through NGOs. In Canada, for instance, there was no distribution by NGOs until the late 1970s. In 1977/8, CIDA was obligated by the Ministry of Agriculture to try to dispose of substantial quantities of surplus skim milk powder. Unable to do so readily in bilateral programs, CIDA offered NGOs the powder to use in their programs, and paid for the transportation costs as well. CIDA also began to fund the transportation costs for foodgrains used by NGOs, which came from voluntary farmer donations through institutions such as the Canadian Foodgrains Bank. Thus the proportion of food aid channelled through NGOs began to increase and continued despite the phasing out of skim milk aid. Table 13.2 suggests the increase was from zero prior to 1977/8 to 7 per cent currently: in fact the increase has been even greater, since CIDA now uses NGOs as executing agencies for some of the bilateral program aid, such that the total share channelled through NGOs was 30 per cent in 1996 (CIDA, 1997a). CIDA issues requests for proposals for specific countries and regions, to which NGOs can respond. It offers foodstuffs and sometimes a limited amount of cash for other project-relevant inputs, as well as permitting a limited amount of monetization of food to cover other essential inputs. Like USAID, CIDA is moving to results-based management and this will devolve more of the day-to-day management of such projects to NGOs.

WHO GIVES FOOD AID?

Of the bilateral programs, the largest is that of the United States. Under PL-480 there are three 'titles,' of which Title I covers concessional sales, Title II covers donations, and Title III covers concessional sales to poorer countries where the counterpart funds are used for development purposes. The Title II component includes donations to the WFP, donations to other governments, and a substantial program administered by NGOs (known as private voluntary organizations (PVOs), in

TABLE 13.2
Channels of Canadian food aid, 1970–1997

Fiscal year	Total food (millions of $Can)	Row percentages		
		Multilateral	Bilateral	NGOs
1970–71	104.2	16.3	83.4	–
1971–72	79.8	19.5	80.8	–
1972–73	112.4	14.5	85.4	–
1973–74	115.7	18.0	81.9	–
1974–75	174.5	9.2	90.7	–
1975–76	222.6	47.4	52.6	–
1976–77	240.1	37.1	62.9	–
1977–78	230.4	39.6	60.4	0.9
1978–79	194.5	50.5	47.9	1.7
1979–80	187.7	52.1	45.7	2.2
1980–81	183.4	58.2	39.9	1.9
1981–82	235.7	48.1	50.2	1.7
1982–83	273.2	44.4	51.8	3.6
1983–84	332.5	43.9	52.9	3.2
1984–85	385.5	38.8	55.6	5.6
1985–86	347.8	43.2	46.9	9.9
1986–87	402.7	41.2	52.3	6.3
1987–88	436.6	39.5	54.4	5.9
1988–89	431.5	43.6	50.4	5.5
1989–90	371.6	46.7	47.0	6.3
1990–91	382.3	47.6	46.2	6.1
1991–92	400.0	52.4	41.4	5.9
1992–93	382.9	56.1	36.5	7.3
1993–94	319.4	59.2	36.0	4.7
1994–95	312.8	59.0	34.5	6.4
1995–96	260.4	48.5	44.0	7.3
1996–97	247.6	66.6	25.9	7.4

Note: Values include shipping costs.
Sources: Charlton (1992) for 1970–91 data; CIDA, FACE *Annual Reports* (various years) for 1992–7 data.

the United States). USAID's current priorities are to use food aid to support agricultural productivity and household nutrition, especially in sub-Saharan Africa and South Asia, and the agency is turning to results-oriented management, devolving more day-to-day management to the PVOs (USAID, 1995).

The Canadian program is similar to that of the other smaller donors (Canada is often the third largest bilateral donor, with Germany or in recent years the European Commission usually in second place). Its evolution up to the end of the 1980s is detailed in Charlton (1992). The program has been periodically reviewed (most recently in CIDA, 1997a), and recent public statements of goals and policies include CIDA (1994b; 1994c; 1994d).

Canada first shipped food aid as part of its aid under the Colombo Plan in 1951, and it became a separate program in 1964/5. When the External Aid Office became CIDA in 1968, food aid was included in CIDA's activities. However, other ministries, particularly Agriculture and Fisheries and Oceans, frequently intervened to use the food aid program to dispose of unwanted surpluses. The desire to maintain support of the provinces resulted in a requirement that 25 per cent of the commodities sent be items other than grain (pulses, oil, canned fish, skim milk, etc.) The establishment of the Food Aid Centre (FACE) in 1978 helped to make the program more consistent and somewhat less vulnerable to interest groups in other ministries. However, since food aid was traditionally only programmed on a biannual basis it was more vulnerable to cuts than other forms of aid, which are programmed on a multiyear basis. Canada's food policy has evolved over time, guided by the results of successive foreign policy reviews (including those in 1970, 1980, 1987, and 1993), as well as evaluations of the food aid program itself (Treasury Board Secretariat, 1977; CIDA, 1983; CIDA, 1997a). These evaluations and reviews have changed policy goals. The 1988 development assistance policy statement *Sharing Our Future* (CIDA, 1987) permitted food aid commitments to be made on a multiyear basis; it continued the trend towards more multilateral food aid and emphasized the role of food aid in agricultural development. Although the 1995 foreign policy statement *Canada in the World* did not contain formal recommendations on food aid, its statement of the six principles guiding aid have had an impact on the program. However, the omission of any discussion of food aid from the policy statement may be indicative of its declining importance and the statement did not provide the Food Aid Centre with a new mandate.

WHO RECEIVES FOOD AID?
The recipients of food aid have also changed over time. Higher income regions, particularly Latin America, now absorb smaller shares of global food aid than in the past.[1] The share of South and Southeast Asia has also declined, as richer countries in Southeast Asia have graduated from their dependence on food aid. The regions

whose shares have increased include sub-Saharan Africa and, in the 1990s, the newly independent states in Europe. These trends reflect in part a greater emphasis on low-income countries but also the increasing share of food aid going to emergencies, which in recent years have been in sub-Saharan Africa and central Europe. Political factors also affect who receives food aid. Australia and Japan support South and Southeast Asia heavily; the United States gives more food aid to Latin America than the global average; and individual countries such as Egypt receive more food aid than their level of income might otherwise predict.

All countries eligible to receive Canadian ODA can also receive food aid for development purposes. In practice only a relatively limited number (twenty or fewer per year) receive bilateral food aid; a somewhat larger group receives multilateral food aid and/or food aid channelled through NGOs. Canada's food aid originally focused on the Colombo Plan members in South Asia: South and Southeast Asia received 72 per cent of Canadian food aid even in 1983/4, but by 1995 this region and sub-Saharan Africa each received 40 per cent. Bangladesh has consistently been the largest recipient, with India and Sri Lanka also included among the major programs, but programs to African countries have become important (Ethiopia, Tanzania in the 1980s, Egypt). One positive feature of food aid is that it tends to be better targeted to the least developed countries. Over the last decade (1986/7 to 1995/6), 54 per cent of Canadian food aid reached these countries, as against only 32 per cent of Canadian ODA.

WHAT COMMODITIES ARE SENT AS AID?
The types of food supplied have likewise changed. Food aid originally evolved out of grain (primarily wheat) surpluses, but has since become more diversified, reflecting both preferences of lobby groups in donor countries and the desires of recipient countries. Wheat represented 78 per cent of global food aid by volume in 1974/5, 71 per cent in 1983/4, but only 52 per cent in 1995/6. The proportion of coarse grains has increased over time, largely in response to recipient preferences. Blended foods and fortified cereals (primarily soy-fortified cereals) are a feature of the U.S. food aid program. Blended foods were designed as nutrient-dense foods suitable for small children (for example, corn-soy-meal, which is fortified with vitamins and minerals). These have predominantly gone to child-feeding programs in South Asia, although more recently there has been a tendency to supply these foods to refu-

gees, a use for which they were not designed. Other foods such as skim milk powder and other dairy products, canned fish, and meat are not well suited as food aid, being much more costly per calorie than grains. Milk is about 5 or 6 times as costly and fish about twenty times as costly per calorie as corn, the cheapest food aid grain. Dairy products, canned meat, and fish have the additional disadvantage that they tend to be consumed more by higher income households, which tends to lead to more 'leakage' to the non-poor. However, producers in donor countries form a vociferous lobby to encourage use of such products as food aid when there are surpluses.

It is noteworthy that as cereal aid has declined drastically in the last couple of years, shipments of non-cereal aid have not declined to the same extent. Non-cereals currently represent around 12 per cent of total food aid volume as against around 3 per cent in 1974/5 and 8 per cent in 1983/4. The share of non-cereals is even higher in value terms, since non-cereals are more costly per ton.

The types of commodities sent by Canada have changed somewhat over the years, following global patterns. The overriding importance of wheat has declined somewhat less than in the global figures (its share of Canadian aid in volume terms was still 83 per cent in 1995), since Canada is less able to supply coarse grains and rice than some other exporters. The second most important commodity after wheat is oil (5 per cent in volume terms in 1995/6). In value terms wheat is less predominant, since it is one of the least costly items (in value terms, excluding transport costs, wheat accounted for 59 per cent of food aid in 1995/6, oil for 19 per cent and pulses – included in other – for 8 per cent; the balance included miscellaneous items such as canned fish). There has been a requirement that at least 25 per cent of food aid is non-cereals, which tends to serve the interests of non-grain exporting provinces.

Different regions receive different types of food aid, and there are differences also by program. Food aid to Europe includes a disproportionate share of the high-cost items (meat and dairy products) and of the medium-cost items (pulses). Likewise Latin America, where almost all countries fall into the 'middle-income' category, receives a disproportionate share of dairy products, fats, and fish. South Asia receives a disproportionate share of the blended foods (largely accounted for by shipments to the Intensive Child Development Services (ICDS) program in India). Poorer countries in sub-Saharan Africa tend to receive lower-valued items such as cereals. This tendency to give higher-valued products to richer countries is somewhat inevitable (based on patterns of consumer demand), but tends to disadvantage poorer recipients.

There are similar biases by type of program. Calculations by one of the authors (in Combs et al., 1994) show that for the U.S. PL-480 Title II program, MCH programs receive disproportionately more of the higher-value items such as blended and soy-fortified foods and oil, whereas emergency programs for refugees receive the lowest value items, whole and processed grains.

The Decline of Food Aid

Previous studies such as Isenman and Singer (1977) and Maxwell and Singer (1979) have commented on the effects of food aid. The most serious criticism is that it can have adverse effects on domestic agriculture in recipient countries, via the depressing effect on farm prices. Food aid may increase dependency on imported foodstuffs that may not be available domestically (wheat imports to urban tropical Africa being a good example). Isenman and Singer (1977) also argue that there is a 'policy effect,' in that food aid permits governments to pursue unsustainable food policies which, in the long run, harm domestic agriculture.

Food aid – like other tied aid – also has the disadvantage of being less valuable to the recipient than untied aid. Food aid shipped from a distant donor may be more costly than food purchased nearby, especially if (as is the case for U.S. food aid) it must be transported in ships of the donor country, whose shipping rates are relatively high. Food aid can also be sent in the form of unfamiliar foods, such as canned fish and skim milk powder. These items may be of low value to the recipients, and in the case of skim milk powder (if mixed with unsafe water or consumed in large quantities by lactose-intolerant populations) may even have detrimental effects. Other criticisms of food aid are that it complicates project logistics, is more costly to administer, and is subject to 'leakage.'

On the other hand, there are particular circumstances in which food aid is very useful, such as humanitarian emergencies, where the adverse effects on agriculture are much less likely. Food aid may be somewhat 'self-targeting,' more likely to reach poorer and vulnerable households, and within households it is better targeted to women and children than other kinds of aid. The strongest argument for food aid is its 'additionality': it is aid that would not otherwise be supplied, and it creates a lobby within donor countries who benefit from the aid supplied and who urge its continuance.

The current decline in food aid is closely related to the Uruguay round of trade negotiations, in which it was agreed to reduce domestic subsidies on agriculture by 20 per cent, to reduce export subsidies from developed countries by 36 per cent in value and 20 per cent in volume over six years, and to move from quantitative import restrictions to tariffs. Several models predict that one consequence will be higher food prices. The World Bank–OECD Development Centre RUNS model predicts that wheat prices will increase by 5.9 per cent, prices of coarse grains by 3.6 per cent, dairy prices by 7.2 per cent, and vegetable oil by 4.1 per cent (Singer, 1995). The reduction of surpluses is expected to reduce the export competition that has been so costly for the European Economic Community and the United States (and other exporters caught in the middle) in the latter part of the 1980s and early 1990s, and in so doing, to decrease the volume of food aid.

The Uruguay agreement on agriculture was accompanied by a 'Decision on measures concerning the possible negative effects of the reform program on least developed and net food importing developing countries.' This decision agreed to 'review' levels of food aid, to provide more food aid on grant terms, to support technical and financial assistance to improve agricultural productivity, and to encourage greater use of existing lending facilities for importers facing problems (such as the IMF and World Bank facilities, with their associated conditionality). The decline in food aid, coupled with increasing difficulties of financing the CGIAR (the international agricultural research) system, suggest that developed countries have so far only paid lip service to this 'Decision.'

It is interesting to note that food aid has actually declined even faster than other types of aid (food aid comprised 10–15 per cent of ODA in the 1970s and is currently less than 5 per cent). The share of food aid in total aid varies by donor, with major agricultural exporters (the United States, Canada, Australia, Germany, and the United Kingdom) having a larger proportion of aid supplied as food (Table 13.3), but in almost all cases the downward trend from the 1980s to the 1990s is evident. One small piece of good news is that the proportion of food aid provided as grants has risen from just over half in 1971 to over 90 per cent in 1992 (Table 13.1).

Canada has in the past been a disproportionately large food aid donor, giving the largest amount of all donors in per capita terms

TABLE 13.3
Percentage share of food aid in ODA of selected major DAC donors, various years

Donor	1978	1980	1982	1984	1986	1988	1990	1992	1994
Australia	6.9	9.6	11.5	15.1	11.2	8.4	9.5	6.9	2.1
Canada	21.2	15.4	17.9	19.2	15.5	17.9	12.5	13.6	7.6
France	2.9	3.0	3.5	3.9	2.4	3.6	0.4	0.5	0.5
Germany	6.9	4.9	9.6	1.9	7.0	6.0	7.2	9.0	5.9
Japan	1.0	7.8	4.6	1.0	1.2	1.6	0.3	0.5	0.4
U.K.	5.5	6.3	8.2	9.9	5.6	6.5	6.3	6.6	4.5
U.S.A.	19.7	18.3	13.8	17.7	15.9	18.0	14.2	11.8	14.1
All DAC	10.2	9.6	8.9	10.4	8.0	8.1	5.8	5.4	3.5

Source: Charlton (1992) based on FAO, *Food Aid in Figures* (various years) for 1978–84; FAO, *Food Aid in Figures* (1994) for 1986–92, OECD (1996a) for 1994.

(CIDA, 1994c). As is the case for other donors however, food aid is declining over time, faster even than overall ODA. Food aid peaked in 1987/8 at Can$437 million, and in 1996/7 had fallen to $248 million (Table 13.2: note that in these tables food aid is valued at domestic prices, which often overstate its value relative to world prices). Wheat shipments, which had reached nearly 1.4 million tons in 1987/8 (including wheat flour), had fallen to only 0.4 million tons in 1995/6, and food aid commitments made under the Food Aid Convention fell from 0.6 million tons in the 1980s to 0.4 million tons in 1995/6. Food aid as a share of ODA has declined quite sharply from 21 per cent in 1978 to 8 per cent in 1994 (Table 13.3). The decline in Canadian food aid is likely to be reflected in a decline in Canada's influence in circles such as the FAO, where it had played a role proportionately larger than its relatively modest total GDP would imply.

Food aid has in the past, and for certain commodities, constituted a significant share of exports, for example 44 per cent of wheat flour exports in 1984/5 (wheat is not usually exported as flour due to higher shipping and storage costs), 16 per cent of canola exports (1984/5), 25 per cent of skim milk exports (1984/5), and 85 per cent of canned fish exports (1993/4). Food aid has also comprised a significant share of production (over 10 per cent) for canned fish and skim milk. Although food aid accounts for only about 3 per cent of total agricultural exports, it is a much larger proportion (often between 15 and 20 per cent) of exports to developing countries.

The Redemption of Food Aid?

Although to the general public improved nutrition may seem an obvious and important goal of food aid, this was not a major consideration in food aid programs until recently. In the United States, the recent food aid policy statement (USAID, 1995) lists nutrition along with agricultural productivity as a main goal. However, it is not mentioned in the recommendations for food aid policy coming out of the Canadian 1988 foreign policy statement *Sharing Our Future* and there are no recommendations on food aid per se in the 1995 statement *Canada in the World*, although it is anticipated that the food aid strategy arising from the program evaluation in 1997 will highlight nutrition. Given the often disappointing track record of food aid for development purposes, now is a good time to re-emphasize its role for nutrition. One food policy expert (Falcon, 1995) evaluates experience thus: 'food aid for famine relief (very important); food aid for development purposes (some successful projects, but few successful programs); and food aid for security support or strategic purposes (virtually always antithetical to longer run agricultural development.)'

Food aid plays a key role in emergencies. Donors have tended to downplay this role, perhaps feeling that it is a temporary 'fix' with no long-term development implications. There are no readily available figures at the global level for the proportion of food aid used for emergencies, although it is possible to infer from the WFP figures that the figure exceeded 25 per cent in 1995/6 (since 82% of WFP aid went for emergencies and WFP accounted for 29% of global food aid in that year). This is however a very conservative estimate, since there are other multilateral agencies – such as the United Nations High Commission for Refugees (UNHCR) – using food for emergencies, as well as NGOs. The importance of emergencies has risen sharply over time. Whereas development programs accounted for 90 per cent of the uses of WFP food aid between 1963 and 1975, they only accounted for 18 per cent in 1995. Emergencies accounted for the rest.

There has been growing concern at the international level that recipients of emergency food aid are not well nourished. Readily preventable deficiency diseases have re-emerged at refugee camps (scurvy in 1984, 1985, 1989, and 1991 in camps in Africa; xerophthalmia in 1985 in Sudan; beri-beri in Thailand in 1985; pellagra in Malawi in 1989 and 1990: Toole, 1993). Acute undernutrition rates in children below five have persisted at high (>20%) levels in some refugee camps for periods as long as six to eight months, and in some cases undernutrition has actually worsened over the period of international assistance.

The reasons for these problems are not hard to identify. Although there is now agreement on a desired minimum intake level for refugees (1,900 calories/person/day), in many cases refugees do not receive their full ration. Also, as we have seen, refugees tend to receive the cheapest calorie-cost items (whole grains), because donors feel this will reach the maximum number of individuals within the budget available. For refugees in closed camps or in remote or drought areas, there is little possibility of exchanging food to obtain some variety in the diet along with much-needed micronutrients. An adequate food ration, with some variety, is obviously the optimal solution for victims of emergencies.

As a second-best option, international research (in which Canada has played a major role) has been directed to fortification of refugee foods. In the United States, consideration has been given to using existing blended foods (originally designed for weaning-age children) in refugee rations (Combs et al., 1994). In Canada, an alternative suggestion has been to custom-design a premix to fortify food at the community or even household level (Beaton, 1995). Generally, national- or regional-level fortification is not an option at this time for many of the sub-Saharan African countries, although there have been some successes. For example, in Malawi the availability of sophisticated local commercial milling capacity permitted the addition of niacin to maize meal, and in some refugee camps vitamin C was added to skim milk powder in cement mixers (Seaman, 1993).

Another alternative is to fortify some donated foods at source. This tends to increase cost (since it requires processing at source, thereby increasing storage and shipping costs) and is not cost effective for rice. Since it is difficult to predict which food aid will be used for refugees, a considerable proportion of food aid may have to be fortified. Canada has made a positive contribution in this area by requiring that all oil for food aid be fortified with vitamin A. This was achieved without additional cost to CIDA; the oil processors agreed to absorb the small additional cost of the fortificant since there is an incentive to sell processed rather than unprocessed oil. Canada has since used its influence to encourage the WFP to accept only fortified oil for its programs.

In the United States, some of the processed grains used for food aid are fortified or enriched (cornmeal, bulgur, and the soy-fortified cereals and blended foods), but – surprisingly – wheat flour is not fortified to domestic standards. Although calcium and vitamin A are added to wheat as per the U.S. Department of Agriculture (USDA) specifications, iron and the B vitamins are not (Combs et al., 1994), despite the minuscule cost savings that this provides. It would seem highly desirable to encourage all food aid donors to fortify or enrich food aid at least up to their own domestic standards. The very small cost savings are unlikely greatly to outweigh the effort of producing a separate mix for food aid use.

In the long run, it would be desirable to provide assistance for domestic fortification in developing countries and there is a potential role here for food aid. At present, it is unlikely that fortification can work in most sub-Saharan African countries (and fortified food is unlikely in any case to reach victims of emergencies), but it is certainly feasible and timely in South Asian countries, where wheat flour is consumed (Pakistan, Bangladesh, and parts of India) and where the incidence of anaemia is very high. Food aid could be supplied to mills during the period of introduction of fortification, to help defray the initial cost of the fortificant or the fortification machinery, until social demand for fortified products is built up. Technical assistance with fortification, supply of fortification equipment, or (even better) assistance with production of such equipment in a developing country would all be very cost-effective uses of ODA, with long-term, sustainable effects. Once introduced, other than limited expenditures for monitoring, governments do not incur expenses for maintaining fortification programs, the costs of which are borne by consumers.

More research on nutritional effects of food aid is desirable. In this regard it is very positive that Canada is helping to fund more work on refugee diets, such as that by Young (1996) on the acceptability of fortified foods among refugee diets, building on the limited number of existing studies of actual food use by refugees (see for example Hansch, 1995). Since 1995/6 CIDA has allotted a proportion of its food aid budget to the Micronutrient Initiative, an international policy research unit based in Ottawa (in 1996/7, 15.2 per cent of the food aid budget went to the Micronutrient Initiative and to WFP 'New initiatives' for women and children). The United States similarly funds the Opportunities for Micronutrient Initiatives (OMNI) program based at John Snow International, which has also undertaken work on food aid.

Another use of food aid, again for the general population and not just for emergencies, would be to support nutrition programs at the community level. In the past food aid has been used to provide incentives for mothers to attend clinics, for girls to attend school, and even to support public sector workers during adjustment programs. International agencies such as UNICEF are promoting the use of community-level volunteers to improve nutrition, building on the successes in countries such as Thailand (Winichagoon et al., 1992) and projects such as that in Iringa, Tanzania. Rather than distributing food to mothers to improve nutrition, it would be cost-effective to use food as an incentive for community nutrition volunteers who would affect nutrition in a sustainable way (assisting health system workers in mobilizing children for growth-monitoring, helping to provide information about the best breastfeeding practices, and educating mothers about healthy diet and hygiene for infants and young children).

There is bad news and good news about trends in food aid. The bad news is that food aid is decreasing and little is being done for the poorest food-deficit countries that are most adversely affected. This is especially bad news for victims of emergencies and for refugees. The good news is that some modest scale efforts are now underway to use food aid in better ways to improve nutrition, and this may serve as a preliminary step in finding an appropriate niche for food aid.

Notes

The authors would like to thank the many people and institutions who provided references, documents and information, including Jenny Cervinskas (Micronutrient Initiative), André Desrosiers (CIDA), Archana Dwivedi (CIDA), Derek Eaton (CIDA), Steven Hansch (Refugee Policy Group), Al Kehler (Canadian Foodgrains Bank), Tom Marchione (USAID), Kevin Perkins (CPAR), Michel Pilote (CIDA), Sonya Rabeneck (WHO), Linda Sherwin (CIDA), Bob Vandenberg (consultant), and Helen Young (Oxfam-UK). Thanks to Gerry Helleiner, Andre Desrosiers, and an anonymous reviewer for helpful comments on earlier drafts. The authors alone are responsible for any remaining errors or omissions.

1 Complete data on disbursements of Food Aid by donors, by region, on WFP commitments, on Canadian Aid to low-income countries, on distribution by commodity type, on commodity composition for Canadian Aid, on commodity composition for global commitments, and on Canadian Food Aid as a percentage of domestic production, exports and agricultural trade, are given in an earlier mimeo version and may be obtained by contacting the authors.

14

Communications and Development: Challenges of the New Information and Communication Technologies

EDNA F. EINSIEDEL AND MELISSA P. INNES

The image of a slum dweller and his family huddled around a small television screen in an urban hovel (or the Aboriginal family in the outback before a similar TV set) came and stayed on as a contemporary cliché for communications and development. Today, this image competes among several others: that of the street vendor in Hong Kong chattering on his cellular telephone; the guerrilla fighter in the hills of Chiapas with his laptop computer, lodging his demands against the government for all the World-Wide-Webbed world to hear; the Russian family enjoying the latest serial of the telenovela from Brazil; or, for that matter, the group of prostitutes in Thailand planning an education campaign to teach other sex workers how to protect themselves from AIDS. In all of these images, the patterns of communication activities in development have evolved in different ways, yet communication as an integral process and tool of development has remained a constant.

That communication processes have been key to development and social change has never been in doubt. As questions are raised about directions for development in the new millennium, and as communications assumes an increasingly important role in development processes in the context of the information age, it is useful to cast a reflective eye on the role played by the new information and communication technologies in development policy and practice.

New Information and Communication Technologies and the 'Leapfrog' Mystique

In the last decade and a half the world has been reconfigured politically and technologically. The ideological walls of the Cold War literally and

figuratively came down and the watchwords increasingly became globalization and open economies; these developments took place against
the backdrop of the 'other revolution' of the new information and communication technologies. As development planners continue to be
faced with problems from the past – meeting basic needs such as clean
water, adequate nutrition, and housing remain major challenges in
many parts of the world – new problems that ignore geographic borders have assumed greater prominence. The experiences of the 'First
World' and those of the 'Second' and the 'Third Worlds' are becoming
increasingly interconnected. The all-embracing markets of transnational capital, massive migration, marginalization, increasing poverty
in industrialized countries, indebtedness, and growing global unemployment have combined to create a situation in which the lines
between First, Second, or Third Worlds, north and south, are increasingly blurred. The AIDS pandemic and global environmental issues
challenge our contemporary methods of addressing national and international crises and require new and different strategies for effective
cooperation and communication across national boundaries. New
information technologies have been seen to assume a prominent role as
a vehicle for change.

The technologies of the information age, which continue to change
rapidly, range from personal communication tools such as cellular tele-
phones to national telecommunication infrastructures, including direct
satellite links. Computers are the nerve centre of the new information
technologies. They have been called the core technology of our times,
'the new paradigm,' 'the new "common sense"' (Forester and Morrison, 1997:11). Convergence is the key development that springs from
the much-heralded mergers of computers with traditional media systems, including broadband and telephone technologies.

In the field of development, information technologies have assumed
an increasingly dominant role in policy priorities and practice. Groups
and organizations from across the development spectrum are increasingly focused on ways in which these technologies may reshape
relations between and across North and South. International donor
agencies and non-governmental organizations (NGOs) have become
involved in information and communication technologies (ICT) initiatives, ranging from Internet connectivity and access to support for the
development of indigenous electronic communication systems to creating networks connecting North and South. Many advocates across
the field are claiming that ICTs are the means by which communities in

the third world will break into the modern era and become full participants in global decision making (IDRC, 1996; PADIS, 1996; CABECA, 1996). There is much discussion about countries across the South 'leapfrogging' the industrial age to join the rest of the world in the information age. 'It is here [in international telecommunication networks] that the technological advances offer developing countries more cost-effective and appropriate technologies still in use in the industrial world' (Amoeka, 1996).

It is further argued that access to 'the information society' via global electronic networks will enable social groups previously excluded from information resources, collaborative initiatives, and decision-making forums to become active participants. These groups will not only receive information from the North but will become equal contributors to the emerging 'global information era' (Amoeka, 1996).

Other development theorists and practitioners contest the potential of ICTs to transform North-South relations (Panos, 1996; Uimonen, 1997). They suggest that contemporary expectations surrounding these technologies need to be considered in relation to a number of significant social, financial, and technological constraints. 'In theory, the means to handle information are increasingly available and democratic. In practice, there is a danger of a new information elitism which further disenfranchises the majority of the world's population' (Panos, 1996: 2). The extent of the constraints was made vivid by South Africa's Deputy President Thabo Mbeki, when he pointed out to the 1995 G-7 conference that 'half of humanity has never made a telephone call' (ibid.). Access to the Internet and the information and networks it contains requires a telephone line, yet forty-nine countries have fewer than one telephone per hundred people, thirty-five of which are in Africa. At a global level, at least 80 per cent of the world's population still lacks basic telecommunications tools (Panos, 1996). The cost of a modem in India is four times its price in the United States, without considering the enormous differences in per capita earnings and standards of living. Furthermore, it is important to distinguish between a technological revolution and a social revolution. New ICTs, although having great potential to be an equalizing force, continue to exist within social power structures in which there are deep divides between haves and have nots. The advent of these technologies by no means guarantees equitable access and utilization of them.

With the perspectives of both the advocate and the critic in mind, it is important to examine how these technologies have been used in development activities before discussing what lies ahead for communication and development. Because of the emergent nature of ICT utilization in many developing countries, it is difficult to present a precise or comprehensive reflection on these activities. What follows is a sample of some of the contemporary initiatives as they exemplify the expectations for these technologies.

Among international aid agencies, there are a number of initiatives aimed at developing, supporting, and coordinating ICT implementation as nation-building tools. The Canadian International Development Agency (CIDA) works in West Africa to assist ten francophone countries to access the Internet and in South Africa to develop the government's telecommunication policy. The agency also provides substantial indirect support to ICT projects being pursued by Canadian NGOs, the International Development Research Center (IDRC), and the North-South Institute. The U.S. Agency for International Development (US AID) has established the Leland Initiative, which intends to bring the benefits of the information revolution through its development strategy proposal, 'Empowering Africans in the Information Age.' It is a five-year $15M effort to extend full Internet connectivity to approximately twenty African countries in order to promote sustainable development (U.S. AID Leland Initiative, 1998).

The World Bank is managing the Information for Development Program (InfoDev), a multilateral donor project to assist the economies in countries across Africa and Latin America to benefit more fully from these technologies. Many of these projects are focusing on Africa because of its enormous telecommunications, information, and development needs. One of these initiatives, the African Information Society Initiative (AISI) is supported by the Economic Commission for Africa, UNESCO, the World Bank, and the International Telecommunications Union (ITU). AISI has been designed to establish broad guidelines for the implementation of and access to ICTs throughout Africa. The AISI guiding principles envision the establishment of an 'African information society' by the year 2010 in which:

- Every man and woman, school child, village, government office, and business, can access information through computers and telecommunications;
- Information and decision support systems are used to support decision making in all the major sectors of each nation's economy;

- Access is available throughout the region to international, regional, and information highways;
- A vibrant private sector exhibits strong leadership in growing information-based economies;
- African information resources are accessible globally, reflecting content on tourism, trade, education, culture, energy, health, transport, and natural resource management; and
- Information and knowledge empower all sectors of society (Amoeka, 1996).

These goals reflect the considerable expectations being placed upon ICTs to revolutionize African society and obliterate exclusionary practices and structures. The investment in ICTs among donor agencies is not without basis. In this information age, developing countries indeed run the risk of being left out or left further behind. The comparative advantage of cheap labour is no longer the norm for many of these countries; what counts today is the currency of knowledge (Drucker, 1994). Thus, using ICTs 'to revitalize and transform traditional, less technologically demanding industries, and to modernize their basic infrastructures and services' has become paramount (Hanna et. al., 1996: 214).

Some cautions remain, however. Despite this proliferation of initiatives,[1] the cost of connectivity remains high and availability is limited primarily to academic and state organizations or larger NGOs with international affiliates. Smaller local organizations and people in rural areas are unable to take advantage of the same opportunities as their urban counterparts. Furthermore, the majority of information and messages about countries in the South and issues on the Internet continues to originate from host computers in Western countries, following traditional unidirectional flows of information from the North to the South. The many Africans, Indians, and Latin Americans overseas, however, are becoming significant as information providers about their countries in the North, using the expanding e-mail connections in their home countries to acquire and subsequently distribute up-to-date information across various websites.

In order to address some of these shortcomings of equity and access, there has been an expanding emergence of initiatives driven by international donors; local, national, and international NGOs; popular education; and civic and rural organizations. Important examples include IDRC's initiative, the Mexicali project in Mexico, the Pan Asian Networking Initiative linking NGOs, and ARSENATE, a FIDOnetwork supported by CIDA. The Acacia Initiative, as another example, seeks to demonstrate how ICTs can enable communities in Africa 'to solve development problems in ways that build upon local goals, cultures, strengths and processes to promote equitable and sustainable development; and build a body of knowledge identifying the policies, technologies, approaches, and methodologies most instrumental in promoting affordable and effective use of ICTs by marginalized communities' (IDRC, 1997). The establishment of networks such as the South African NGO Network (SANGONet) and the South Asian Network for Alternative Media (SANAM) are intended to empower local communities through access to ICTs. In this context, 'the purpose and end of electronic networking is to make popular initiatives and popular interventions more effective. That is, it is not efficiency but an agenda of social transformation and a pro-people developmental paradigm, which must be the driving force of the networking system' (Centre d'études et de resources sur L'Asie du Sud, 1995:89).

Although these projects have been made possible with funding from international donor agencies, some popular, civic and non-governmental organizations see ICTs as tools to help redress the global imbalance of power brought about by imbalances in information flows. They consider these technologies as a central component to the building of stronger civil societies and as tools to 'empower the disempowered' by providing links to regional, national and international networks pursuing radical social change (SANGONet documentation, 1996). NGOs active in popular education and literacy movements in India argue that 'an alternate electronic communication network that enables larger areas of cooperation and pooling of resources is a prerequisite for an alternate ideology' (CERAS, 1995).

Another function of ICTs is to link organizations horizontally for information exchange and to bring about a more critical mass in the efforts to represent particular causes or interests. Women's organizations across southern Africa are currently working to establish a women's network in collaboration with SANGONet to connect various women's groups in the region and to connect the region with women's organizations across the globe (Esterhuysen, 1996).

The provision of technical know-how to overcome barriers of time and space is also afforded by networks. HealthNet links health centres across the region with health professionals worldwide via satellite. Doctors working in rural areas are able to rapidly receive information, enabling them to address health problems in local emergencies. Ground stations are currently operating in eighteen countries (Australia, Brazil, Cameroon, Canada, Congo, Cuba, Ethiopia, Gambia, Ghana, Kenya, Mali, Mozambique, Sudan, Tanzania, Uganda, the United States, Zambia, and Zimbabwe). The network enables medical publications, which include a weekly newsletter featuring abstracts and articles with current medical information, and an AIDS Bulletin, to be accessed by rural health centres within these eighteen countries (HealthNet, 1997).

Education and training are similarly promoted via these technologies. For example, telecentres or 'telecottages,' popular in remote regions of Scandinavia where they combine functions of training centre, library, post office, telecommunication shop, and communication centre, are now being adopted in parts of Africa (Berendt, 1996–7).

In addition, the linkage of organizations for the promotion of common economic interests has also been highlighted. For example, the Mexicali project grew out of a 1995 workshop that included ninety representatives from farmers' associations across the Rio Colorado Valley in Mexico. By June of 1996, twelve farm organizations were connected and were using the system, which includes several World Wide Web information services. Plans are underway to expand the number of participating organizations in the next few years. With seed money from the Food and Agriculture Organization, the farmers' organizations bought computer equipment which is currently being used to compile and distribute a directory for each organization, its agricultural activities and production figures, and information about local growing conditions and production plans. This project is working to develop strategies for expanding farmer access to information related to marketing and the development of national and international trading links (see Richardson, 1996).

It is clear from these examples that the investment in ICTs for development has become a donor priority. In the context of declining aid dollars (World Bank, 1998), allocations to ICTs become significant, particularly when viewed in the context of basic needs. When it is recognized that ICTs have an impact on practically every sector, interest in this development tool may be easier to justify.

Having said that, in the efforts to push the development process along on the ICT foundation a number of critical questions – controversies even – emerge. While the goals clearly spell out the need for universal access, the provision of infrastructure is equally important.

In this context, the precise roles of the private sector, the state, and NGOs in insuring this accessibility remains unclear and will need to be given careful consideration (Mansell and Wehn, 1998).

Second, as we pointed out above, the cost of connectivity remains high and availability remains mostly limited to academic and state organizations or larger NGOs with international affiliates. Smaller local organizations and people in rural areas are unable to take advantage of the opportunities available to their urban counterparts.

Third, unless appropriate training is made available for the technical as well as the social uses of these technologies, they will remain underutilized if not rejected.

Thinking through the Technological Terrain

As development policies and practices have undergone significant transformations in the last few decades, so has communication. We are standing at a point that evokes *déjà vu*. The late 1940s and 50s promised mass media as an important tool for development; today we stand on a similar promontory, full of promises for the new information and communication technologies. And yet, the promontory we stand on today overlooks a world that is different from that of a half century earlier. It is no longer a world of two ideological camps and economic borders are open, even dangerously so, rather than closed. In this new world order, communications and information have even more dominant roles to play.

Does history have any lessons, any cautionary tales to recall?

Let us revisit the debates that took place throughout the late 1970s and the first half of the 80s over the idea of a New World Information and Communication Order (NWICO) within the United Nations. These debates revolved around the issues of cultural and ideological domination by the more powerful and technologically developed countries through dominance of global communication technologies and media production, resulting in one-way flows of information and consequent harm to local cultures and identities (MacPhail, 1987). What developing countries argued for was an international system that allowed more autonomy and control over the information products and resources and the opportunity to develop their own media resources.

The objectives of this new world information and communication order included:

1 The elimination of imbalances and inequities characterizing the situation at that time;
2 The elimination of negative effects of certain monopolies, public or private, and excessive concentrations;
3 Removal of internal and external obstacles to a free flow and wider and better balanced dissemination of information and ideas;
4 Plurality of sources and channels of information; and
5 The capacity of developing countries to achieve improvement of their own situations via access to equipment, training, and enhancement of infrastructure suitable to their needs and aspirations, with assistance from the North (MacBride et al., 1983).

The issues raised in this debate around equity, control, and cultural integrity remain relevant today. The 'technological fix,' then as now, remains the paramount concern; that is, the key to redressing the imbalances was simply to ensure that all mankind [sic] was within easy reach of a telephone by the early part of the next century. Contemporary discussions of the role of the new ICTs in development likewise assume uncritically the benefits of the technologies and concern themselves with the how and when to 'connect' communities in the South instead of with the why, who, under what conditions, and with what implications. It is to these issues that we now turn.

Technologies are more than artifacts and tools. They are what Boulding has called 'ways of doing things' (Boulding, 1969). If we conceive of them as ways of living, or as social practices, they cannot be isolated from the web of values that inevitably surround them. As social practices, they undoubtedly have a significant cultural link. The consequence here is to pose *the other question*: what can we do with the technology that accommodates who we are and where we may wish to go?

This question assumes a greater challenge in the context of the competing forces of globalization and cultural specificities. If social allegiances in the world were once cast in political-ideological terms, they seem now to be drawn along cultural terms. The conflicts of Jihad versus McWorld (Barber, 1993) have become all too familiar in the last decade and they do not seem to be abating. As Barber has warned, 'Just beyond the horizon of current events lie two possible political futures – both bleak, neither democratic. The first is a retribalization of large swaths of humankind by war and bloodshed ... The second is being borne in on us by the onrush of economic and ecological forces that demand integration and uniformity and that mesmerize the world with fast music, fast computers, fast food' (23). Thus we see the rise of movements such as the Taliban in Afghanistan and neo-Nazis in Europe at the same time as the prolific spread of influences such as Saatchi and Saatchi[2] and CNN in diverse communities across the globe.

In this world, the question of identity looms larger even as globalization promotes homogenization. While the examples of China or Malaysia trying to block satellite signals against Western cultural invasions are illustrative, Canadians also need only look inward to appreciate the nuances behind Quebec's language and cultural laws and the country's capitulation to the lost battle of blocked satellite signals as reminders that issues of identity are not so easily resolved. The challenges of identity in the face of cultural homogenization remain, and the new technologies offer similar promises and pitfalls, as the more traditional media did (and still do), of extending and re-emphasizing these problems. The signals of homogenization remain the same whether delivered through the airwaves or through cyberspace.

The questions of access and equity similarly loom large. While electronic connectivity continues at a frenetic pace, large inequities still remain in terms of access to various information technologies, as Table 14.1 clearly demonstrates. The same warning that Jane Parpart issues in Chapter 12 regarding the uncritical acceptance of participatory development applies here to the embrace of information technologies: while dissolving some hierarchies, information technologies may simultaneously create new ones. The ways in which these issues of equity are addressed will be critical in determining whether the new ICTs deepen or bridge the gaps between information haves and have-nots. South Africa has shown uncommon sensitivity. The South African Broadcasting Corporation's decision to rely on analogue rather than digital technology for its satellite broadcasting venture was based on the desire 'to connect *with the rest of the continent* as well as the rest of the world' (Berendt, 1996–7: 4).

In our zeal to connect every man, woman, child, every business organization and government agency, particularly in African countries, have we ignored the other development challenges in basic needs, education, or human rights? As Uimonen graphically states, the 1.3 billion people who live in absolute poverty across the globe 'cannot eat information, nor does it keep them warm. How can the Internet reach out to these people, and help them in their daily struggle?'

TABLE 14.1
The information age

Country	Daily newspaper per 1,000 people, 1994	Radios per 1,000 people, 1995	TV sets per 1,000 people, 1996	Mobile phones per 1,000 people, 1996	Fax machines per 1,000 people, 1995	Personal computers per 1,000 people, 1996	Internet hosts per 1,000 people, July 1997
Bangladesh	6.0	48.0	7.0	0.0	0.0	–	0.0
Burkina Faso	0.0	30.0	6.0	0.0	–	0.0	0.0
Canada	189.0	–	709.0	114.0	23.6	192.5	228.0
Guatemala	23.0	–	122.0	4.0	1.0	2.8	0.79
India	31.0	120.0	64.0	0.0	0.1	1.5	0.05
Peru	86.0	–	142.0	8.0	0.6	5.9	2.6
South Korea	404.0	–	326.0	70.0	8.9	131.7	28.8
Syria	18.0	–	91.0	0.0	0.3	1.4	0.0
Sweden	483.0	–	476.0	282.0	45.3	214.9	321.5
Thailand	48.0	208.0	167.0	28.5	2.4	16.7	2.1
Uganda	2.0	124.0	26.0	0.0	0.1	0.5	0.0
United States	228.0	–	806.0	165.0	64.6	362.4	442.1

Source: World Bank, *World Development Indicators – 1998*. Washington, D.C.: International Bank for Reconstruction and Development, 1998.

(Uimonen, 1997). We also need to ask whose voices are to be heard. The Internet has already demonstrated its capacities to provide channels that circumvent those of the more powerful (Frederick, 1993); will the forces of commercialization or the forces of state power overtake the opposing voices? And yet 'The biggest obstacle to the survival of a free and democratic Internet is that the telecommunications companies own the infrastructure on which the Internet operates' (Baran, 1996: 17). Many remain unaware that the Internet, once run by government and universities, who provided much of the funding for operation of its 'backbone' lines (the major transcontinental phone lines that carry the Internet traffic), has now been turned over to communication giants and long-distance telephone companies such as AT & T, Sprint, and MCI in the United States; British Telecom; Deutsch Telecom; and Japan's NTT (Baran, 1996). The increasing private sector role in setting international standards and providing content is unlikely to diminish and the challenge remains for establishing viable partnerships among the private sector, the state, and civil society organizations to work towards mutually beneficially goals. Leaving the ICT development to the devices of the marketplace will surely result in important gaps, particularly from the point of view of equitable access. This will constitute one of the key challenges for donor agencies interested in supporting ICT development efforts.

Perhaps most important in considering these technologies and their impact on the field of development is that they be understood as social tools, whose potential and limitations are only realized within their local or global contexts. Thus, the potential of ICTs as tools for authentic participation, as a means to catapult countries in the South into the information age and to help address existing power imbalances depends on the extent to which they adequately address the issues of North-South relations, divisions of power and control, and equitable access for participation in the information society. For international aid efforts, balancing support of ICT programs between investments in technological and social capabilities will be critical.

We need to remind ourselves that in the end, communications are not just technologies; they are reflections of the values and cultures within which they occur. Communities and societies aspire for just and equitable societies; their use of information and communication technologies for development should have the same goal. Communications are ultimately the discourses of individual and community. The individual negotiates his or her way through the shoals of modernity and post-modernity via this discourse just as communities – national and local – do. Only by reflecting on the ways in which these discourses are carried out, how they are mediated by technology, and by actively shaping these ways might we arrive at more authentic forms of human life – the way we conceive of what development ultimately means.

Notes

1 In addition to these activities, the UN Economic Commission for Africa created the Pan-African Development Information System (PADIS) in 1980 as a cooperative regional development information system to serve Africa (PADIS, 1996). Since then, PADIS has linked more than eighteen African organizations to a FIDOnet-based network. Its overall objective is the promotion of development management information in the African region. PADIS is currently working with IDRC to install electronic networks in an additional twenty-four African countries through the Capacity Building for Electronic Communication in Africa (CABECA) project (CABECA, 1997). As of 1994, all CABECA nodes were located in national universities, research centres, international NGOs, and government offices, although many emerging initiatives, such as IDRC's Acacia project, are currently working towards more universal and diverse access.

2 One of the largest multinational advertising firms.

Conclusion

JIM FREEDMAN

Foreign aid is a common good in the political trade between states. It is no surprise that recent changes in the global arena have radically altered the way foreign aid is perceived. Presently, this arena is changing rapidly, from an orderly game between two large teams to a much less orderly free-for-all led by a state whose interests are unfailingly self-serving. The question here is whether this transition to a more liberal, U.S.-led economic environment will entail a decline in civic responsibility, as it has in the transition to market-led economies throughout the globe. If it does, then foreign aid has a crucial role, and this is to preserve a measure of civic responsibility in the affairs of states.

A foreign aid philosophy at the turn of the century should be a manifesto for global responsibility. Ideally it would include many of the arguments found in this book, such as, for example, a justification for why a humanitarian-focused regime must be preserved, an appeal to respect the political integrity of needy states for both economic and political reasons, and innovative ways for financing development assistance that do not rely on the largest of donor states. It would support measures to reduce the reckless flow of capital. It would recognize the notion of social capital, and it would argue that the management of assistance to communities be embedded in the communities themselves.

But first it will have to respond to a chorus of detractors for whom the notion of foreign aid is passé.

There is a shrill, Chicken Little tenor to the argument about the end of foreign aid, and it goes something like this. As long as the foreign aid arena pitted two ideologies against one another, foreign aid was part public relations and part social engineering intended to showcase one or another competing ideology. The Cold War arena has now been replaced by one that promotes the liberalization of economies by encouraging more foreign investment and by making liberal reforms the condition for continued aid. If foreign aid's beneficiaries were once held hostage to a low-level conflict, they are now hostage to an ideological commitment to propagate the message of the market. Aid now promotes a 'transition' to an export-oriented, market-respecting economic environment, and this re-orientation of aid tends to favour those regimes which are more plausibly poised on the verge of making such a transition. The poorer countries, because of their political and economic foibles, are considered less and less to be viable investments. As a consequence, foreign aid veers from its idealist course, away from assistance to the poor and towards support for emerging entrepreneurs and for the opening of economic environments. Foreign aid has been conscripted into a purpose that benefits affluent traders more than the dispossessed.

The Chicken Little litany furthermore insists that foreign aid is heir to a 'modernist agenda,' a bias towards remaking the developing economies in the image of the affluent ones, who too proudly tout their own history as a state's only imaginable path to well-being. The argument is that the foreign aid agenda is not only out of step with a rapidly changing world, but that it also carries the quasi-colonial burden of bearing a naive view about what constitutes economic development and change (see Cowen and Shenton 1996 and Crush 1995). A recent review of the 'global crisis in foreign aid' (Grant and Nijman 1998: 193) finds the modernist paradigm ever stronger in an era when the only acceptable dénouement for emerging states is a liberal economy carrying the victory banner from the Cold War. Here is even more evidence for the end of aid: not only are the coffers of foreign aid emptying fast, but aid is wrong-headed and morally bankrupt as well.

This book recognizes that the real-politick of international relations has often forced the humanitarian impulse among states into the shadows, making it difficult to discern, and even more difficult to institutionalize. But it is up to those less seduced by the harsh logic of interstatal relations or the academics' discoveries of nefarious hegemonic constructions to revive aid, perhaps with a different reading of the logic or with a more eloquent rendition of the possibilities for the altruistic impulse. The curious feature about understanding interstatal relations is how easy it is to locate the worst of human motives in them: self-seeking sorts of behaviour make more sense, they are more conspicuous, and academics find them more compelling subjects.

The humanitarian credo, therefore, needs an eloquent spokesperson. While any of the contributors in this book could serve, there is one who has for years insisted that the essence of foreign aid is and should be the foundation of a global civic consciousness: Professor Cranford Pratt. His own essay is the moral compass of the volume. It charts the lamentable decline of the humanist perspective in Canada alongside the ascending importance of Canadian economic competitiveness and security. He argues, in the second chapter, that the threat of world poverty to Canadian security, the degradation of the global environment, and Canada's business interests abroad are all addressed by contributing to the creation of a global common weal: 'There is something artificial and unreal,' he says, 'in discussing the rationale for Canadian aid as if the choice is in fact between humanitarian objectives or advancing common security.' Cranford Pratt has done more than anyone to rescue humanitarian internationalism from the disdain of those who preach, disingenuously, that tending exclusively to Canada's market advantage is what is best for Canada in the world.

Once markets pervade an economy, very little is sacred, neither local authority, nor landlords nor families of high caste nor monarchies nor national pride. The fierce individualism that a market economy introduces into a social sphere has a salutary effect, but like a stubborn cleanser, it washes away the principles of right or privilege or authority and leaves only the spare commitment to trade. The market ethos scrubs away political ideologies, but it also scrubs off any inclination towards humanitarian intervention, leaving the raw pursuits of financial power to govern most affairs. In an era of pervasive global markets, political principles of right and justice tend to become afterthoughts, adjuncts to the exercise of financial wealth, where the only place for political right or social equity is in the shadows. There is the temptation to regard social or political configurations as obstructions in the affairs of merchant nations, and to forget that social configurations always affect economic growth, even if their presence is denied and in spite of the rather obvious truth that some social configurations may be better or worse for economic growth.

This is worrisome because it risks neglecting an important insight about development assistance. Communities, like nations, produce more when the social conditions are right. Democracy in some form – one might call it good governance if the phrase were not already so oversold – is a precondition for making productive environments more so, which is to say conducive to growing more rice, selling more life insurance, or cutting more hair. And it follows that one of the most promising strategies for making humanitarian aid work is to establish some ground rules for creating the social and political conditions for productive activity in communities.

The phrase social capital embodies this insight. Setting the social stage appropriately is a precondition for energizing economies, and this applies at a national as well as a village level. Norman Uphoff has done as much as anyone to lay the groundwork for a science of social capital, for identifying the social conditions that allow people to make the best use of physical capital. Collective action, based on some version of social equity and community sovereignty, makes watercourses work better, makes farmers more productive, and encourages communities to take sensible action on a range of important political issues. When communities maintain an equitable social environment, they are able to act successfully on a number of common endeavours. They are able to take effective action for preserving their forests or protecting other common resources. They are able to take stock of their well-being, carry out surveys, or hold meetings in which they identify needs of a community, accept them, and act on these needs effectively. Nations can do the same with fiscal policies. In generating and spending state revenue, states make choices about the distribution of national wealth among social strata or occupational groups, and in doing so, shape a society and influence its productivity.

The concept of social capital gives this book, implicitly and explicitly, one of its main theoretical moorings and is the backdrop for its message. The majority of these essays identify social or political conditions for realizing economic ends. Economics and politics are determinants of each other, and there is a broad message here for those who are concerned about the prospects for social justice as the global economy changes. Economic stability, or even prosperity, is a mirage unless there is some institutional provision for keeping the excesses of poverty and other social injustices from generating political chaos. In the international arena, social capital includes the formal and informal provisions for resolving social conflict, for protecting the poor against the excesses of deprivation, and for preserving the freedom of those with the initiative to generate wealth. Development assistance must take responsibility for building social capital in the economy of nations.

Global prosperity, which after all is the fondest wish of all our contributors, is inseparable from the social responsibility that each of the national players assumes in promoting a climate of social security. Every nation state can assume a portion of this responsibility, donor nations and beneficiaries alike, and they do so inside the enterprise, however maligned it has been, of the give and take of foreign aid. If foreign aid contributes to preserving this climate of social and civic responsibility, it is utterly indispensable.

References

ACC/SCN. 1997. Report on the Nutrition Situation of Refugee and Displaced Populations. Geneva:
ACC/SCN of the World Health Organization, 8 March.

Adams, J.S. 1963. Toward an Understanding of Inequity. *Journal of Abnormal and Social Psychology* 67 (July), 422–36.

– 1965. Inequity in Social Exchange. In L. Berkowitz, ed., *Advances in Experimental Social Psychology.* New York: Academic Press, 43–90.

Adelman, Irma. 1991. What Is the Evidence on Income Inequality and Development? In Donald J. Savoie and Irving Brecher, eds., *Equity and Efficiency in Economic Development.* Montreal and Kingston: McGill-Queen's University Press.

Akram-Lodhi, A.H. 1997. The Structure of Rural Markets in Northern Pakistan. In J. Freedman and A.H. Akram-Lodhi, eds., *Water, Pipes and People: The Social and Economic Impact of the Salinity Control and Reclamation Project in Northern Pakistan.* Ottawa/Hull: Canadian International Development Agency.

Alesina, Alberto, and Roberto Perotti. 1994. The Political Economy of Growth: A Critical Survey of the Recent Literature. *World Bank Economic Review* 8, no. 3, 351–71.

Altimir, Oscar. 1994. Income Distribution and Poverty Through Crisis and Adjustment. *CEPAL Review* 52, 60–74.

Amoeka, K. 1996. Keynote Address, Conference on the Information Society and Development. African Information Society Initiative. http://www.bellanetorg/aisi.

Anyanwu, C.N. 1988. The Technique of Participatory Research in Community Development. *Community Development Journal* 23, no. 1, 11–15.

APIC. 1997. Africa on the Internet: Starting Points For Policy Information. http://www.igc.apc.org/apic.

Ashby, J.A., and L. Sperling. 1995. Institutionalizing Participatory, Client-Driven Research and Technology Development in Agriculture. *Development and Change* 27, 753–70.

Baba, Marietta L. 1994. The Fifth Subdiscipline: Anthropological Practice and the Future of Anthropology. *Human Organization* 53, no. 2, 174–86.

Bairoch, Paul. 1975. *The Economic Development of the Third World since 1900*. London: Methuen.

Baran, N. 1996. Privatizing Cyberspace. *New Internationalist* (December), 16–17.

Barber, B. 1993. *Jihad vs. McWorld*. New York: Times Books.

Bauer, Peter. 1976. *Dissent on Development*. Cambridge: Harvard University Press.

Beaton, G.H. 1995. *Fortification of Foods for Refugee Feeding: Executive Summary and Recommendations*. Report submitted to CIDA. Toronto: GHB Consulting.

Berendt, A. 1996–7. Grassroots Movements For Appropriate Technology. *InterMedia* 24, no. 6 (December–January), 22–7.

Berg, Elliot. 1993. Rethinking Technical Cooperation: Reforms for Capacity-Building in Africa. New York: UNDP.

Berry, Albert. 1988a. Comments on Problems, Development Theory and Strategies of Latin America. In Gustav Ranis and T. Paul Schultz, eds., *The State of Development Economics: Progress and Perspectives*. Basil Blackwell.

– 1988b. When Do Agricultural Exports Help the Rural Poor? A Political Economy Approach. Unpublished mimeo.

– 1997. The Inequality Threat in Latin America. *Latin American Research Review* 32, no. 2, 3–40.

Black, Ira B. 1991. *Information in the Brain: A Molecular Perspective*. Cambridge, Mass.: MIT Press.

Bonilla, Victor Daniel. 1972. *Serfs de dieu et maitres d'Indiens. Histoire d'une mission capucine en Amazonie*. Paris: Fayard. Coll. Anthropologie Critique.

Boulding, K. 1969. Technology and the Changing Social Order. In D. Popenoe, ed., *The Urban-Industrial Frontier*. New Brunswick, N.J.: Rutgers University Press.

Bound, J., and G. Johnson. 1992. Changes in the Structure of Wages in the 1980s: An Evaluation and Alternative Explanations. *American Economic Review* 82, 371–92.

Bulmer-Thomas, Victor. 1996. *The New Economic Model in Latin America and Its Impact on Income Distribution and Poverty*. New York: St Martin's Press in association with the Institute of Latin American Studies, University of London.

CABECA. 1997. Capacity Building for Electronic Communication in Africa: Introduction, 1995. http://www.sas.upenn.edu/African_Studies/Hornet/CABECA.

CERAS. 1995. Electronic Communication Networking Among NGO's In India: A Feasibility Study Of Its Impact On Indian Popular Education Movement. Unpublished conference proceedings.

CIDA. *Annual Reports*. Ottawa: Supply and Services Canada, various years.

– 1983. *Evaluation Assessment: Canadian Food Aid Program*, vols. 1 and 2. Hull: CIDA, Policy Branch, Evaluation Division.

– 1987. *Sharing Our Future: Canadian International Development Assistance*. Hull: CIDA.

– 1994a. *Netherlands Ministry of Foreign Affairs and Norway Royal Ministry of Foreign Affairs, Evaluation of the World Food Program*. Abridged version. Norway: Chr. Michelsen Institute.

– 1994b. *Food Aid: What Canada Supplies and Why*. Hull: CIDA, Communications Branch.

– 1994c. *Canada's Food Aid Policy and Program: The Need for Food Aid*. Hull: CIDA, Communications Branch.

– 1994d. *Emergency Food Aid: Learning the Lessons of History*. Hull: CIDA, Communications Branch.

– 1994e. *Food Aid Program 1993/4, Annual Statistical Report*. Hull: CIDA, Multilateral Program Branch, Food Aid Centre.

– 1997a. *CIDA's Food Aid Program: A Comparative Profile*. Ottawa: CIDA, Performance Review Division.

– 1997b. *Lessons Learned from the Implementation of Food Aid*. Hull: CIDA, Performance Review Division.

CIDA, FACE (Food Aid Co-ordination and Evaluation Centre). *Annual Report*, various years.

Cassells, Philip. 1993. *The Giddens Reader*. Stanford, Cal.: Stanford University Press.

Centre d'études et de resources sur l'Asia du Sud. 1995. *Information Technologies in South Asia*. Delhi: New Delhi Press.

Ceron, Solarte B. 1985. *Contexto socio-economico de las migraciones internas en Narino*. Pasto: Universidad de Narino, Colombia.

Chambers, R. 1983. *Rural Development, Putting the Last First*. Essex: Longman Scientific and Technical.

– 1994a. The Origins and Practice of Participatory Rural Appraisal. *World Development* 22, no. 7, 953–69.

– 1994b. Participatory Rural Appraisal (PRA): Analysis of Experience. *World Development* 22, no. 9, 1253–68.

– 1994c. Participatory Rural Appraisal (PRA): Challenges, Potentials and Paradigm. *World Development* 22, no. 10, 1437–54.

Charlton, M.W. 1992. *The Making of Canadian Food Aid Policy*. Montreal and Kingston: McGill-Queen's University Press.

Chen, Shaohua, Gaurav Datt, and Martin Ravallion. 1994. Is Poverty Increasing in the Developing World? *Review of Income and Wealth*. Series 40, no. 4 (December), 359–76.

Cohen, Jack, and Ian Stewart. 1994. *The Collapse of Chaos: Discovering Simplicity in a Complex World*. New York: Viking Books.

Coleman, James S. 1988. Human Capital in the Creation of Social Capital. *American Journal of Sociology* 94, Supplement, 95–120.

Combs, G.F., P.B. Dexter, S.E. Horton, and R. Buescher. 1994. *Micronutrient Fortification and Enrichment of PL 480 Title II Commodities: Recommendations for Improvement*. Arlington, Va.: OMNI/John Snow International.

Cooper, F., and R. Packard, eds. forthcoming. *International Development and the Social Sciences*. Berkeley: University of California Press.

Copans, Jean, dir. 1975. *Anthropologie et Impérialisme*. Paris: Maspero.

Cornia, Giovanni Andra, Richard Jolly, and Frances Steward, eds. 1987. *Adjustment with a Human Face: Protecting the Vulnerable and Promoting Growth*. Oxford: Clarendon Press.

Coveney, Peter, and Roger Highfield. 1995. *Frontiers of Complexity: The Search for Order in a Chaotic World*. New York: Fawcett Columbine.

Cowen, M.P., and R.W. Shenton. 1996. *Doctrines of Development*. London: Routledge.

Craig, C., and M. Mayo, eds. 1995. *Community Empowerment*. London: Zed.

Crush, J., ed. 1995. *Power of Development*. London: Routledge.

Drucker, P. 1994. The Age of Social Transformations. *Atlantic Monthly* (November), 53–80.

Dubinsky, Alan, and Michael Levy. 1989. Influence of Organizational Fairness on Work Outcomes of Retail Salespeople. *Journal of Retailing* 65, no. 2 (Summer), 221–52.

Elias Ortiz, Sergio. 1946. The Modern Quillacinga, Pasto, and Coaiquer. In Julian H. Steward, ed., *Handbook of South American Indians*, vol. 2. Washington: Smithsonian Institute. Bureau of American Ethnology, Bulletin 143.

Emmanuel, A. 1972. *Unequal Exchange: A Study of the Imperialism of Trade*, trans. Brian Pierce. New York: Monthly Review Press.

Escobar, Arturo. 1995. *Encountering Development; The Making and Unmaking of the Third World*. Princeton, N.J.: Princeton University Press.

Esman, Milton J., and Norman Uphoff. 1984. *Local Organizations: Intermediaries in Rural Development*. Ithaca, N.Y.: Cornell University Press.

Esterhuysen, A. 1996. Empowering Women in the Information Society: Building a Women's Information and Communication Network for South Africa. SANGONet, Unpublished manuscript.

European Commission. 1996. *EC Food Security and Food Aid Program*. Brussels: European Commission Information Unit. April.

– n.d. *Food Aid of the European Union in 1995*. Brussels: European Commission Directorate General for Development, Food Security and Food Aid Unit.

FAO. various years. (Food and Agriculture Organization of the United Nations). *Food Aid in Figures*. Rome: FAO.

– 1975. *Water Management for Irrigated Agriculture (Gal Oya Irrigation Scheme)*. Sri Lanka: Project Findings and Recommendations. Rome: Food and Agriculture Organization.

– 1994a. *FAO Yearbook: Production 1993*. 47. Rome: FAO.

– 1994b. *FAO Yearbook: Trade 1993*. 47. Rome: FAO.

– 1995. *FAO Yearbook of Fishery Statistics:* Commodities 1993. 77. Rome: FAO.

– 1996. *Food for All: Report on the World Food Summit*. Rome: FAO.

FAO/WFP. 1997. Food Aid/Food Aid Shipments. In FAOSTAT Statistics Database. http://apps.fao.org/lim500/nph-wrap.pl?FoodAid&Domain= FoodAid. 12 March.

Falcon, W.P. 1995. Food Policy Analysis, 1975–95: Reflections by a Practitioner. Washington, D.C.: International Food Policy Research Institute Lecture Series no. 3.

Fals-Borda, Orlando. 1991. Algunos ingredientos basicos. Orlando Fals-Borda and M. Anisur Rahman, dirs., *Accion y conocimiento: como romper el monopolio con investigacion-accion-participacion*. Bogota: CINEP, 7–19.

Feder, Gershon. 1982. On Exports and Economic Growth. *Journal of Development Economics* 12, nos. 1–2.

Ferguson, J. 1991. *Anti-Politics Machine*. Minneapolis: Minnesota University Press.

Fields, Gary. 1991. Growth and Income Distribution. In George Psachropoulos, ed., *Essays on Poverty, Equity and Growth*. Washington, D.C.: Pergamon Press for the World Bank.

Fisher, Julie. 1994. Is the Iron Law of Oligarchy Rusting Away in the Third World? *World Development* 22, no. 2, 129–43.

Forrester, B., and P. Morrison. 1997. *Computer Ethics: Cautionary Tales and Ethical Dilemmas*. Cambridge: MIT Press.

Frank, A. Gunder. 1969. *Capitalism and Underdevelopment in Latin America*. New York: Monthly Review Press.

Frederick, H. 1993. Computer Networks and the Emergence of Global Civil Society. In L. Harasim, ed., *Global Networks: Computers and International Communication*. Cambridge, Mass.: MIT Press.

– ed. 1986. *SCARP Mardan Evaluation Baseline Study*. Ottawa/Hull: Canadian International Development Agency.

Freedman, Jim, and Haroon Akram-Lodhi. 1997. Introduction. *Water, Pipes and People; The Social and Economic Impact of the Salinity Control and Reclamation Project in Northern Pakistan*. Ottawa/Hull: Canadian International Development Agency.

Freire, Paulo. 1974. *Pedagogie des opprimes*. Paris: Maspero.

Gell-Mann, Murray. 1994. *The Quark and the Jaguar: Adventures in the Simple and the Complex*. Boston: Little Brown.

Ghai, Dharam, and M.A. Rahman. 1981. The Small Farmers' Groups in Nepal. *Development* 1, no. 2, 23–8. Rome: Society for International Development.

Gleick, James. 1987. *Chaos: Making a New Science*. New York: Viking Books.

Goetz, M.A. 1995. Institutionalizing Women's Interests and Gender-sensitive Accountability in Development. *IDS Bulletin* 26, no. 3, 1–10.

Gombay, Christie. 1997. Eating Cities: The Politics of Everyday Life in Kampala, Uganda. Dissertation, University of Toronto.

Goodwin, Brian. 1994. *How the Leopard Changed Its Spots: The Evolution of Complexity*. New York: Charles Scribner's.

Grant, Richard, and Jan Nijman. 1998. *The Global Crisis in Foreign Aid*. Syracuse, N.Y.: Syracuse University Press.

Greenberg, Jerald. 1988. Equity and Workplace Status: A Field Experiment. *Journal of Applied Psychology* 73, no. 4 (November), 606–13.

Gupta, Dipak K. 1990. *The Economics of Political Violence*. New York: Praeger.

Halleck, D. 1994. Zapatistas on-line. *NACLA Report on the Americas*. 28, no. 2 (Sept.–Oct.), 30–2.

Hanna, N., S. Boysen, and S. Gunaratne. 1996. The East Asian Miracle and Information Technologies: Strategic Management of Technological Learning. World Bank Discussion Papers, no. 326, Washington, D.C.: World Bank.

Hansch, S. 1995. Mitigating micronutrient malnutrition in humanitarian crises. Washington, D.C.: Refugee Policy Group, draft. (mimeo)

HealthNet. 1997. HealthNet Documentation and Resources. http://www.healthnet.org.

Heilbroner, R.L. 1992. *Twenty-First Century Capitalism*. Toronto: Anansi Press.

Helleiner, G.K., et al. 1995. Report of the Group of Independent Advisers on Development Cooperation Issues Between Tanzania and its Aid Donors. Royal Danish Ministry of Foreign Affairs.

Hennessy, Rosemary. 1993. *Materialist Feminism and the Politics of Discourse*. New York: Routledge.

Hettne, B. 1995. *Development Theory and the Three Worlds*. 2nd ed. London: Longman.

Hewitt, Adrian, ed. 1994. *Crisis or Transition in Foreign Aid*. London: Overseas Development Institute.

Hirschman, A.O. 1963. *Journeys toward Progress: Studies in Economic Policy-Making in Latin America*. New York: Twentieth Century Fund.

– 1967. *Development Projects Observed*. Washington, D.C.: Brookings Institution.

– 1977. *The Passions and the Interests: Political Arguments for Capitalism before Its Triumph*. Princeton, N.J.: Princeton University Press.

– 1984. *Getting Ahead Collectively: Grassroots Experiences in Latin America*. New York: Pergamon Press.

Hook, Steven. 1995. *National Interest and Foreign Aid*. Boulder, Col.: Lynne Rienner Publishers.

– ed. 1996. *Foreign Aid toward the Millennium*. Boulder, Col.: Lynne Rienner Publishers.

Hyden, Goran, and Bo Karlstrom. 1993. Structural Adjustmant as Policy Process: The Case of Tanzania. *World Development* 21 (September), 1359–1401.

IDRC. 1997. Acacia Initiative: An Overview. http://www.idrc.ca/acacia/5_e.htm.

IGC (International Grains Council). 1996. International Grains Council: Grain Trade and Food Security Co-operation. http://www.int-grains-council.org.uk/broeng.html. 27 September.

IMCA (Instituto Mayor Campesino). 1990. Proyecto micro-regional de desarrollo rural. In F. Bernal, dir. *El campesinado contemporaneo. Cambios recientes en los pa'ses andinos*. Bogota, Tercer Mundo Editores, 440–50.

Ilchman, Warren F., and Norman Uphoff. 1997. *The Political Economy of Change*. New Brunswick, N.J.: Transaction Books. Originally published by the University of California Press.

Independent Commission for World-Wide Telecommunications Development. 1985. The Missing Link: Unpublished Report. Geneva: ITU.

Isenman, P.J., and H.W. Singer. 1977. Food Aid: Disincentive Effects and Their Policy Implications. *Economic Development and Cultural Change* 25, 205–37.

Jackson, C. 1997. Post-Poverty, Gender and Development? *IDS Bulletin* 28, no. 3, 145–55.

Jantsch, Erich. 1980. *The Self-Organizing Universe: Scientific and Human Implications of the Emerging Paradigm of Evolution*. New York: Pergamon Press.

Jayarajah, Carl, and William Branson. 1995. *Structural and Sectoral Adjustment: World Bank Experience, 1980–92*. Washington, D.C.: World Bank.

Johnson, Harry G. 1967. *Economic Policies toward Less Developed Countries*. Washington, D.C.: Brookings Institution.

Johnson, John H., and Sulaiman S. Wasty. 1993. Borrower Ownership of Adjustment Programs and the Political Economy of Reform. *World Bank Discussion Paper 199*. Washington, D.C.: World Bank.

Kabeer, N. 1995. *Reversed Realities: Gender Hierarchies in Development Thought*. London: Verso.

Kapur, D. 1997. The New Conditionalities of the IFIs. *International Monetary and Financial Issues for the 1990s*. Vol 8. New York: United Nations.

Katz, L., and K. Murphy. 1992. Changes in Relative Wages, 1963–1987: Supply and Demand Factors. *Quarterly Journal of Economics* 107 (February), 35–78.

Kawakami, Takao. 1993. Aid in the Post Cold War Era. *Japan Views Quarterly* (Spring), 14–17.

Kearney, Michael. 1996. *Reconceptualizing the Peasantry: Anthropology in Global Perspective*. Boulder, Col.: Westview Press.

Kelly, P., and W. Armstrong. 1996. Villagers and Outsiders in Cooperation: Experiences from Development Praxis in the Philippines. *Canadian Journal of Development Studies* 12, no. 2, 241–259.

Khan, Akhtar Hameed. 1996. *Orangi Pilot Project: Reminiscences and Reflections*. Karachi: Oxford University Press.

Killick, Tony. Donor Conditionality and the Improvement of Economic Policies. Unpublished manuscript.

Kindleberger, Charles P. 1996. *World Economic Primacy: 1500–1990*. London: Oxford University Press.

Korten, David. 1980. Community Organizations and Rural Development: A Learning Process Approach. *Public Administration Review* (September/October), 480–511.

Korten, Frances F., and Robert I. Siy. 1988. *Transforming a Bureaucracy: The Experience of the Philippine National Irrigation Administration*. West Hartford, Conn.: Kumarian Press.

Krishna, Anirudh, Norman Uphoff, and Milton J. Esman, eds. 1997. *Reasons for Hope: Instructive Experiences in Rural Development*. West Hartford, Conn.: Kumarian Press.

Krueger, Anne O. 1988. The Relationship Between Trade, Employment and Development. In Gustav Ranis and T. Paul Schultz, eds., *The State of Development Economics: Progress and Perspectives*. Oxford: Basil Blackwell.

Krugman, Paul. 1987. Is Free Trade Passé? *Journal of Economic Perspectives*, no. 2, 131–44.

Kuhn, Thomas. 1962. *The Structure of Scientific Revolutions*. Chicago: Chicago University Press.

Kuznets, Simon. 1955. Economic Growth and Income Inequality. *American Economic Review* (March), 1–28.

Labrecque, Marie France. 1996. The Study of Gender and Generational Hierarchies in the Context of Development: Methodological Aspects. In Parvin Ghorayshi and Claire Belanger, eds., *Women, Work, and Gender Relations in Developing Countries*. Westport, Conn.: Greenwood Press, 3–13.

– 1997. *Sortir du labyrinthe: femmes, developpement et vie quotidienne en Colombie andine*. Ottawa: Presses de l'Universite d'Ottawa.

Leibenstein, Harvey. 1965. X-Efficiency vs. Allocative Efficiency. *Economic Development and Cultural Change* 56, no. 2, 392–415.

– 1976. *Beyond Economic Man: A New Foundation for Microeconomics*. Cambridge, Mass.: Harvard University Press.

Leland. 1997. The Leland Initiative. http://www.info.usaid.gov/regions/afr/leland/project.htm.

Lenin, V.I. 1966. *Imperialism and the Split in Socialism*. Moscow: Progress Publishers.

Lewin, Roger. 1992. *Complexity: Life on the Edge of Chaos*. New York: Macmillan.

Lewis, W. Arthur. 1978. *Growth and Fluctuations: 1870–1913*. London: G. Allen & Unwin.

Lipton, Michael, and John Toye. 1990. *Does Aid Work in India? A Country Study of the Impact of Official Development Assistance*. London: Routledge.

List, Friedrich. 1827. *Outlines of American Political Economy*.

– 1841. *The National System of Political Economy*.

Little, Ian M.D., Tibor Scitovsky, and Maurice Scott. 1970. *Industry and Trade in Some Developing Countries*. Oxford: Oxford University Press.

Lumsdaine, David Halloran. 1993. *Moral Vision in International Relations: The Foreign Aid Regime, 1949–1989*. Princeton: Princeton University Press.

MacBride, S., et al. 1983. *Many Voices, One World*. Paris: UNESCO.

MacPhail, T. 1987. *Electronic Colonialism: The Future of International Broadcasting and Communication*. Beverly Hills, Cal.: Sage.

Mahoney, M. 1996. The Problem of Science in Feminist Psychology. *Feminist Studies* 22, no. 3, 603–25.

Mander, Jerry, and Edward Goldsmith. 1996. *The Case against the Global Economy and for a Turn toward the Local*. San Francisco: Sierra Club Books.

Mansell, R., and V. Wehn. 1998. *Knowledge Societies, Information Technologies and Sustainable Development*. New York: Oxford University Press.

Marchand, M., and J. Parpart, eds. 1995. *Feminism/Postmodernism/Development*. London: Routledge.

Maxwell, S.J., and H.W. Singer. 1979. Food Aid to Developing Countries: A Survey. *World Development*, 7.

Mayoux, L. 1995. Beyond Naivety: Women, Gender Inequality and Participatory Development. *Development and Change* 26, 235–58.

Michels, Robert. 1959. *Political Parties*. Originally published 1915. Glencoe, Il.: Free Press.

Mill, John Stuart. 1848. *Principles of Political Economy*. 2 vol.

Mittleman, J. 1997. *Globalization: Critical Reflections*. Boulder, Col.: Lynne Rienner.

Mohammed, Azizali. 1997. Notes on MDB Conditionality on Governance. *International Monetary and Financial Issues for the 1990s*. Vol. 8. United Nations.

Moore, Barrington. 1966. *Social Origins of Dictatorship and Democracy.* Boston: Beacon Press.

Moore, Mick, and Mark Robinson. Can Foreign Aid be Used to Promote Good Government in Developing Countries? 1995. In J. Rosenthal, ed., *Ethics and International Affairs: A Reader.* Washington, D.C.: Georgetown University Press.

Morris, Morris D. 1979. *Measuring the Condition of the World's Poor: The Physical Quality of Life Index*. New York: Pergamon Press, for the Overseas Development Council.

Moser, C. 1993. *Gender Planning and Development: Theory, Practice and Training*. London: Routledge.

Mosse, David. 1994. Authority, Gender and Knowledge: Theoretical Reflections on the Practice of Participatory Rural Appraisal. *Development and Change* 25, 497–526.

Murray-Rust, D. Hammond. 1983. Irrigation and Water Management in Sri Lanka: An Evaluation of Technical and Policy Factors Affecting Operation of the Main Channel System. PhD dissertation, Department of Agricultural Engineering, Cornell University.

OECD. 1992. *DAC Principles for Effective Aid.* Paris: OECD.

– 1995. *Development Cooperation, Efforts and Policies of the Members of the Development Assistance Committee.* Paris: OECD.

– 1996a. *Development Cooperation, Efforts and Policies of the Members of the Development Assistance Committee.* Paris: OECD.

– 1996b. *Efforts and Policies of the Members of the Development Assistance Committee.* Paris: OECD.

– 1996c. Paris: OECD Development Assistance Committee, Development Cooperation Review Series no. 12.

– 1996d. New Sources of Finance for Development. *Briefing Paper No. 1.*

– 1997. *Development Cooperation: Efforts and Policies of the Members of the Development Assistance Committee.* Paris: OECD.

– 1998. *Development Cooperation: Efforts and Policies of the Members of the Development Assistance Committee.* Paris: OECD.

Pack, Howard. 1992. Learning and Productivity Change in Developing Countries. In Gerald K. Helleiner, ed., *Trade Policy, Industrialization and Development, New Perspectives*. Oxford: Clarendon Press.

Padis. 1996. PADIS Newsletter. UNDP Website: www.undp.org/popin/regional/africa/journals/PADIS.

Panos. 1996. The Internet and the South: Superhighway or Dirt Track? The Panos Institute. http://www.oneworld.org/panos/panos_internet_press.html.

Parpart, J. 1993. Who Is the 'Other'? A Postmodern Feminist Critique of Women and Development Theory and Practice. *Development and Change* 24, no. 3 (July), 439–64.

Patel, I.G. 1971. Aid Relationships for the Seventies. In Barbara Ward, Lenore D'Anjou, and J.D. Runnalls, eds., *The Widening Gap: Development in the 1970s.* New York: Columbia University Press.

Pearson, Lester B., et al. 1969. *Partners in Development, Report of the Commission on International Development.* New York: Praeger.

Pomfret, R. 1997. *Development Economics.* Hemel Hempstead: Prentice Hall.

Popper, Karl. 1972. *Objective Knowledge: An Evolutionary Approach.* Oxford: Clarendon Press.

Porter, Michael. 1990. The Competitive Advantage of Nations. New York: Free Press.

Pratt, Cranford. 1994. Canadian Development Assistance: A Profile. In Cranford Pratt, ed., *Canadian International Development Assistance Policies: An Appraisal.* Montreal and Kingston: McGill-Queen's University Press.

Prebisch, Raul. 1950. *The Economic Development of Latin America and its Principal Problems.* New York: United Nations.

Prigogine, Ilya, and Isabelle Stengers. 1984. *Order Out of Chaos: Man's New Dialogue with Nature.* New York: Bantam Books.

Putnam, Robert D., et al. 1993. *Making Democracy Work: Civic Traditions in Modern Italy.* Princeton: Princeton University Press.

Rahman, Anisur M., and Orlando Fals-Borda. 1991. Un repaso de la investigacion-accion-participacion. In Orlando Fals-Borda and M. Anisur Rahman, dirs., *Accion y conocimiento. Como romper el monopolio con investigacion-accion-participation.* Bogota: CINEP, 39–50.

Ranis, G. 1987. Comment on Hla Myint's 'The Neo-Classical Resurgence in Development Economics': its Strength and Limitations. In G. Meier, ed., *Pioneers in Development.* Washington, D.C.: World Bank.

Rahnema, M. 1990. Participatory Action Research: The 'Last Temptation of Saint Development.' *Alternatives* 15, 199-226.

Ribot, J.C. 1996a. *Participation without Representation: Indirect Rule in Sahelian Forestry.* Rutgers University: Center for the Critical Analysis of Contemporary Culture.

– 1996b. 'Participation without Representation: Chiefs, Councils and Forestry Law in the West African Sahel.' *Cultural Survival Quarterly* (Fall), 40–4.

Richardson, D. 1996. The Internet and Rural Development: Recommendations for Strategies and Activities. http://www.fao.org/waicent/faoinfo/sustdev/Cddirect/CDDO.

Riddell, Roger. 1996. *Aid in the 21st Century: Towards a Research Agenda to Strengthen the Case for Aid.* UNDP. Office of Development Studies. Discussion paper series, 6.

Robinson, J. 1996. Searching for the 'Community' in Community-Based Conservation: A Case Study of A Zimbabwe Campfire Project. Masters in Environmental Studies thesis, Dalhousie University.

Sabelli, Fabrizzio. 1993. *Recherche anthropologique et developpement.* Neuchatel: Éditions de l'Institut d'ethnologie; Paris: Éditions de la Maison des sciences de l'homme.

Salmen, Lawrence, F. 1992. *Reducing Poverty, An Institutional Perspective.* Poverty and Social Policy Series, Paper No. 1. Washington, D.C.: World Bank.

SANGONET. Women's Pages. http://wnapc.org/women, 1996.

Schumpeter, Joseph. 1934. *The Theory of Economic Development.* Cambridge, Mass.: Harvard University Press.

Schuurman, F. 1993. *Beyond the Impasse: New Directions in Development Theory.* London: Zed Press.

Seaman, J. 1993. Comments on Toole (1993). In *Nutritional Issues in Food Aid.* Geneva: ACC/SCN Symposium Report, Nutrition Policy Discussion Paper no. 12.

Serageldin, Ismail, ed. 1996. *Sustainability and the Wealth of Nations: First Steps in an Ongoing Journey.* Environmentally Sustainable Development Studies and Monographs Series No. 5. Washington, D.C.: World Bank.

Shettima, Kole. 1996. Participation, Gender and Politics in Institutions of Rural Reform: A Comparative Study in Northern Nigeria. Dissertation, University of Toronto.

Singer, H.W. 1950. The Distribution of Gains between Investing and Borrowing Countries. *American Economic Review* 40, 473–85.

– 1995. The Future of Food Trade and Food Aid in a Liberalizing Global Economy. Keynote address to the Hunger Briefing and Exchange, Brown University. http://netspace.org/hungerweb/HW/WHP/briefing/keynote.html. 4 August 1995.

Slocum, Rachel, L. Wichhart, D. Rocheleau, and B. Thomas-Slayter, dirs. 1995. *Power, Process and Participation: Tools for Change.* London: Intermediate Technology Publications.

Smith, Adam. 1776. *An Inquiry into the Nature and Causes of the Wealth of Nations.* 2 vol.

Staudt, K. 1990. *International Development and Politics: The Bureaucratic Mire.* Philadelphia: Temple University Press.

Stokke, Olav. 1996. *Foreign Aid towards the Year 2000: Experiences and Challenges.* London: Frank Cass.

Sundar, Aparna. 1997. Sea Changes: Organizing Around the Fishery in a South Indian Community. Unpublished paper.

Sunkel, O. 1969, National Development Policy and External Dependence in Latin America. *Journal of Development Studies* 6, 23–48.

– 1973. The Pattern of Latin American Dependence. In V. Urquidi and Rosemary Thorp, eds., *Latin America in the International Economy.* London: Macmillan.

Suski, L. 1997. *Voices and Absences: The Subjects of Development Discourse.* Newfoundland: Canadian Association for Studies in International Development.

Taussig, F.W. 1893. *State Papers and Speeches on the Tariff.* Cambridge, Mass.: Harvard University Press.

Thomas-Slayter, B., et al. 1995. *A Manual for Socio-Economic and Gender Analysis: Responding to the Development Challenge.* Worcester, Mass. Mimeographed report.

Thomson, J. 1995. Participatory Approaches to Government Bureaucracies: Facilitating the Process of Institutional Change. *World Development* 23, no. 9, 1521–54.

Tiessen, R. 1997. A Feminist Critique of Participatory Development Discourse: PRA and Gender Participation in Natural Resource Management. International Studies Association, 19 March.

Toole, M. 1993. Protecting Refugees' Nutrition with Food Aid. In *Nutritional Issues in Food Aid.* Geneva: ACC/SCN Symposium Report, Nutrition Policy Discussion Paper no. 12.

Treasury Board Secretariat. 1977. *Evaluation of the Canadian Food Aid Program.* Ottawa: Government of Canada.

Tyler, William. 1981. Growth and Export Expansion in Developing Countries. *Journal of Development Economics* 9, no. 1, 121–30.

Uimonen, P. 1997. Internet as a tool for Social Development. Paper presented to the UNRISD INET Conference '97.

USAID (United States Agency for International Development). 1995. Food Aid and Food Security Policy Paper. Washington, D.C.: USAID 1995. Mimeo.

USAID Leland Initiative. 1998. Africa Global Information Infrastructure Project. www.info.usa.gov/leland

Uphoff, Norman. 1986. *Local Institutional Development: An Analytical Sourcebook with Cases.* West Hartford, Conn.: Kumarian Press.

– 1988. Assisted Self-Reliance: Working with, rather than for, the Poor. In John C. Lewis, ed., *Strengthening the Poor: What Have We Learned?*, 47–59. New Brunswick, N.J.: Transaction Books.

- 1990. Distinguishing Power, Authority and Legitimacy: Taking Max Weber at His Word, Using Resource-Exchange Analysis. *Polity* 22, no. 2, 295–322.
- 1992, 1996. *Learning from Gal Oya: Possibilities for Participatory Development and Post-Newtonian Social Science.* London: Intermediate Technology Publications. Originally published by Cornell University Press.
- 2000. Understanding Social Capital: Learning from the Analysis and Experience of Participation. In P. Dasgupta and I. Serageldin, eds., *Social Capital, A Multifaceted Perspective.* Washington, D.C.: World Bank.

Uphoff, Norman, Milton J. Esman, and Anirudh Krishna, eds. 1998. *Reasons for Success: Learning from Instructive Experiences in Rural Development.* West Hartford, Conn.: Kumarian Press.

WFP (World Food Program). 1995. *Annual Report 1995.* Rome: WFP.

WFP/INTERFAIS. 1996. Global Food Aid Statistics. Special Edition of the Food Aid Monitor: Food Aid Flows 1995. April.http://www.wfp.org/InfoServs_INTERFAIS_Monitor_Faf4home.html. June 21, 1996b.

WFP. WFP in Statistics. 1995. http://www.wfp.org/InfoServs_Stats_Stats95_Home.html. 16 October 1996 (23 September 1996 for some tables).

Wade, Robert. 1985. The System of Administrative and Political Corruption: Canal Irrigation in South India. *Journal of Development Studies* 18, no. 3, 287–328.

Waldrop, Mitchell M. 1992. *Complexity: The Emerging Science at the Edge of Order and Chaos.* New York: Simon and Schuster.

Weekes-Vagliani, W. 1994. Participatory Development and Gender: Articulating Concepts and Cases. Technical Paper no. 95 (OCDE/OD, 94, 15. Paris: UN/OECD.

Weiermair, Klaus, and Mark Perlman, eds. 1990. *Studies in Economic Rationality: X-Efficiency Examined and Extolled.* Ann Arbor: University of Michigan Press.

Welbourn, A. 1991. RRA and the Analysis of Difference. *RRA Notes* 14, 14–23.

White, S.C. 1995. Depoliticising Development: The Uses and Abuses of Participation. *Development and Practice* 6, no. 1, 6–15.

Wieringa, S. 1994. Women's Interests and Empowerment: Gender Planning Reconsidered, *Development and Change* 25, 11–27.

Wijayaratna, C.M., and Norman Uphoff. 1997. Farmer Organization in Gal Oya: Improving Irrigation Management in Sri Lanka. In Krishna, et al. *Reasons for Hope*, 166–83.

Williamson, Jeffrey G. 1996. Globalization, Convergence and History. *Journal of Economic History* 56 (June), 277–306.

Winichagoon, P., K. Kachandam, G.A. Attig, and K. Tontisirin. 1992. *Integrating Food and Nutrition into Development: Thailand's Experiences and Future Visions.* Bangkok: UNICEF EAPRO and Institute of Nutrition, Mahidol University.

Wood, A. 1994. *North-South Trade, Employment and Inequality.* Oxford: Clarendon Press.

– 1995. Does Trade Reduce Wage Inequality in Developing Countries? Institute of Development Studies, University of Sussex.

Wood, Hugh. 1995. Ouellet Illustrates 'Traditional' Style. *Globe and Mail,* 8 April.

Wood, Robert. 1996. Rethinking Aid. In S. Hook, ed., *Foreign Aid toward the Millenium.* Boulder, Col.: Lynne Rienner Publishers.

World Bank. 1995a. *Pakistan Poverty Assessment. Report No. 14397-PAK.* Washington, D.C.: World Bank.

– 1995b. *Strengthening the Effectiveness of Aid: Lessons for Donors.* Washington, D.C.: World Bank.

– 1996a. *Partnership for Capacity Building in Africa.* Washington, D.C.: World Bank.

– 1996b. *Global Economic Prospects and the Developing Countries.* Washington, D.C.: World Bank.

– 1997. *World Development Report 1997.* New York: Oxford University Press.

– 1998. *World Development Indicators.* Washington, D.C.: International Bank for Reconstruction and Development.

Young, H. 1996. The Acceptability and Use of Fortified Foods as a Source of Essential Micronutrients Among Nutritionally at Risk Refugee Populations. Oxford: Oxfam mimeo: research proposal.

Zimmerman, R., and S. Hook. 1996. The Assault on U.S. Foreign Aid. In Steven Hook, ed., *Foreign Aid toward the Millenium.* Boulder, Col.: Lynne Rienner Publishers.

Contributors

Jonathan S. Barker teaches political science at the University of Toronto. He has written on the politics of rural change in Africa (*Rural Communities under Stress: Peasant Farmers and the State in Africa*, 1989). His recent book, *Street-Level Democracy: Political Settings at the Margins of Global Society*, presents a novel research method and includes colourful case studies by five collaborators.

Albert Berry is professor of economics at the University of Toronto. His research focuses on Latin America in the areas of labour markets and income distribution, small and medium enterprise, and the impact of structural adjustment and globalization on these aspects of the economy. Recent publications include 'The Income Distribution Threat in Latin America,' *Latin American Research Review* (Summer 1997) an edited book, *Poverty, Economic Reform, and Income Distribution in Latin America* (1997); *SME Competitiveness: The Power of Networking and Subcontracting* 1997; and 'Agrarian Reform, Land Distribution and Small Farm Policy as Preventive of Humanitarian Emergencies,' for a volume on complex humanitarian emergencies to be published by the WIDER Institute. He is research director of the Latin American Studies Programme at the Centre for International Studies, University of Toronto, and recently team leader of Pakistan 2010, a planning exercise funded by the Asian Development Bank to identify promising economic strategies for Pakistan over the medium term.

Roy Culpeper was born in Karachi and has lived in Canada since 1959. He received his PhD in economics from the University of Toronto in 1975. Culpeper joined the North South Institute in 1986 and was vice-president and coordinator of Research from 1991 until 1995, when he was appointed president. His previous work experience included positions in the Manitoba government's Cabinet Planning Secretariat, the federal Department of Finance, and the Department of External Affairs. From 1983 until 1986, Culpeper was adviser to the Canadian executive director at the World Bank in Washington. At the Institute he has conducted research on a broad range of issues relating to international finance. From 1993 to 1995, he directed the Institute's largest-ever project, a comprehensive study of four regional development banks. Culpeper is the author of numerous publications, including *Titans or Behemoths?: The Multilateral Development Banks and Canada and the Global Governors: Reforming the Multilateral Development Banks*, and co-author of *High Stakes and Low Incomes: Canada and the Development Banks*. He was co-editor (with Albert Berry and Frances Stewart) of *Global Development Fifty Years After Bretton Woods*.

Edna F. Einsiedel is professor of communication studies at the University of Calgary. She also serves as coordinator of the undergraduate Development Studies Program. Dr Einsiedel's research interests in development include gender issues, communications planning, and program evaluation. She headed an IDRC-supported project on the enhancement of undergraduate international development studies programs in Canadian universities, leading to the formation of the Canadian Consortium for University Programs in International Development Studies (CCUPIDS) and the development of an on-line network linking students and faculty in this consortium (IDSNet). She is also currently involved in an international collaborative project on biotechnology and the public with participation from countries in the European Union, the United States, Canada, and Japan.

Jim Freedman is currently a program analyst for the office of the Iraq Programme, United Nations, in New York and Baghdad. He has taught courses on development issues in the Department of Anthropology at the University of Western Ontario, and has served as a consultant for a number of international development organizations. He received his PhD in anthropology from Princeton University. Freedman has published extensively on development related topics, ranging from evaluation methodology to public administration reform, farm systems, population growth, and the management of landmine removal. Most recently, he has co-authored *Water, Pipes and People*

(1997), a study of a salinity control and reclamation project in Northern Pakistan. Other publications include a novel and popular works of non-fiction.

Anne Germain is currently a Junior Program Officer at CIDA. A graduate of the University of Toronto at Scarborough's International Development Studies Programme, her interest in questions of food and nutrition was triggered during her work with BIDANI, a Nutrition-in-Development Programme based at the University of the Philippines Los Banos. She is currently pursuing work on issues pertaining to women, knowledge, and food security in development policy and practice.

Keith Griffin is professor of economics at the University of California, Riverside. He was formerly president of Magdalen College, Oxford. He has served as adviser and consultant to various governments, international agencies, and academic institutions in Asia, Africa, Latin America, and Eastern Europe and was a member of the World Commission on Culture and Development. Griffin is the author of *Studies in Globalization and Economic Transitions* and *Alternative Strategies for Economic Development* and co-author (with Terry McKinley) of *Implementing a Human Development Strategy,* among other books.

Gerry Helleiner is professor emeritus of economics at the University of Toronto. Until 1999 he also served as the research coordinator of the developing countries' intergovernmental Group of Twenty-four on matters of their concern arising at the International Monetary Fund and the World Bank. He is the author and editor of many books on international trade, finance, and the developing countries.

Susan Horton is professor of economics at the University of Toronto and supervisor of studies of the undergraduate International Development Studies Programme. Her research focuses on labour markets, health, and nutrition in developing countries, and she has worked in a wide range of countries, including Bangladesh, Bolivia, Ghana, Jamaica, Nepal, the Philippines, and Tanzania. She has also served as a consultant for UNICEF, UNDP, FAO, the World Bank, the Asian Development Bank, the Micronutrient Initiative, and the Planning Institute of Jamaica. She has served as vice-chair of the board of trustees of the International Food Policy Research Institute.

Melissa P. Innes is a graduate student in Communication Studies at the University of Calgary. Before initiating her graduate work Innes spent a significant amount of time living and working overseas. She was involved with women's small-scale loan and income generating projects in Lesotho and development education projects across Canada. She is currently working on her thesis research in Lusaka, Zambia, with the support of a Canadian Bureau of International Education (CBIE) award. She is exploring the socio-economic, political, and cultural relations that frame the use of new ICTs as tools for progressive civic organizations in achieving their development goals.

Marie France Labrecque received her PhD in 1982 from City University of New York. She is professor of anthropology at Laval University, Quebec. Her particular interest has been in economic anthropology and the study of peasantry in Mexico and Colombia. Labrecque's recent work deals with a critique of the 'women and development' approach in international development, including income-generating projects and participatory methodologies. Her present research deals with the gendering of production and the expansion of the *maquiladoras* in the rural areas of the state of Yucatan, Mexico. She has edited and authored a number of books, including, *L'égalité devant soi: rapports sociaux de sexe et développement international* (1994) and *Sortir du labyrinthe: femmes, développement et vie quotidienne en Colombie andine* (1997). Her recent work in English includes a chapter in Parvin Ghorayshi and Claire Bélanger, eds., *Women, Work, and Gender Relations in Developing Countries: A Global Perspective* (1996).

David R. Morrison is director of the International Program and professor of political studies at Trent University. He is author of *Aid and Ebb Tide: A History of CIDA and Canadian Development Assistance* and several articles on Canada's North-South relations. He is a former president of the Canadian Association for the Study of International Development (CASID). The founding chair of Comparative Development Studies at Trent, he also served as the university's dean of arts and science and vice-president (academic).

Jane L. Parpart is professor of history, international development studies, and women's studies at Dalhousie University. She is the author of numerous articles on women and development, with a particular focus on Africa. She co-edited *Feminism/Postmodernism/Development* with Marianne Marchand (1995) and has just completed a collection on teaching Africa in the twenty-first century, *Great Ideas for Teaching about Africa* (1999), with Misty Bastian.

Cranford Pratt is emeritus professor of political science at the University of Toronto. He has worked in Uganda and in Tanzania and is the author of several books and numerous articles on African political and development issues, including *The Critical Phase in Tanzania, 1945–68* (1976). Since 1980 Pratt has concentrated on Canada's relations with the Third World. He first edited, with Robert Matthews, *Human Rights in Canadian Foreign Policy* (1988); he then edited and contributed to *Internationalism under Strain: The North-South Policies of Canada, the Netherlands, Norway and Sweden* (1989), *Middle Power Internationalism: The North-South Dimension* (1990), and *Canadian International Development Assistance Policies: An Appraisal* (1994 and 1996).

Ian Smillie has thirty years of experience in the field of international development, as an administrator, evaluator, and writer. He has managed large development enterprises in Canada, Africa, and Asia, was a founder of the Canadian non-governmental development organization, Inter Pares, and was director of one of Canada's largest NGOs, CUSO. As consultant to a wide range of government and non-governmental organizations for fifteen years, he has been involved in the creation, advancement, or expansion of a range of development initiatives in South Asia and Africa. Smillie has written extensively on various aspects of development; his most recent books are *The Alms Bazaar: Altruism under Fire – Non Profit Organizations and International Development*, and *Stakeholding: Government-NGO Partnerships for International Development* (ed. with Henny Helmich).

Norman Uphoff is director of the Cornell International Institute for Food, Agriculture and Development and a professor of government and international agriculture at Cornell University. He previously served as chair of the Rural Development Committee at Cornell from 1971 to 1990. Uphoff spent a sabbatical year at the Agrarian Research and Training Institute (ARTI) in Sri Lanka in 1978–9, studying rural communities and their capacity for initiating and managing local development. While there he became involved with the planning and implementation of the Gal Oya Water Management Project funded by USAID; he then helped establish a similar participatory irrigation management program for USAID in Nepal, on the border with the Indian state of Bihar. Uphoff is the author *Learning from Gal Oya* (1996) and of numerous articles on development.